Mad at School

Corporealities: Discourses of Disability

David T. Mitchell and Sharon L. Snyder, editors

Books available in the series:

Revels in Madness: Insanity in Medicine and Literature
by Allen Thiher

Points of Contact: Disability, Art, and Culture
edited by Susan Crutchfield and Marcy Epstein

A History of Disability
by Henri-Jacques Stiker

Disabled Veterans in History
edited by David A. Gerber

Narrative Prosthesis: Disability and the Dependencies of Discourse
by David T. Mitchell and Sharon L. Snyder

Backlash Against the ADA: Reinterpreting Disability Rights
edited by Linda Hamilton Krieger

The Staff of Oedipus: Transforming Disability in Ancient Greece
by Martha L. Rose

Fictions of Affliction: Physical Disability in Victorian Culture
by Martha Stoddard Holmes

Foucault and the Government of Disability
edited by Shelley Tremain

Bodies in Commotion: Disability and Performance
edited by Carrie Sandahl and Philip Auslander

Moving Beyond Prozac, DSM, *and the New Psychiatry: The Birth of Postpsychiatry*
by Bradley Lewis

Disability in Twentieth-Century German Culture
by Carol Poore

Concerto for the Left Hand: Disability and the Defamiliar Body
by Michael Davidson

Disability Theory
by Tobin Siebers

The Songs of Blind Folk: African American Musicians and the Cultures of Blindness
by Terry Rowden

Signifying Bodies: Disability in Contemporary Life Writing
by G. Thomas Couser

Disability Aesthetics
by Tobin Siebers

Stumbling Blocks Before the Blind: Medieval Constructions of a Disability
by Edward Wheatley

Mad at School: Rhetorics of Mental Disability and Academic Life
by Margaret Price

Mad at School

Rhetorics OF *Mental Disability* AND *Academic Life*

MARGARET PRICE

The University of Michigan Press ❦ *Ann Arbor*

For my family ❧

Published in the United States of America by
The University of Michigan Press
Manufactured in the United States of America
♾ Printed on acid-free paper

2014 2013 2012 2011 4 3 2 1

A CIP catalog record for this book is available from the British Library.

Library of Congress Cataloging-in-Publication Data

Price, Margaret, 1969–
Mad at school : rhetorics of mental disability and academic life / Margaret Price.
p. ; cm. — (Corporealities)
Includes bibliographical references and index.
ISBN 978-0-472-07138-8 (cloth : alk. paper) — ISBN 978-0-472-05138-0 (pbk. : alk. paper)
1. College students—Mental health. 2. College teachers—Mental health. 3. Mentally ill—Employment. 4. Mentally ill—Education (Higher) I. Title. II. Series: Corporealities.
[DNLM: 1. Mentally Disabled Persons—psychology—Personal Narratives. 2. Communication—Personal Narratives. 3. Faculty—Personal Narratives. 4. Stereotyping—Personal Narratives. WM 302]
RC451.4.S7P735 2010
616.89'00835—dc22 2010033748

ISBN 978-0-472-02798-9 (e-book)

Cover illustrations: top, © iStockphoto.com/vm; bottom, photo by John Zhuang.

Acknowledgments

I am deeply grateful to the network of readers, thinkers, friends, and family who have helped bring this book to completion. At the University of Massachusetts–Amherst, Anne Herrington, Cathy Luna, and Donna LeCourt directed my early work in disability studies with generosity and rigor. Also at UMass, my community at Learning Disabilities Support Services, especially Kathy Weilerstein, provided continual support and challenge. At Wayne State University, Ellen Barton took the time to meet and ask after the nervous new adjunct in the halls. At Spelman College, I have been welcomed by an energetic community of teacher-scholars; I am especially grateful for the mentorship of Donna Akiba Sullivan Harper, Anne Bradford Warner, Pushpa Parekh, and Veta Goler, and for the astute fellowship of my colleagues across all departments. My students are a continual source of delight and pondering. I want to particularly thank Timile Brown, who taught me a great deal about pedagogical accessibility.

Spelman College has provided many forms of support, including a Faculty Research Grant, a Junior Faculty Research Leave, and a project grant from the Office of the Provost, all of which provided time and resources needed to complete this project. The Comprehensive Writing Program, Department of English, and Ethel Waddell Githii Honors Program have also provided support for travel, materials, and conversations with many distinguished visitors. The Community of Practice with Spelman's Office of Disability Services, led by Merrine McDonald, provides welcome opportunities for everyday activist efforts—and always a fantastic lunch.

The Conference on College Composition and Communication (CCCC) and the Society for Disability Studies Conference (SDS) have brought warm friendship and stimulating ideas from many people, including Elizabeth Brewer, Brenda Jo Brueggemann, Susan Burch, Mel Chen, Jay Dolmage, Rosemarie Garland-Thomson, Alison Kafer, Stephanie Kerschbaum, Cynthia Lewiecki-Wilson, Kristin Lindgren, Carol Moeller, Amy Vidali, Sophia Wong, Cynthia Wu, and Melanie Yergeau. I'm especially grateful to the members of the Disability Studies Special Interest Group and the Committee on Disability Issues within CCCC, and the Queer Caucus within SDS. My visit to the Centre for Disability Studies at the University of Leeds opened a new world of accessible pedagogy and theory; I thank Colin Barnes, Alison Sheldon, Mark Priestley, and all students and staff at the Centre for their generous welcome and uproarious seminar. The Future of Minority Studies Project and Mellon Foundation provided a fellowship for a two-week institute that introduced me to new ideas and permanently changed my thinking on minority studies. I am also grateful to the National Coalition of Independent Scholars and the Center for Independent Study: Barbara Currier Bell and Katalin Kádár Lynn listened to my questions, sent me piles of material on independent scholarship, and kindly encouraged my work.

At the University of Michigan Press, LeAnn Fields dedicated a tremendous amount of time and energy to shaping this book into its current form, offering feedback and encouragement every step of the way. She and her editorial assistant, Scott Ham, are editors in the best sense: allies and sharp readers.

Reading and feedback on various portions of this project have been provided by Ellen Barton, Timile Brown, Susan Burch, Stephanie Kerschbaum, Petra Kuppers, Marian Lupo, Leah (Phinnia) Meredith, Cal Montgomery, Ty Power, Tobin Siebers, Cindy Wu, and anonymous reviewers for University of Michigan Press. For their insightful comments and for the gift of their time, I am deeply grateful. All errors and all mushiness of theory or evidence are my responsibility. I am also grateful for the friendship and support of Jeanette Beal, Jeff Brune, Eli Clare, Jennifer DiGrazia, Nirmala Erevelles, Kim and Glenn Goldsmith, Michelle Hite, Andy Inkster, Marisa Klages, Bradley Lewis, Sara Lewis, Katherine Mancuso, Mary Martone, Matt Rice, Lauren Rosenberg, Amy Small, Bethany Stevens, Cole Thaler, Russell Turknett, Sharon Wachsler, and Joe Wear, as well as my thriving online communities on Facebook, LiveJournal, MindFreedom, and Ravelry.

Kennan Ferguson has known me since I was nineteen years old, when I used to stomp around and say things like "Theory is crap." I cannot thank him enough for his companionship and support over decades. JD

Dykes has provided love, chihuahuas, carrot soup, and the question "What do you need?" I'm grateful to my mom, dad, and brothers—Mary, Rick, Richard, and Dan Price—for their humanity, and for their willingness to listen.

Portions of the introduction and chapter 1 appeared in "Mental Disability and Other Terms of Art," part of a cluster of articles addressing the theme of disability and language, in *Profession* 2010. Portions of the research on "kairotic space" and conference accessibility appeared in "Access Imagined: The Construction of Disability in Conference Policy Documents," *Disability Studies Quarterly* (2009). Chapter 4 appeared in slightly different form as "'Her Pronouns Wax and Wane': Psychosocial Disability, Autobiography and Counter-Diagnosis," *Journal of Literary & Cultural Disability Studies* (2009). All are reprinted here with permission.

Contents

Foreword

TOBIN SIEBERS

Many of us, Margaret Price argues, are mad at school. We are crazy in the classroom. *Mad* and *crazy* are offensive terms, but they are also rhetorical indicators, useful both to expose discrimination against people with mental disabilities and to chart the road not yet taken to arrive at classrooms attentive to the mental diversity of students and teachers in higher education. Price's goal is to apply the theory and activism of disability studies to transform the way that academic thinking is understood. Disability studies values neurodiversity inside and outside the classroom. It views different kinds of thinking as a critical resource for higher education, not as a form of deviancy that obstructs learning or needs to be eliminated from academic life.

Higher education has a strong interest in purging people with mental disabilities, but Price uncovers a secret population of teachers, students, and staff who think differently. Here the disabled mind goes to college, and there meets other disabled minds, and these minds are numerous and variable. Price demonstrates how little we understand these minds, how quickly our response to them turns sour, how easily we give up on teaching them, how predictably we label them as unteachable. More important, Price exposes how inadequate are the models with which we understand mental disability in higher education. Academic lore converts the people inhabiting the classroom into fictional personalities designed to cover up the distrust of thinking differently in academic life. In the guise of "the eccentric teacher," "the absent-minded professor," "the clueless undergraduate," and "the nervous graduate student" exist individuals whose minds must be dismissed from the classroom if they pass beyond the "amusing" stage.

Consider the spectrum of familiar student personalities and how easily they drift toward pathology. Teachers are happy when students actively participate in class. But how quickly some of these vocal students are thought to slide in another direction, from being articulate and smart to dominating the conversation and showing off, becoming inconsiderate and prone to outbursts, narcissistic, perhaps violent. Teachers are unhappy when students seem unable or unwilling to participate in class. How quickly some of these quiet students seem to display other behaviors, from being silent and missing class, appearing unmotivated, lazy, or dumb, to turning sullen, withholding, and disturbed, perhaps violent. There is no question of reversing the direction in these spectrums, for once the slippery slope toward pathology appears—and it always does—it becomes obvious that the spectrum itself relies on medical diagnosis. Teachers may insist that they are not therapists or doctors, that they are being asked to do things beyond their training, but their feelings of inadequacy and suspicion in the classroom actually reveal a hidden agenda of classroom teaching—what is being diagnosed in persistent and determined ways is the mental health of students.

The intersection between academic and medical discourse, how the medical world schools the classroom, is Price's most stunning revelation. Rationality, participation, independence, coherence, and collegiality are educational standards, Price claims, used to measure teachers and students, but they also serve a medical purpose because individuals who fail the standards are not only considered unfit for the classroom, they are suspected of being unfit for life. Teachers do see their students, despite protests to the contrary, from the point of view of the therapist. The reliable, likable, sensible, independent, and smart student is judged fit for school; other students need help badly, but not help that teachers can provide—for "we are not therapists"—and so these students are exiled from the classroom. Medical judgments determine who is teachable, who should or should not be in school.

Teachers are subject to the same judgments by students and other teachers. The best teachers have the best interpersonal skills. The best teachers have the most energy. They move around the classroom when they speak. They know how to use the blackboard. They gesture approvingly. They make their students laugh. What of the teacher who has chronic fatigue? What of the teacher who is manic? What of the teacher who has agoraphobia or panic disorder? The best teachers are supposed to be good and productive colleagues. They always have a piece of scholarship on their desk, a research project going at the lab, a conference paper to prepare. They offer helpful suggestions to colleagues. What of the teacher who has depression? What of the teacher who has memory loss? What of the teacher who has anxiety and cannot tolerate department meetings or academic conferences? Teachers with these and other mental disabilities are often driven out of the classroom; they exist at the margins of the schools in adjunct positions or as independent scholars, finding entry to higher education barred by the fact that they do not measure up to narrow and unspoken standards of mental health.

All of these problems Price addresses in great detail, but her most daring and courageous contribution is her analysis of school shootings. Despite the fact that school shootings are extremely rare, continued reminders of their possibility exist everywhere. For Price, school shootings garner such attention because they represent the fearsome consequence at the heart of the greatest myth about mental disability—that the mad are violent. In this scenario, violence represents the probable outcome of all mental disability, which explains why the smallest displays of mental diversity in the classroom invite paranoia. Price overturns, with the greatest delicacy and sympathy to victims, the false idea that the mentally disabled are always violent and that school shooters are monsters. Her case studies are difficult. Seung-Hui Cho killed 32 persons and himself at Virginia Tech. Steven Kazmierczak, a 27-year-old graduate student, opened fire on a crowded auditorium at Northern Illinois University, wounding 24 people, of whom six died, including himself. In a heart-breaking and powerful account, Price demonstrates that discussions of school shootings repeat the same patterns of explanation, providing a limit case of the myths surrounding mental disability in higher education. The refusal to understand school shooters trickles down as the justification to avoid the shy lab partner or the unfriendly colleague, to stay out of the path of anyone whose mind seems remotely different.

Price defines single-handedly a new direction in disability studies by providing incisive analyses of different minds, not only those connected to autism and attention deficit disorder (which are the most familiar examples) but many other forms of cognitive and mental disability for which we do not yet have names. Price gets inside the heads of people of diverse thought in the classroom. She imagines differently the thoughts of the shy sophomore, the fidgety undergraduate, the awkward graduate student. She gives us the perspective of the unfriendly office mate, the nervous lecturer, the panicky job candidate, the cranky older colleague. She gets inside their heads because they all are or will be in our heads. This book is more than a report on mental disability in higher education. It is a book brimming with ideas about how to change thinking about thinking in the classroom.

Introduction

Bodily decay is gloomy in prospect, but of all human contemplations the most abhorrent is body without mind.

—*Thomas Jefferson,*
letter to John Adams, 1816

If you are crazy, can you still be of sound mind?

This is not an idle question: I am crazy (although I don't usually use that word to refer to myself), and I make my living by using my mind. I'm a professor of composition and rhetoric. I spend most days thinking, talking, and writing.

Some of my students have been crazy. Colleagues too. Most of us are good at academic work, although the opportunity—or rather, the privilege—we have to engage in that work varies widely.

When you hear that someone is "crazy," a host of stereotypical images may come immediately to mind. For instance, you may picture a homeless person muttering on a bus; a figure lying restrained on a hospital gurney; or a dull medicated gaze.[1] You might also think of danger, for a common assumption about mental illness is that it goes hand in hand with violent behavior. Often, when I talk about madness with colleagues or friends, they mention film and television images of violent insanity; they associate madness and threat. Or they may refer to the recent shootings on college campuses: Virginia Tech, Northern Illinois, the University of Alabama–Huntsville (UAH). They might even say—as one commenter on a *Chronicle of Higher Education* blog did—that we seem to be in a new age of threat from "academic psycho-killers." In the face of such images, it is rarely persuasive to point out that madness is usually not threatening—at least not in the immediate physical sense. People with mental disabilities do move in an aura of constant violence within institutions, but as several scholars have observed, most of the violence comes not from these individuals but is instead directed at them.[2]

Alternatively, the image that springs to mind may be that of the extraordinary mad person, a star like Nobel Prize–winning mathematician John Forbes Nash Jr. as portrayed in the film *A Beautiful Mind.* That film upholds a truism about mental illness, namely, its link to creative genius. (It also upholds another truism, which is that in order to overcome one's madness, one must simply refuse to tolerate it—"Just Say No" as cure—but that's another story.) The commonsense link between madness and genius arises again and again, in stories about real people like composer Robert Schumann, who is said to have been bipolar ("Portrait"), as well as fictional characters like Sherlock Holmes, whose meticulous attention to detail has been suggested to indicate Asperger's syndrome (Sanders).

This book focuses on manifestations of madness—what I call "mental disability"—in the academic realm. I'm interested in the ways that mental disability affects the lives of students, faculty, and staff in U.S. higher education. I am also interested in the ways that mental disability is identified and valued (or, more often, devalued) in this space. Although I do refer to studies that make use of empirical data such as the prevalence of mental disabilities among college students, my concern is focused more upon the ways that we decide *who* is mentally disabled in the first place, and *what we do* once we have decided a person should be labeled as such. Put simply, I am interested in the stories that are told about mental disability in U.S. higher education. Who tells the stories? Who is privileged or deprivileged through the telling? In what ways might we want to change the stories we are telling, the ways we are imagining the proper place of the disabled mind in college? Indeed, do we even know what it means to have a disabled (unsound, ill, irrational, crazy) mind in the educational realm, a realm expressly dedicated to the life of the mind?

In U.S. higher education, both the "creative genius" and the "violent" stereotypes are referred to regularly. Faculty members who display "quirky" behavior are sometimes regarded with affection: think of funny Professor X, who mumbles in the hallways and perhaps wears outlandish outfits. (For what it's worth, my anecdotal observation indicates that quirks are more welcome in academe when displayed by a person who is white, male, and/or tenured; but that is only my observation.) Sometimes, less benignly, faculty members are labeled "difficult" and become the object of administrative hand-wringing, or even formal sanctions. In this case we might think of Professor Y, who is notorious for her outbursts in faculty meetings and who is whispered to be "unbalanced." Students as well as professors populate the stories about madness in academe: in recent decades, stories about faculty "quirks" or "difficulty" have been joined by more urgently worded stories about violence. So, in addition to Professors X and Y, we now also have Student Z, whose writing contains violent themes and who, it is feared, may "go off" at any moment. Faculty and staff are encouraged to be alert for signs of imminent violence in student writing, in an atmosphere that Benjamin Reiss has called "quasi-psychiatric surveillance" (27), and many campuses have instituted "security" measures such as those outlined in the lurid (and expensive) DVD titled *Shots Fired on Campus: When Lightning Strikes.* With the relatively recent addition of UAH biologist Amy Bishop to the roster of "academic psycho-killers," writing by university faculty may soon draw the same level of attention and scrutiny.

I believe we must pay attention to this proliferation of stories, for several reasons. First, the abundance of stories indicates that mental disability is not now—if it ever was—a rare occurrence. Although the *Diagnostic and Statistical Manual of Mental Disorders* (DSM) announces in its title that it identifies "disorder[ed]" states of mind, and thus implicitly deviations from the "normal," or at least more ordered, realm, its array of diagnoses is so copious that it seems to suggest that "human life is a form of mental illness" (Lawrence Davis). It's no coincidence that anecdotal stories about crazy people have proliferated along with the number of diagnoses in DSM, for a diagnosis is in essence a story—*especially* in DSM, which relies mainly upon descriptive criteria. Some, like Lawrence Davis, have argued that the explosion of DSM diagnoses is approaching the absurd. Davis wrote in a 1997 *Harper's* article, "Once the universe is populated with enough coffee-guzzling, cigarette-puffing, vigorous human beings who are crazy precisely because they smoke, drink coffee, and move about in an active and purposeful manner, the psychoanalyst is placed in the position of the lucky fellow taken to the mountaintop and shown powers and dominions." However, I argue that, while remaining skeptical of the motivations that have brought the enormous DSM into being,[3] we might also take this proliferation of stories as evidence of two important truths about disorderly minds. First, such minds show up all the time, in obvious and not-so-obvious ways; and second, recognizing their appearance is not a yes-no proposition, but rather a confusing and contextually dependent process that calls into question what we mean by the "normal" mind.

That realization, that minds are best understood in terms of variety and difference rather than deviations from an imagined norm, is aligned with a theoretical and activist stance called disability studies (DS). According to DS scholars and activists, disability is popularly imagined as a medical "problem" that inheres in an individual, one that needs to be fixed ("cured") and is cause for sorrow and pity. DS countermands this dominant belief by arguing that disability is a mode of human difference, one that becomes a problem only when the environment or context treats it as such. To take a frequent example, using a wheelchair is not in and of itself a problem unless one must navigate a built environment, such as a bus, airplane, or building, which assumes stairs are the best and only way to ascend from one level to another.

In *Claiming Disability,* Simi Linton offers this description of DS:

> While retaining the word *disability,* despite its medical origins, a premise of most of the literature in disability studies is that disability is best understood as a marker of identity. As such, it has been used to build a coalition of people with significant impairments, people with behavioral or anatomical characteristics marked as deviant, and people who have or are suspected of having conditions, such as AIDS or emotional illness, that make them targets of discrimination. . . . When disability is redefined as a social/political category, people with a variety of conditions are identified as *people with disabilities* or *disabled people,* a group bound by common social and political experience. (12)

Adopting a DS perspective is not simple. The ramifications of the premise described by Linton are many, and often require a disorienting shift away from presumptions of tragedy, courage, or brokenness. Moreover, since the publication of *Claiming Disability* in 1998, DS scholars have continued an energetic debate about what DS is, how it manifests in various fields, and how it signifies differently for different kinds of impairments. Although DS is concerned with individual experience, it is foremost a social and political perspective. As such, it shifts the "problem" of disability away from individuals and toward institutions and attitudes. Strongly indebted to postmodern ways of knowing, DS generally understands the institution as a system that produces human oppression (as well as privilege). This book examines the impact of one particular set of institutional discourses—those of U.S. higher education—on persons with disabilities of the mind. It is both an attempt to broaden the field of DS and a critique of the field's long-standing emphasis on physical and sensory impairments.

My analysis of academic discourse[4] focuses on certain commonplace beliefs, or topoi. Lawrence J. Prelli explains topoi (singular *topos*) as "lines of thought that bear on a [person's] credibility in this or that rhetorical situation" (90). A topos contributes to the construction of a rhetor's ethos, or perceived character. It is often an issue or theme with which she must contend in the process of presenting herself as a credible and persuasive person. Because common topoi are generally recognized by a rhetor and her audience, they can serve as points from which to begin arguments. However, when they are shared by an in-group, they also tend to be unexamined; thus, as Sharon Crowley explains, "commonplaces are part of the discursive machinery that hides the flow of difference" (73). Common topoi are often invoked when rhetors wish to reinforce dominant values or "challeng[e] the beliefs/practices of miscreants and outsiders" (Crowley 73).[5] This gives topoi great power, especially power on the part of dominant groups to exclude or punish marginalized groups or persons.

I argue that some of the most important common topoi of academe intersect problematically with mental disability. These include

- Rationality
- Criticality
- Presence
- Participation
- Resistance
- Productivity
- Collegiality
- Security
- Coherence
- Truth
- Independence

For instance, what does "participation" in a class mean for a student who is undergoing a deep depression and cannot get out of bed? Or a student who experiences such severe anxiety, or obsession, that he can barely leave his dorm room or home? What about a student on the autism spectrum who has difficulty apprehending the subtle social cues that govern classroom participation, the difference between "showing engagement" and "dominating the conversation," the sorts of spontaneous oral performances that are considered "smart"? What does "collegiality" mean for a faculty member who has these same difficulties? What happens to the "productivity" of an academic writer who struggles to achieve the linear coherence that most academic writing demands? Or whose disability affects the many self-directed stages of writing and revising—initiation, organization, seeking and applying feedback, completion? Why, indeed, is "coherence" one of the most-often emphasized features of a thesis-driven academic argument; does the demonstration of coherence indicate a stronger mind? How do the new requirements for "security" in U.S. academic environments resonate with (or against) our cherished values of free speech and independence? Finally, what are we to make of the ever-growing number of "independent" scholars in the United States, many of whom occupy that "independent" status because their mental impairments or disabilities make a securely affiliated academic job impossible?

To a great extent, we don't know the answers to these questions, for academics (which I define, for the purposes of this study, to include students, staff, administrators, and independent scholars as well as faculty) with mental disabilities are largely excluded from academic discourse. The instruments of exclusion are not visible or dramatic—men in white coats dragging people away—but quiet, insidious: We flunk out and drop out. We fail to get tenure. We take jobs as adjuncts rather than tenure-track faculty. We transfer schools; we find a way to get a job or a degree elsewhere. Or not. Earlier, I said that mental disabilities are better understood in terms of variety and difference rather than "yes/no" diagnoses. That's true; but another truth exists alongside, which is that, in the institutional terms of academic discourse, a sharp rhetorical divide exists between those who are allowed in and those who are not. The fondly regarded "absent-minded" or "quirky" professor is a noticeable figure, but less noticeable is the student with severe depression who drops out of school; the adjunct with autism who never manages to navigate a tenure-track job interview successfully; or the independent scholar whose written works are widely cited but who cannot adhere to the social requirements of teaching in a classroom.

Those of us who do function successfully in academe tend to pass much of the time. Sadly, the necessity of passing for survival perpetuates the conventional view of academe as an "ivory tower"—an immaculate location humming with mental agility and energy, only occasionally threatened (from the outside) by the destructive force of insanity. Recently, this destructive force is often represented as a violent student or faculty member who is assumed to have gone mentally haywire, like a bad cog in an otherwise smoothly operating machine. But things are going to change, not least because those with atypical minds are entering academe in unprecedented numbers. (Or, as some arguments suggest, we are simply being noticed more often.) According to the U.S. Department of Education, in the year 2003–4, 22 percent of students with disabilities in college reported having "mental illness or depression"; 7 percent reported learning disabilities; and 11 percent reported attention deficit disorder ("Profile" 133). Results published in the *Archives of General Psychiatry* put the numbers even higher: according to analysis of data from the 2001–2 National Epidemiologic Survey on Alcohol and Related Conditions, nearly half (46 percent) of college students reported having experienced some psychiatric disorder in the year the survey was conducted (Blanco et al.).[6] Meanwhile, between 1994 and 2004, the percentage of students in K–12 schools labeled as having autism rose 525 percent (Monastersky).[7] Indeed, in particular locations, things *are* changing, and often for the better, as shown by programs such as "College Camp," which is designed to introduce students with intellectual differences to college life (Sunderland). This is a book about the violence of exclusion, but also about the ongoing negotiations and successes achieved by academics with mental disabilities—not through heroic feats of "overcoming," but through microrebellions, new forms of access and cooperation, a gradual reshaping of what academe is and might be.

My aim in this book is to use the activism and theory of disability studies to argue for changes to the ways that academic discourse is understood, taught, written, and evaluated. I believe that DS has much to offer academic discourse, ranging from our ways of understanding classroom practices, to our ways of gathering (at conferences and meetings), to our communication with audiences who have a stake in our work. Such audiences include students, families of students, legislators and public officials, alumni of colleges and universities, and, of course, instructors and professors—all of us who are concerned, one way or another, with the life of the mind. One of my grounding assumptions is that *school matters*—how we learn, how we teach, how we work to develop new ideas that point toward a better society for all.

Why academic discourse in particular? In part, this is my focus because I have a personal stake in it. I am a professor, and I have observed firsthand how difficult it can be to negotiate academe with a disorderly mind. But there is a deeper urgency to this project as well: I perceive a theoretical and material schism between academic discourse and mental disabilities. In other words, I believe that these two domains, *as conventionally understood,* are not permitted to coexist. Academic discourse operates not just to omit, but to abhor mental disability—to reject it, to stifle and expel it. For thousands of years academe has been understood as a bastion of reason, the place in which one's rational mind is one's instrument. But what does that mean for those of us with atypical (some would say "impaired" or "ill") minds who work, learn, and teach in this location? In order to answer this question, we need to unpack not only the practices that characterize academic discourse, but also the attitudes and ways of knowing that underlie those practices.

Catherine Prendergast has asked, "Does some kind of al/chemical transformation need to occur before the mentally ill can be heard? And in whom does it need to take place?" ("Rhetorics" 203). Her question inspires me to follow with another: What transformation would need to occur before those who pursue academic discourse can be "heard" (which I take to mean "respected"), not *in spite of* our mental disabilities, but *with* and *through* them? What would have to happen to the dominant understanding of academic discourse, driven as it is by Aristotelian notions of rationalism, and largely "head-centered" (Garland-Thomson, "Shape" 120)? In the rest of this book, I examine the discursive processes by which academic discourse abhors mental disability. I also discuss ways that persons with mental disabilities *have* gained what Prendergast calls "rhetoricity" ("Rhetorics" 202) in various genres and spaces—through defiant writings, small victories, and our simple daily survival—thus pointing a way toward a more inclusive, and thereby enriched, academe.

My purpose is not only to offer new insights into the rhetoricity of mentally disabled people, but also into ways that we might reconstruct "normal" academic discourses to become more accessible for all. Far from being an altruistic project, this is an effort that will strengthen our current system of academic discourse generally, for ableism impairs all of us. Ableism contributes to the construction of a rigid, elitist, hierarchical, and inhumane academic system. We have already heard many calls for ways that this system should be overhauled. Adjusting our practices for the thoughtful inclusion of mental disabilities will improve the ways all of us *treat* one another (pun intended). Put another way, I am not arguing that mentally disabled persons can measure up to current "standards" of academic discourse. I am arguing that academic discourse needs to measure up to us.

Naming and Definition

Who am I talking about? So far I've used a variety of terms to denote impairments of the mind, and I haven't yet exhausted the list. Contemporary language available includes *psychiatric disability, mental illness, cognitive disability, intellectual disability, mental health service user* (or *consumer*), *neurodiversity, neuroatypical, psychiatric system survivor, crazy,* and *mad.* "No term in the history of madness is neutral," Geoffrey Reaume argues, "not *mental illness, madness,* or any other term" (182). Moreover, as Ian Hacking has pointed out, particular names may thrive in a particular "ecological niche"—for instance, the intersection of the diagnosis "neurasthenia" with nineteenth-century French stories of the "Wandering Jew" (2, 120) or the diagnosis "drapetomania," applied to African American slaves who attempted to escape (Jackson 4). Keeping this dynamism in mind, the following analysis does not aim to accept some terms and discard others. Rather, I want to clarify the different areas they map and show that each does particular kinds of cultural work in particular contexts. Although I use *mental disability* as my own term of choice, I continue to use others as needed, and my overall argument is for deployment of language in a way that operates as inclusively as possible, inviting coalition, while also attending to the specific texture of individual experiences. In doing so, I follow the urging of Tanya Titchkosky, who argues that the aim of analyzing language about disability should not be to mandate particular terms but rather "to examine what our current articulations of disability are saying in the here and now" ("Disability" 138). The problem of naming has always preoccupied DS scholars,[8] but acquires a particular urgency when considered in the context of disabilities of the mind, for often the very terms used to name persons with mental disabilities have explicitly foreclosed our status *as* persons. Aristotle's famous declaration that man is a rational animal (1253a; 1098a) gave rise to centuries of insistence that to be named mad was to lose one's personhood.

Mad is a term generally used in non-U.S. contexts, and has a long history of positive and person-centered discourses. MindFreedom International, a coalition of grassroots organizations, traces the beginning of the "Mad Movement" to the early 1970s, and reports on "Mad Pride" events that continue to take place in countries including Australia, Ghana, Canada, England, and the United States. MindFreedom and other groups organize activist campaigns, sponsor exhibits and performances, and act as forums and support networks for their thousands of members. *Mad* is less recognizable in the United States, which can be to its advantage, since its infrequency helps detach it from implication in medical and psychiatric industries. In addition, *mad* achieves a broad historical sweep. Psychiatry, with its interest in brains, chemistry, and drugs, arose only in the last couple of centuries; however, writings on madness can be found in pre-Socratic discourse, and their historical progression through centuries spans medicine, philosophy, and literature, as Allen Thiher shows in *Revels in Madness: Insanity in Medicine and Literature.*

> The center of our discourses on madness has had many names: *thymos, anima,* soul, spirit, self, the unconscious, the subject, the person. Whatever be the accent given by the central concept, access to the entity afflicted with madness is obtained through a language game in which these concepts or names play a role, organizing our experience of the world even as the world vouchsafes criteria for correct use of these notions. (3)

Thiher does not discuss at length his choice of *mad,* but it is evident from the far-reaching scope of his study that this term achieves a flexibility that *mental illness* and *cognitive disability* do not: it unites notions of that "central concept" through time and across cultures. As with *queer,* the broad scope of *mad* carries the drawback of generality but also the power of mass.

Many persons in the mad movement identify as psychiatric system survivors. According to MindFreedom, psychiatric system survivors are "individuals who have personally experienced human rights violations in the mental health system." A more inclusive term is *consumer/survivor/ex-patient* (*c/s/x*). Drawing upon the work of Linda J. Morrison, Bradley Lewis argues that this term "allows a coalition among people with diverse identifications" while also indicating that the relationship between the three positions is neither exclusive nor linear (157). Lewis goes on to suggest that we might add *patient* as well, making the abbreviation into a quatrad (p/c/s/x), to represent the fact that some persons within the psychiatric system are forced into this objectified and passive role (157).

When I first encountered the term *survivor,* I felt hesitant. It seemed to have unsettling similarities to "cure": a survivor, I thought, implicitly had *had* a traumatic experience and come out the other side. This doesn't describe my experience. I make regular use of the psychiatric system, and I consider myself the agent and director of my treatments; for example, I interviewed and discarded psychiatrists until I found one who agrees with my approach to my bodymind.[9] However, there is no avoiding the fact that he, not I, wields the power of the prescription pad. In addition, I possess the economic and cultural privilege that permits me to try out and reject various caregivers, a privilege not open to many in the c/s/x group. And finally, like any "patient," I am subject to my caregivers' power over information. For example, when my psychiatrist and my therapist conferred and arrived at one of my diagnoses, they chose not to share that diagnosis with me until some months later (their stated reason being that I had been in the midst of a crisis and was not ready to process the information). As it happens, I think they made an appropriate decision, but the fact remains that regardless of what I thought, the outcome would have been the same; I had no say in the matter.

In her ethnographic study *Talking Back to Psychiatry,* Linda J. Morrison interviewed activists in the c/s/x movement, which she defines as "people who have been diagnosed as mentally ill and are engaged in different forms of 'talking back' to psychiatry and the mental health system," as well as allies including "dissident mental health professionals, lawyers, advocates, and family members" (ix). Morrison found that they made use of the term *survivor* in various ways, and that a "heroic survivor narrative" is deeply influential in the movement, both through published accounts (such as Kate Millett's *The Loony-Bin Trip*) and in individuals' processes of identity formation vis-à-vis psychiatric discourse (101). Participants' survivor narratives "exist in a range of intensity, from high drama to muted skeptical observations" (129), but the narrative as a whole, Morrison argues, plays a crucial role in the movement, helping to build solidarity and empower resistant voices. Significantly, this narrative, and the term *survivor,* have also been singled out for denigration by critics (Morrison 152–53).

My own thinking on *psychiatric system survivor* was deepened when I discussed it with my colleague Petra Kuppers. One evening at a conference, sitting on the bed in her hotel room and chewing over my thoughts, I said that I didn't feel I "survived" the psychiatric system so much as worked within it, negotiating and resisting as I went. "But," Petra said simply, "that *is* survival." Her insight has shifted my view of the term: rather than thinking of a survivor as one who has undergone and emerged from some traumatic experience (such as incarceration in a mental institution), it can also denote one who is actively and resistantly involved with the psychiatric system on an ongoing basis.

Mental illness introduces a discourse of wellness/unwellness into the notion of madness; its complement is *mental health,* the term of choice for the medical community as well as insurance companies and social support services. This well/unwell paradigm has many problems, particularly its implication that a mad person needs to be "cured" by some means. One material consequence of this view is that mental health insurance operates on a "cure" basis, demanding "progress" reports from therapists and social workers, and cutting off coverage when the patient is deemed to have achieved a sufficiently "well" state. For instance, although the American Psychiatric Association recommends that persons with my diagnoses remain in long-term talk therapy, my insurance company (CIGNA) determined in 2006 that I was "well enough" and terminated my mental-health coverage, except for brief pharmaceutical consultations with my psychiatrist. During a months-long battle with the "physician reviewer" employed by CIGNA, my therapist's and psychiatrist's requests for continued coverage (which, according to CIGNA's rules, I was not permitted to make directly) were repeatedly turned down. Ultimately, my therapist was informed that the decision would stand unless I "actually attempt[ed] suicide," at which point I would be deemed unwell enough to resume therapy. This "well/unwell" paradigm reflects the larger tendency of American medical systems to intervene in "problems" rather than practice a more holistic form of care.

However, an advantage of *mental illness* is that it can be allied with the substantial—and sometimes contentious—conversation within DS on the intersections between illness and disability. In a 2001 *Hypatia* article, "Unhealthy Disabled: Treating Chronic Illnesses as Disabilities," Susan Wendell points out that activists in the disability rights movement in the United States have often sought to "distinguish themselves from those who are ill" (18). This has led to a schism between those she calls the "healthy disabled," whose impairments "are relatively stable and predictable for the foreseeable future" (19), and those who are chronically ill. Because those with chronic illnesses are often exhausted, in pain, or experiencing mental confusion, their very identities as activists come into question:

> Fluctuating abilities and limitations can make people with chronic illnesses seem like unreliable activists, given the ways that political activity in both disability and feminist movements are structured. . . . Commitment to a cause is usually equated to energy expended, even to pushing one's body and mind excessively, if not cruelly. (25)

Wendell acknowledges that "healthy disabled" and "unhealthy disabled" are blurry categories: a person with cerebral palsy, for example, may also experience exhaustion, pain, or mental confusion; indeed, a person with a physical impairment may also have a chronic illness. Usually, however, "disabled" implicitly means "healthy disabled," and full inclusion of the unhealthy disabled must involve "changes in the structure, culture, and traditions of political activism," with new attitudes toward "energy and commitment, pace and cooperation" (Wendell 26). As yet, such changes are largely unrealized. Consider the last conference you attended: did events run from 9:00 a.m. until late at night? Consider the "tenure clock," or activist efforts that call for attendance in public places for hours at a time: do such occasions assume each participant will have the ability to meet people, interact, and function for hours on end? Consider the persons who did not attend. Do you know who they are?

Andrea Nicki's theory of psychiatric disability picks up Wendell's point about energy and health, but reshapes it to critique the implicitly rational mind of the "good" disabled person—or, as Quintilian might have put it, the "good disabled person speaking well" (see Brueggemann, *Lend*). Not only must this person be of rational mind, Nicki argues; he must also adhere to a "cultural demand of cheerfulness," which is particularly insidious because in some cases—for a person with depression, for example—this would involve not just an attitude *toward* his illness but a direct erasure *of* his illness (94). Like Wendell, Nicki calls for redesign of our social and work environments, emphasizing the importance of interdependence as a means to achieve this goal. Anne Wilson and Peter Beresford have argued that the project will be difficult, and will involve not just surface-level changes, but a full reworking of the social model of disability (145).

One part of this reworking will be the acknowledgment that, although discursive alliances can be drawn between physical and mental illness, important differences exist as well. For example, while members of the disability rights movement, including myself, proudly call ourselves "disabled," many members of the c/s/x movement view the term *disabled* with more suspicion. In the view of the c/s/x movement, when psychiatry assigns a diagnosis of "mental illness" to a person, that person is marked as permanently damaged, and as one whose rights may be taken away—unless, of course, she complies with psychiatry's requirements for "care," which may include medication, incarceration, or electroshock. Morrison makes this point by contrasting psychiatric diagnosis with the diagnosis of a cold:

> In modern psychiatry, a person who has been diagnosed with a serious and persistent mental illness (SPMI) is rarely considered "cured" or completely free of illness. The implied expectation is that mental illnesses are chronic. They may remit but they are likely to recur. Compare, for example the yearly cold symptoms with congestion and cough that many people experience, followed by recovery to a "normal" state. In psychiatric illness, recovery from the symptoms would not be considered the end of the problem. The likelihood of a return to a symptomatic state, with resultant need for medical intervention, would be assumed . . . [A] former patient is always expected to become a future patient and the sick role is ongoing. In fact, if a patient believes otherwise, this can be considered a symptom of exacerbated illness. (5)

This paradox, in which belief of one's own wellness may *in itself* be considered evidence of unwellness, lies at the heart of psychiatric diagnosis. To accept the psychiatric profession's definition of oneself as sick is considered a key move toward getting well; the technical term for acceptance of a psychiatric label is "insight." Although members of the c/s/x movement occupy a range of perspectives, generally the movement resists psychiatry's efforts to place its "patients" into the "sick role." Like Deaf activists, c/s/x activists have much in common with disability activists, but strong differences as well—one of which is the issue of whether or not to self-identify as *disabled.*

One thing c/s/x and disability activists agree upon, however, is the deeply problematic nature of modern psychiatric discourse. Working in concert with the gigantic forces of for-profit insurance companies and the pharmaceutical industry, mainstream psychiatry places ever-increasing emphasis on a biological and positivist definition of mental illness, all while claiming to remain "theory-neutral" (Bradley Lewis 97). However, dissident voices can be heard within psychiatry as well. As Morrison shows, some medical professionals are members of the c/s/x movement. Groups that bring together critical psychologists and psychiatrists and the c/s/x movement have proliferated since the 1990s, and include the Critical Psychiatry Network; Psychology, Politics and Resistance; the Mental Health Alliance; and Radical Psychology Network. This resistant strain of psychiatry is sometimes called *postpsychiatry,* a theory/practice that views "mind" philosophically and socially as well as biologically.

Postpsychiatrist medical philosophers Patrick Bracken and Philip Thomas argue that, once Descartes had established the now-conventional body/mind split (as well as valorization of the individual subject), subsequent theories of mind continued to perpetuate this belief, extending into nineteenth- and twentieth-century psychiatry, which expanded its effects still further. Bracken and Thomas identify three outcomes of this philosophy: the beliefs that "madness is internal"; that madness can be explained neurologically and treated (solely) with pharmaceuticals; and that psychiatrists have the "right and responsibility" to coerce their patients ("Postpsychiatry" 725). Postpsychiatry offers an alternative path, Bracken and Thomas suggest, not by replacing old techniques with new ones, but rather by "open[ing] up spaces in which other perspectives can assume a validity previously denied them"—especially the perspectives of those labeled "mentally ill" ("Postpsychiatry" 727). In addition to centering the agency of mad people, Bracken and Thomas argue for replacing the conventional separation of body and mind with an emphasis on social context, ethical as well as technical (chemical) modes of care, and an end to the claim that coercive "treatments" are applied for "objective" or "scientific" reasons. In a later, briefer article, Bracken and Thomas clarify the relationship of Cartesian dualism to postpsychiatry: human mental life, they argue, is not "some sort of enclosed world residing inside the skull," but is constructed "by our very presence and through our physical bodies" ("Time to Move" 1434).

Bradley Lewis offers an in-depth account of postpsychiatry in *Moving Beyond Prozac, DSM, & the New Psychiatry: The Birth of Postpsychia-*

try. Describing himself as a "hybrid academic," Lewis holds both an M.D. in psychiatry and a Ph.D. in interdisciplinary humanities (ix). From this unusual position, Lewis makes a call for postpsychiatry that is both pragmatic and theoretical: cyborg theory, neurophysiology, and the governing structure of the APA all occupy significant parts of his attention. *Moving Beyond Prozac* describes "a theorized postpsychiatry," which would "take seriously the role of language and power" as well as "work without the pseudo-foundations and pseudo-certainties of modernist science and reason" (17). Lewis does not wish to do away with psychiatrists and clinics, but rather to reform them. The reformed "clinical encounter," for example, would include "not only the modernist values of empirical diagnosis and rational therapeutics but also additional clinical values like ethics, aesthetics, humor, empathy, kindness and justice" (17; see also Lewis, "Narrative Psychiatry"). While pragmatic, Lewis's argument is not individualistic, but aimed at discourses and structures of power. Individual psychiatrists and practices do need to change, Lewis suggests, but the core project is revision of the psychiatric profession to become more democratic, less positivist, less capitalistic, and to include the voices and concerns of *all* its stakeholders, including the c/s/x group.

Neuroatypical and *neurodiverse* mark a broader territory than psychiatric discourse: these terms include all whose brains position them as being somehow different from the neurotypical run of the mill. *Neuroatypical* is most often used to indicate persons on the autism spectrum, including those with Asperger's syndrome (AS), but has also been used to refer to persons with bipolar disorder (Antonetta) and traumatic brain injuries (Vidali). In her "bipolar book" (13) *A Mind Apart,* Susanne Antonetta argues that neurodiversity acts a positive force in human evolution, enabling alternative and creative ways of thinking, knowing, and apprehending the world.

A potential problem with the rhetoric of neurodiversity is that it can read as overly chipper (like a "Celebrate Diversity!" bumper sticker); its optimism can flatten individual difference. However, it also carries a complement, *neurotypical* (or NT), which destabilizes assumptions about "normal" minds and can be used to transgressive effect (Brownlow). For example, Aspies For Freedom has used *NT* to parody the rhetoric of "cure" propagated by the organization Fighting Autism. Until very recently, Fighting Autism published and maintained a graphic called the "autism clock" (fig. 1) which purported to record the "incidence" of autism for persons aged three to twenty-two and the supposed

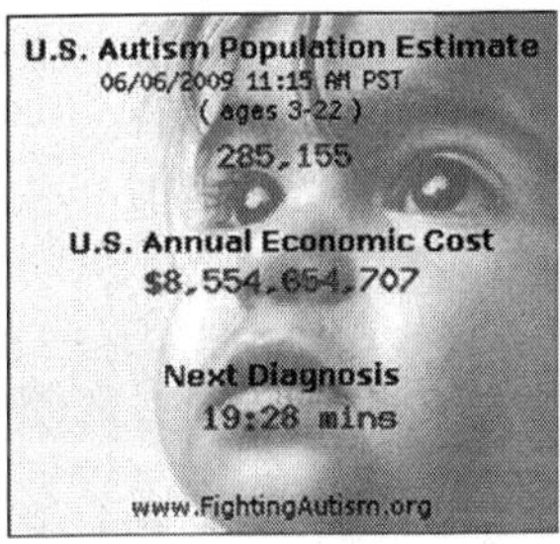

The "autism clock" (captured on June 6, 2009) published by Fighting Autism. This image was taken down in July 2010 in response to activists' protests.

Parody of the "autism clock" published by Aspies For Freedom.

economic "cost" of this incidence.[10] In response, Aspies For Freedom published a parody of the autism clock (fig. 2), which pathologizes neurotypicals and suggests that for the onrush of diagnoses ("1 every minute"), there will be "2 to take them."

While Fighting Autism viewed autism as a disease that must be battled and cured, Aspies For Freedom takes the stance that autism is a form of neurodiversity, that is, of difference, not something that should be eradicated. Although public opinion of autism tends to be dominated by the disease/cure model, resistant voices of neurodiversity have proliferated, especially through web-based communities, blogs, and webtexts (see, for example, Yergeau, "Aut(hored)ism").

Some DS scholars, including Cynthia Lewiecki-Wilson, have called for a coalition of those with psychiatric and cognitive disabilities; she suggests that the term *mental disability* can be used to denote the rhetorical position of both groups:

> For the purposes of this paper, I group mental illness and severe mental retardation under the category *mental disabilities*. Despite the varieties of and differences among mental impairments, this collective category focuses attention on the problem of gaining rhetoricity to the mentally disabled: that is, rhetoric's received tradition of emphasis on the individual rhetor who produces speech/writing, which in turn confirms the existence of a fixed, core self, imagined to be located in the mind. (157)

In other words, according to Lewiecki-Wilson, the notion that one's disability is located in one's mind unites this category, not because such a thing is inherently true, but because persons with these kinds of disabilities share common experiences of disempowerment as rhetors—a lack of what both Prendergast and Lewiecki-Wilson call "rhetoricity." My own struggles for adequate terminology follow Lewiecki-Wilson's call for coalition politics. Although it is important to note the differences between specific experiences, in general I believe we need *both* local specificity *and* broad coalitions for maximum advantage. Persons with impaired bodyminds have been segregated from one another enough.

For a while, I used the term *psychosocial disability.* I like its etymology, the fact that it bumps *psych* (soul) against social context; I like its ability to reach toward both mind and world. Its emphasis on social context calls attention to the fact that psychosocial disabilities can be vividly, and sometimes unpredictably, apparent in social contexts. Although it's common to describe psychosocial disabilities as "invisible," or "hidden," this is a misnomer. In fact, such disabilities may become vividly manifest in forms ranging from "odd" remarks to lack of eye contact to repetitious stimming.[11] Like queerness, psychosocial disability is not so much invisible as it is apparitional, and its "disclosure" has everything to do with the environment in which it dis/appears.[12] *Psychosocial disability* announces that it is deeply intertwined with social context, rather than buried in an individual's brain.

Although *psychosocial* has been used in narrow ways that comply with a medical model of disability, it also has considerable traction within disability studies. In her introduction to a 2002 special issue of *Disability Studies Quarterly,* Deborah Marks argues that a psychosocial perspective can "challenge the disciplinary boundary between psychological and social paradigms." Taking up her point, Patrick Durgin has amplified the term's radical possibilities:

> A "psycho-social formulation" is, in short, the none-of-the-above option in the diagnostic pantheon. It is the excluded middle or liminal space where impairment meets world to become disability. To use clinical language, it does not "present" clinically because it resists being given diagnostic surmise; and yet it won't "pass" as normal. (138)

Durgin goes on to argue that, although *psychosocial* may seem a kind of "golden mean" between medical and social paradigms, it too must undergo critical examination; not least, I would add, because this term can and has been used in medicalized and positivist projects. For example, in the third and fourth editions of the *Diagnostic and Statistical Manual of Mental Disorders,* the authors have made a great show of considering social factors in their new classification of "mental disorders," and also of having involved a broad base of patients and clinicians in developing the manual. Yet, as Lewis points out, that show is largely illusory; the central developers of the landmark DSM-III (and inventors of its categories) numbered just *five persons,* and the overarching rationale for the manual is increasingly positivist and biological. Despite this history, I value the potential of *psychosocial* for reappropriation. In a sense, Durgin is saying to the authors of the DSM, "You want social? We'll give you social."

My appreciation of *psychosocial* has been affirmed by philosopher Cal Montgomery, who pointed out its usefulness in terms of sensory as well as cognitive disabilities, saying, "I do think we need a way of talking inclusively about people for whom access to human interaction is problematic." (See chapter 6 for elaboration of this point.) However, having spent the last couple of years trying this term out—on the page, in conference presentations, at dinner with friends—I've become increasingly uncomfortable with it, because in most cases it seems to provoke puzzlement rather than connection. Explaining my experiences to Cal, I wrote: "I've been using the term 'psychosocial disability' in various settings for over a year—at conferences, in casual conversations, in my writing, etc.—and it seems that, *unless* I'm writing an article where I can fully explain what I'm getting at, people just kind of go blank when I use the term. I have started to feel like, what's the point of using a term that no one gets but me?" Put simply, in most social contexts, *psychosocial* failed to *mean.*

So I have taken another tack. Following Lewiecki-Wilson, these days I'm using *mental disability.* As Lewiecki-Wilson argues, this term can include not only madness, but also cognitive and intellectual dis/abilities of various kinds. I would add that it might also include "physical" illnesses accompanied by mental effects (for example, the "brain fog" that attends many autoimmune diseases, chronic pain, and chronic fatigue). And, as Cal suggests, we should keep in mind its potential congruence with sensory and other kinds of disabilities—that is, its commonalities with "people for whom access to human interaction is problematic."

Finally, while I respect the concerns of those who reject the label *disabled,* I have chosen to use a term that includes *disability* explicitly. In my own experience, claiming disability has been a journey of community, power, and love. Over the last twenty years, I have migrated from being a person who spent a lot of time in hospitals, who was prescribed medications and prodded by doctors, to a person who inhabits a richly diverse, contentious, and affectionate disability community. Let me tell a story to explain this migration: On a December day in 2008, I arrived in a fluorescent-lit hotel room in San Francisco to listen to a panel of scholars talk about disability. I had recently made a long airplane journey and felt off-balance, frightened, and confused. I sat beside disability activist and writer Neil Marcus, and when he saw my face, he opened his arms and offered me a long, hard-muscled hug. That hug, with arms set at awkward angles so we could fit within his wheelchair, with chin digging into scalp and warm skin meeting skin—that, to me, is disability community. Neil may or may not know what it is like to wake with night terrors at age forty, I may or may not know what it feels like to struggle to form words, but the reaching across those spaces is what defines disability for me. We write, we question and disagree, we are disabled. Simi Linton has said of the term *disability* that "We have decided to reassign meaning rather than choose a new name" (31).

And so, in naming myself a crazy girl, neuroatypical, mentally disabled, psychosocially disabled—in acknowledging that I appear (as a colleague once told me) "healthy as a horse" yet walk with a mind that whispers in many voices—I am trying to reassign meaning. In the best of all possible worlds I would refuse to discard terms, refuse to say which is best. I believe in learning the terms, listening to others' voices, and naming myself pragmatically according to what the context requires. I believe that this is language.

Overview of Chapters and a Note on Style

Many of us are mad at school. This includes not only those of us with mental disabilities who work and learn in academic settings; it also includes those who are *mad at school* in the other sense—frustrated, critical, and concerned. Such persons may include clinicians and social workers; the friends and family members of students, staff, and faculty with mental disabilities; and researchers of educational settings or mental disabilities from a great variety of disciplines. In other words, many different people, coming from many different backgrounds, have a stake in this book. For this reason, I have attempted to write in a manner that is accessible to a wide variety of readers. I've tried to imagine audiences including my students; my colleague who specializes in mathematical datamining; my mother (a retired administrator in higher education); my father (a psychology professor); and my friend Sarah, whose youngest son has Down syndrome. This book contains stories about my own experience, because I believe stories are one way of accessing theory. It also contains stories told by others, those I've worked with and engaged in research with. And it does contain a fair amount of "academic jargon"—reviews of studies, speculation on theories, writing by teachers and researchers. I hope that you, as the reader, will pick and choose the parts of this book that are meaningful to you. I want to offer it as a kind of smorgasbord, not a single sustained argument that must be read from beginning to end.

Chapter 1 addresses the question of academic discourse itself—what it is, and how it intersects with the discourses of mental disability. Beginning with classical rhetoric, it explores the significance of topics including "rationality" and "the critical." This chapter also introduces my methodology, which is an adaptation of critical discourse analysis (CDA) and pays particular attention to rich discursive features (Barton) including juxtaposition, interdiscursivity, pronouns, and key terms.

Chapter 2 focuses on the classroom. I begin by introducing my theory of *kairotic space,* which I define as the less formal, often unnoticed, areas of academe where knowledge is produced and power is exchanged. Drawing upon rhetorical theories of *kairos* as well as DS theories of "crip time," I analyze topoi including "presence," "participation," and "resistance." Through close reading of students' writing, as well as teachers' accounts of their classroom experiences, I explore the role these features play in the exclusion of persons with mental disabilities from academic discourse, and consider digital as well as face-to-face pedagogical spaces. The chapter concludes with a series of concrete suggestions for creating more inclusive classroom spaces.

Chapter 3 examines professional kairotic spaces, including conferences and job searches. Such gatherings generally assume various abilities, including the ability to operate in crowds, to navigate unfamiliar geographies, and to cope with fast-moving and often agonistic exchanges (for instance, the question-and-answer session after a conference panel). Drawing upon published guidelines from professional organizations such as the Modern Language Association and American Psychological Association, as well as written accounts by faculty (including non-tenure-track faculty), I analyze these texts in terms of the topoi "collegiality" and "productivity." As with chapter 2, I conclude with concrete suggestions for creating a more inclusive professional infrastructure.

Chapter 4 shifts focus from the everyday spaces of academe to its representation in crisis—specifically, in the context of school shootings. Because the shooting at the University of Alabama–Huntsville occurred just as this book was going to press, my focus is on two other sites—Virginia Tech and Northern Illinois University. However, I stress that the myths and representations that played out in stories of students Seung-Hui Cho and Steven Kazmierczak are being reiterated in stories of faculty member Amy Bishop. This chapter argues that representations of school shootings usually presume that madness was the *cause* of the shooters' actions. But in such representations, madness tends to operate as the *mechanism* through which the shooters are placed in a deviant space separate from everyone else ("normals"). In this way, an attempt is made to construct academe as a "safe zone" that must be protected from the violent incursions of madness. Accounts of Cho and Kazmierczak can be read as medicalized case studies that perpetuate dominant discursive formations in which the topos of security is used to buttress myths of race, class, and violence.

Chapter 5 turns its focus to textual sites of microrebellion in which rhetors with mental disabilities find ways to speak on their own terms. This chapter analyzes *A Mind Apart: Travels in a Neurodiverse World,* by Susanne Antonetta; *Lying: A Metaphorical Memoir,* by Lauren Slater; and "Her Reckoning: A Young Interdisciplinary Academic Dissects the Exact Nature of Her Disease," by Wendy Marie Thompson. Using the rich feature of pronouns as a window into the larger dynamics of power and personhood that play out in these texts, I show that they subvert the conventional imperatives of autobiography by engaging in a strategy I call *counterdiagnosis.* Counter-diagnosis refuses a confessional position and refigures key topoi of autobiographical prose including "rationality," "coherence," and "truth." These texts claim cultural and academic capital not in spite of, but *through,* their authors' neuroatypicality.

Chapter 6 exists because, quite simply, I could not bear to publish this book without careful attention to those who operate outside the privileged borders of academe, whether by choice or by exclusion. The chapter is a small-scale qualitative study involving interviews with three independent scholars, Leah (Phinnia) Meredith, Cal Montgomery, and Ty Power. Given the shocking statistics about academics with mental disabilities—for example, that 86 percent of students with psychiatric disabilities withdraw from college before completing their degrees (Collins and Mowbray 304)—I felt that there were important stories to be told by those who operate from contingent and marginal positions. In addition, I wanted to apply the principles of accessible design to qualitative research, exploring the ways that access must shift and stretch when participants and researcher have mental disabilities. The primary topos investigated in this chapter is independence itself: what does it mean to be an "independent" scholar in a social and academic system rife with the inequities of ableism? Ty, Cal, and Phinnia offer important correctives to my own thinking as well as provocative insights about how academic discourse and qualitative research might be reformed to become more accessible for all.

End Note

Much of this book is a story, or rather, a series of stories. I believe that incorporating narratives of experience is one way to improve access to academic prose. (Also, and admittedly, it's just the way I write.) Among the stories I like best are those that render their own occasions of telling—that is, the ones that explain how and why they came about, what the writer was thinking, what impelled the ideas to come into form. And so I begin my own storytelling with the tale of how this book began.

I can mark the moment with some precision, because—typically—I was taking notes. The moment occurred at the Conference on College Composition and Communication in early April 2008. I was sitting in a chilly conference room at the New Orleans Riverside Hilton for an afternoon session titled "Teaching Writing through the Lens of the Body: Disability in the Composition Classroom." Although the panel title implied a focus on physical disability, I knew from the presentation titles that there would be significant focus on mental disabilities: Muffy Walter Guilfoil was presenting "The Mad Hattress in the Composition Classroom," and George Williams was presenting "Depression, Anxiety and Empathy in First-Year Writing Courses." At some point while listening to the speakers, I opened my notebook and scribbled this:

Psychosocial Disability and Academic Discourse ~~Mental~~ ~~Psychosocial Disability~~

~~Ghosts in the Machine; Acad.~~

~~Rhetorically Reading Mental Illness~~

~~Rhetorical Compositions~~

We are in need of an extended study into the impact of mental disabilities upon academic discourse. Current conversations on issues including ~~university culture~~, the increasing awareness and presence ~~proliferation~~ of disabled students and faculty following the ADA; the problematics of the T&P system; ~~school~~ violence in schools; and the "global turn" toward international trauma? are all ~~key sites for~~ sites in which such disabilities are repeatedly mentioned. Yet we — DS and other disciplines — have not yet fully theorized mental disabilities in relation to historical, social and political models. Nor have we ~~even~~ made much of a dent in the tremendous implications for practice such theorizing would create.

Much of the existing work is narrative; theoretical work is scattered across disciplines.

A focus on mental disabilities calls into question some of our most cherished ~~academ~~ tropes of acad. discourse, including ~~rationality~~, productivity, collegiality & rationality.

The page of notes that became this book. From author's files.

The result is the book you hold in your hands, are reading from a screen, or are listening to. Simply put, I wrote this book because I could not go any longer without writing it.

CHAPTER 1

Listening to the Subject of Mental Disability

Intersections of Academic and Medical Discourses

All our writing is spun out of our guts, whatever kind of writer we are, but we arrange many codes of indirection to avoid letting our guts be seen in our academic articles and books.

—*Donald Wesling,*
"Scholarly Writing and Emotional Knowledge"

What is it about feelings that causes critics to flee?

—*Elspeth Probyn,*
Blush

I teach writing at a four-year college, and in pretty much every class I teach—first-year composition, argumentation, research methods, even creative nonfiction—I use the word *rhetoric* a lot. My students often ask me what it means. I could offer them one of Aristotle's classical definitions—"Rhetoric is the counterpart of dialectic" (1354a), for instance, or "Rhetoric is the ability to discern the available means of persuasion" (1355b). However, I prefer to put my definition in terms that are, in my students' parlance, more *relatable*—so I usually end up saying something like, "Rhetoric is the ways we communicate with each other, not only in writing or by speaking, but also in visual ways, like pictures, or even in subtle ways like the expressions on our faces or the attitudes we bring to each other." I generally have to restrain myself from going on and on about it—emphasizing that I don't *just* mean communication, for instance, or blabbing about the Sophists and Kenneth Burke—because I want my students to focus on one simple feature of my definition: rhetoric is already part of their lives, already something they know about and are skilled in. I hope to lead them away from the notion that rhetoric is necessarily negative ("empty rhetoric," "mere rhetoric") and also to demystify the term. Sometimes I tell them this story: A few days before I began a Ph.D. program called "Rhetoric and Composition," I pulled my dictionary off the shelf and looked up *rhetoric.* I didn't know what it meant either, not really, and I was afraid someone might ask me. My point is that rhetoric is both familiar and unfamiliar; it is the water in which we all swim, but a term rarely used in everyday life. With this in mind, I'll begin by explaining my approach to mental disability, which I call a rhetorical approach, and why it's important to consider mental disabilities in terms of rhetoric.

Rhetoric is a persuasive endeavor, not just in the obvious sense (e.g., trying to convince Dad to give you the car keys for the evening) but in subtler senses as well: Are you coming across as a reliable person? A likable person? Are you *making sense*? Your words, gestures, appearance, the authorities you call upon—do they inspire others? Do they give you credibility? Is your audience motivated to action, or to contemplation, or at least to *receive* your message, to take it seriously? This is rhetoric. So then, what does it mean when a person with a mental disability—schizophrenia, for instance—bumps up against this basic human need to be received, listened to, understood? In "On the Rhetorics of Mental Disability," Catherine Prendergast explains why rhetoric poses a particular problem for persons with mental disabilities: a diagnosis as mentally ill "necessarily supplants one's position as rhetor" (191). Those with mental disabilities, Prendergast argues, exist in a "rhetorical black hole" (198). We speak from positions that are assumed to be subhuman, even nonhuman; and therefore, when we speak, our words go unheeded. "To be disabled mentally," Prendergast concludes, "is to be disabled rhetorically" (202). In concrete terms, this means that persons with mental disabilities are presumed not to be competent, nor understandable, nor valuable, nor whole. We are placed in institutions, medicated, lobotomized, shocked, or simply left to survive without homes. The failure to make sense, as measured against and by those with "normal" minds, means a loss of personhood. Prendergast marks this oppression with the term *rhetoricity* (202): that is, the ability to be received as a valid human subject. Persons with mental disabilities lack rhetoricity; we are rhetorically disabl*ed.*

This might not seem like such a big deal, until we consider the depth and reach of rhetoric in our lives. To lack rhetoricity is to lack all basic freedoms and rights, including the freedom to express ourselves and the right to be listened to. Moreover, as Cynthia Lewiecki-Wilson has shown, some rhetors—including the "severely mentally retarded and mentally ill" (157)—are denied these basic freedoms and rights even by the most liberal measures. Liberal humanists, including those in the disability rights movement, Lewiecki-Wilson argues, fight for the rights of people with many kinds of disabilities, including mobility and sensory impairments. But at the level of rhetoricity, the system breaks down. While the disability rights movement has made tremendous gains in legal and social areas, Lewiecki-Wilson shows, these benefits have accrued to "those disabled who can meet the tests of liberal subjectivity"—which generally does not include those with severe cognitive or psychiatric disabilities (159). And the touchstone for this system of internal oppression, Lewiecki-Wilson suggests, is communication itself:

> Each assumption of liberal subjectivity—autonomy, intention, the essential stability of something called intelligence linked to a core self, and language as reflection of that inner core—is brought to crisis when mentally disabled people have moved from having little or no language toward communicating complexly using collaborative practices such as facilitated communication. (160)[1]

In other words, if one can communicate and *be received* as a valid communicator, one can be included in various humanist projects, including disability rights. However, if one lacks that particular ability, one is generally overlooked—or rather, *obliterated* as a speaking subject, placed into Prendergast's "black hole" (198). Nirmala Erevelles, also writing about facilitated communication, makes a similar point about the intimate relationship between rhetoric and status as human. Echoing Lewiecki-Wilson, Erevelles argues that debates within disability studies are "brought to crisis" when forced to consider "deviant" subjects, including those classified as mad, for such subjects upend both "positivist rules" and "humanist rationality" ("Signs of Reason" 53). Thus, if I did take more time to discuss rhetoric with my students, I would say this: Rhetoric is not simply the words we speak or write or sign, nor is it simply what we look like or sound like. It is who we are, and beyond that, it is *who we are allowed to be.*

This brings me to discourse; for if rhetoric governs who we are allowed to be as persons, discourse is a primary tool of that process of government. I draw this argument in part from Michel Foucault, who has defined discourse as "the group of statements that belong to a single system of formation" (*Archaeology* 107), which he amplifies to mean "discursive formation," or statements that are grouped together and "institutionalized, received, used, re-used, combined together, the mode according to which they become objects of appropriation, instruments for desire or interest, elements for a strategy" (*Archaeology* 117). Discourse, in Foucauldian terms, is a web of human phenomena that are plied in an ongoing struggle for power and knowledge, two entities he viewed as so intertwined he often wrote them as one (*power/knowledge*). In his later works, Foucault revised his view of power/knowledge to embrace the term *governmentality,* which he described as part of "a triangle" of power/knowledge entities. Naming the points of the triangle "sovereignty-discipline-government," Foucault argued that this mechanism of power/knowledge "has as its primary target the population and as its essential mechanism the apparatuses of security" ("Governmentality" 102). *Security* here refers not only to more literal and explicit instances of security, such as the moves toward "campus security" described in chapter 4; it also refers to a "web of social control" plied by the modern state that "generate[s] an increasing specification of individuality" ordered around the concept of normality (Tremain, "Foucault" 6). One effect of governmentality, therefore, is the creation and maintenance of the disabled subject—the figure around whom structures including asylums, "assistive" technologies, and telethons are constructed (Tremain, "Foucault" 5). In this book, I pay attention to the structures that govern educational contexts, including not only those structures explicitly marked as being "for" disabled people, such as "special education," but also those that are implicitly marked as being "for" everyone, including the "normal" operations of spaces such as classrooms, conferences, and academic writing.

Foucault has been criticized for his rather nihilistic view toward power/knowledge and the limp role he assigns to subjects, although some DS scholars have argued that his later works offer a more nuanced form of agency through theories of ethics (see, for example, Allan). It has also been suggested that, while Foucault identified the shift of medical discourse toward the domain of empirical clinical "findings," he underestimated its significance for individual patients—perhaps because of his skepticism about individual agency in the first place. For example, H. Tristram Engelhardt Jr. argues that Foucault discounts the importance of patients' power to define their own ailments, which was degraded by the rise of medical discourse, as their complaints "came to be understood as bona fide problems only if they had a pathoanatomical or pathophysiological truth value" (183). Other critics, such as Bradley Lewis, use Foucauldian theory to argue that we can, as individual subjects, wreak change even within powerful discursive formations such as psychiatric discourse. Lewis argues that "there is always room to shape, reshape, and resist within discursive formations" (46).

One such resistant strain of theory/methodology, which grew alongside Foucauldian theory, is critical discourse analysis (CDA). Norman Fairclough's theory of discourse, in contrast to Foucault's, is explicitly activist:

> This is not a matter of reducing social life to language, saying that everything is discourse—it isn't. . . . I see discourse analysis as "oscillating" between a focus on specific texts and a focus on what I call the "order of discourse," the relatively durable social structuring of language which is itself one element of the relatively durable structuring and networking of social practices. (*Analysing* 2–3)

For Fairclough, then, attention to discourse is foremost an *activist* goal. Identifying the workings of governmentality through texts[2] is not an end in itself, but rather a means to intervene in such practices to effect social change. I argue that CDA is a theory/method particularly well suited to DS for a number of reasons, including their shared investment in recognizing social relations in terms of power and difference as manifested through language (Price, "Access Imagined"). Ruth Wodak has explained this investment as follows: "Power is about relations of difference, and particularly about the effects of differences in social structures . . . CDA takes an interest in the ways in which linguistic forms are used in various expressions and manipulations of power" (11). Like CDA, DS concerns itself with human difference, and emphasizes the ways that people with disabilities are ostracized, medicalized, heroized, and otherwise pushed out of the societally defined space of the "normal." And like CDA, DS has a long history of interest in the ways that language is used to construct formations of power and difference.

In my analysis of academic discourses, I will rely on methods drawn from CDA, not often in the microlinguistic style applied by Fairclough and others, but in a broader way that draws upon Ellen Barton's theory of discourse analysis. Barton defines discourse analysis as follows:

> Discourse analysis involves looking at texts, inductively identifying their rich features and salient patterns, and then using these features and patterns as examples in an argument in support of some generalization(s) or claim(s) about the meaning relations between features, texts, and their contexts. (23)

Barton further clarifies what she means by "rich features" by defining them as "linguistic features that point to the relation between a text and its context" (23). In other words, a rich feature offers a cue to the reader, who can then make a connection between a text and the context from which it arises. The use of *wheelchair-bound* versus *wheelchair user* is an example of one such rich feature: *wheelchair-bound,* usually adjectival, imagines a person who is confined to the wheelchair, "bound" to it, while *wheelchair user* explicitly names the person ("user") and deploys *wheelchair* as a single, nonconfining, feature of that person.[3] Such linguistic differences may seem subtle until one is in a position to begin noticing how ubiquitously wheelchair users are described in popular discourse as being "bound" or "confined" to their wheelchairs.

Barton emphasizes that this form of analysis, even at its most qualitative, does not consist of simply trawling through a text and picking out features at will. Rather, a systematic inductive process must govern the selection of rich features. Such features must possess, according to Barton, both "linguistic integrity and contextual value" (24). That is, they must appear often enough in the text to warrant the formation of generalizations, and they must contribute in a "significant" (24) manner to the way that text makes meaning. In my own analyses, I pay close attention to linguistic formations including pronouns, active or passive voice, genre, definition, intertextuality, and interdiscursivity, applying to each of Barton's criteria for rich feature analysis. Analysis of these formations has led to the identification of topoi including rationality, criticality, presence, participation, productivity, collegiality, security, coherence, truth, and independence.

Generally speaking, the topoi I am interested in circulate around theories of *reason.* The rise of academic discourse in the United States has been deeply enmeshed with the Enlightenment ideal of reason, which in turn is steeped in classical rhetorical dualisms such as right/wrong and good/bad. From Plato to Aristotle and on through modernist rhetorics, descriptions of rhetoric tend to presuppose a particular kind of rhetor—what Quintilian called the "good man speaking well."[4] This view assumes that goodness, rightness (in the sense of moral rightness), and truth are universal and inseparable, as in Cicero's announcement, "There is a true law, a right reason, conformable to nature, universal, unchangeable, eternal, whose commands urge us to duty, and whose prohibitions restrain us from evil." Now, the Sophists, most famously Isocrates, took a somewhat wilder view of "truth," and by no means is classical Greek rhetoric the only tradition that merits attention (see "Beyond Greco-Roman Rhetorics"; Glenn, *Rhetoric Retold;* Lipson and Binkley). However, it is generally agreed that contemporary U.S. education has been heavily, if not primarily, influenced by the dominant Greek rhetorical theories dating from Plato and beyond. An often-cited example of the valorization of reason comes from Aristotle's *Nichomachean Ethics.* In his introduction to that volume, Jonathan Barnes glosses *eudaimonia,* or "happiness," as a function of reason: a happy man "frequently performs with some success the most perfect of typically human tasks . . . [which is] rational activity" (xxxiv). I want to pause here for a moment and unpack this claim, for its implications are complex. At first glance, it seems to be a simple valorization of reason as abstract entity. However, more careful study indicates that Aristotle's "reason" can be interpreted more flexibly. And yet, I argue, even in our more postmodern readings of Aristotle's reason, the omission of rhetors with mental disabilities continues to persist.

Aristotle's statement could be taken as an argument for a dry, abstract form of reason (more like Plato's), but numerous scholars have argued that Aristotle's notion of "reason" is in fact more complicated. This is the case made by James S. Baumlin and Tita French Baumlin in "Psyche/Logos: Mapping the Terrains of Mind and Rhetoric." They suggest that, far from being separate realms, rhetoric and psychology are deeply implicated with one another: Platonic dialogue is a form of "healing through language" (247), and an Aristotelian appeal to ethos is "a radically psychological event situated in the mental processes of audience" (251). The authors' eventual point is that, along with the three traditional rhetorical appeals outlined by Aristotle (*ethos, pathos,* and *logos*), we ought to pay attention to a fourth, *mythos,* a community-based form of truth/persuasion, which gives due consideration to the role of audience and "reaches beyond conventional logic" (257). *Mythos* would allow us to move beyond conventional notions of reason as logical proof and to recast it as "a means of participation in the rhythm of the universe, its contrasting joys and pains" (257). It would seem, according to the history presented by Baumlin and Baumlin, that reason and emotion reside together quite comfortably, and hence, that there is ample space to theorize rhetoricity for those with mental disabilities.

However, as I read "Psyche/Logos," I am most struck by the fact that this analysis retains one fixed point: namely, that all rhetors will possess some baseline of *health,* whether that be defined as mental health or, in more classical terms, "the health of the soul" (Baumlin and Baumlin 247). It is true that Aristotle's version of health requires a "harmonious" relationship among rationalism, emotionalism, and appetite (248). That is, a careful reading of Aristotle does give some space to emotion and community discourse as legitimate factors in rhetoric. But even as Baumlin and Baumlin celebrate the power of mythos to move beyond a conventional model of individual rationalism, this model remains, as they put it, "a healing story" (257). The possibility that a mind might be radically *unhealed,* unwell (in conventional terms), that it might be crazy or neuroatypical—this possibility is not offered space even in the expanded version of rhetorical appeals suggested by "Psyche/Logos." Thus, although the boundaries of rhetoric are broadened by Baumlin and Baumlin to allow more space for rhetorics of emotion, "emotion" is carefully circumscribed in a way that disallows the mad subject. Rhetoricity is still denied.

Much contemporary work on classical rhetoric continues the habit I have identified in "Psyche/Logos." Although scholars have earnestly tried to include consideration of emotion, irrationality, and even specific mental disabilities (such as post-traumatic stress disorder), into their analyses, this fixed point seems to persist: rhetoric exists as a healing property; its role is to socially integrate the mad subject; and "healing" *is* social integration. For example, the definition of "healing" offered by the editors of *Writing and Healing* is "change from a singular self, frozen in a moment of unspeakable experience, to a more fluid, more narratively able, more socially integrated self" (Anderson and MacCurdy, "Introduction" 7). Note the elision of *narratively able* with *socially integrated.* This definition suggests that social integration is key to narrative ability, which would seem to foreclose the possibility of a mad rhetor, for what is madness but a radical disunity of perception from that held by those who share one's social context? Despite many attempts to refigure rhetoric through multiracial, feminist, poststructural, sophistic, and other theories, the underlying presumption of reason-as-normality has remained largely unchanged. Even when our stated beliefs would urge us to do otherwise, we continue to practice academic discourse (in classrooms, in writing, at conferences) as a project of social hygiene. Our practice continues to circulate around the imperatives to diagnose, cure, contain, or expel the mad subject.

Rhetorical Approaches to Psychiatric Discourse

We are accustomed to thinking of medical rhetoric as a realm far removed from academic rhetoric—except in the appearance of "scientific" findings, "objectively" presented in journals such as *Science* or *Nature*. Psychiatric rhetoric, as a subcategory of medical rhetoric, is governed away from academic life with particular care. Perhaps because of the popular conception that unsound minds have no place in the classroom, academic and especially pedagogical research seem almost obsessed with the diagnosis of sound and unsound minds. The impulse underlying this predilection, I argue, is a desire to protect academic discourse as a "rational" realm, a place where emotion does not intrude (except within carefully proscribed boundaries), where "crazy" students are quickly referred out of the classroom to the school counseling center, and where "unstable" or "difficult" teachers are triaged out by means of the tenure-and-promotion system. This impulse is explored in more detail in the two following sections. First, however, we must understand the ways that psychiatric discourse *itself* facilitates this divide.

Psychiatric discourse positions itself as natural, scientific, and objective, a system through which human minds may be reliably measured as "crazy" or "normal," and through which human bodies can therefore be sorted into their appropriate spaces: the educational institution or the mental institution. Yet it is, like any communicative endeavor, a rhetorical project: as J. Fred Reynolds argues, "As more and more people are declared to have and are then treated for an ever-expanding list of mental illnesses, more and more will become dependent on and vulnerable to the rhetoric, particularly the recorded rhetoric, of the mental health care professions" (152). It is crucial to understand psychiatric discourse *as* a rhetorical endeavor, not least because this discourse often claims to operate in ways that transcend rhetorical concerns such as context and audience. I focus my discussion of psychiatric discourse upon the *Diagnostic and Statistical Manual of Mental Disorders,* a text whose importance to the field of mental health "cannot be overstated" (Aho 245). I argue that this manual's claims to objectivity, its implication with capitalist structures including the pharmaceutical and insurance industries, and especially its efforts to conceal the rhetorical processes of its own revision and publication, help sustain the complementary impulse from teachers and scholars across the disciplines to regard mental disability as something radically "other" to everyday life, including the everyday life of university culture. To put it in simpler terms, both psychiatrists and teachers are interested in governing the mad subject in academic discourse, and the two groups' efforts feed each other.

The DSM was first published in 1952 by the American Psychiatric Association. Its appearance was fueled by American psychiatrists serving during World War II, who advocated outpatient treatment of servicemen and veterans. The manual has since undergone a series of revisions, each designated by a Roman numeral: DSM-II (1968), DSM-III (1980), and DSM-IV (1994).[5] A new revision, DSM-5, is expected in 2013. Each revision includes changes to the system of classifying mental disorders, sometimes dramatic ones; one of the most often-cited shifts between DSM-II and DSM-III was the removal of homosexuality as a mental disorder (although it was replaced, at the time of that specific 1973 revision, by the diagnosis of "Sexual Orientation Disturbance"). Most analysts agree that the publication of DSM-III was a watershed event. According to the manual's authors, "DSM-III introduced a number of important methodological innovations, including explicit diagnostic criteria, a multiaxial system, and a descriptive approach that *attempted to be neutral* with respect to theories of etiology" (DSM-IV-TR xxvi; emphasis added). However, critics of the manual place this revision in strikingly different terms. According to a discourse analysis conducted by Lucille Parkinson McCarthy, a rhetorician, and Joan Page Gerring, a psychiatrist, DSM-III "represents not an incremental development of its two predecessors but, rather, a dramatic shift in psychiatry toward the biomedical model and away from competing models, which dominated the field before 1980" (157). In other words, revisions of DSM have represented an increasing adherence to a model of mental disability as a measurable and biological phenomenon, and DSM-III was a turning point in this process.[6]

The outcomes of this turn have been dramatic. Mitchell Wilson's 1993 critique points out two important ones: first, the power base of psychiatry shifted, with researchers replacing clinicians as the most powerful voices in the psychiatric profession (400); and second, DSM-III's claim of objectivity allowed the manual to begin to seem "natural—not made by human hands" (408). Citing Habermas, Wilson argues that DSM-III's claim of objectivity "serves, rhetorically, as the most persuasive argument on its own behalf" (408). This second tactic has been critiqued by numerous philosophers of science, including Sandra Harding: by setting itself up as "objective" or "neutral," scientific discourse provides a simultaneous argument for its stance while also insulating itself against the possibility of alternative arguments. Donna Haraway calls this strategy a "god-trick" (189), and Thomas Nagel the "view from nowhere": that is, it claims a gaze that comes from nowhere and everywhere all at once, omniscient and unlocatable, and therefore shielded from any countergaze.[7]

Wilson's analysis, published in the *American Journal of Psychiatry*, is relatively mild; critiques from outside psychiatry are more pointed. For example, Anne Wilson and Peter Beresford, identifying as psychiatric system survivors, state flatly that "From our perspectives, having been on the receiving end of [psychiatry's] diagnostic process, the categorization and classification of our mental and emotional distress has served no useful purpose" (146). McCarthy and Gerring argue that DSM-III represents not only a shift toward the biomedical model, but also "works to maintain the dominance of psychiatry among mental health disciplines [and] enhances its prestige in relation to other medical specialties" (186). Aho emphasizes the "market forces" involved in the revision of DSM-III, tracing the relationship between the manual's biomedical approach and its "marriage" to the pharmaceutical industry and the concomitant growth of privately "managed" health care in the United States (244). Lennard J. Davis, writing on obsession, calls DSM an "obsessive text" (10) and notes that the in-group of researchers on obsessive-compulsive disorder (OCD) are shored up by each other's material privileges—that is, they publish, cite, and fund one another—and are also "well-funded by the drug companies" that sell drugs that purport to "cure" obsession (220). One of the most sustained and radical readings comes from Bradley Lewis. In *Moving Beyond Prozac, DSM, and the New Psychiatry*, Lewis summarizes both the "bad science" (102–5) and "bad rhetoric" (105–9) that went into the making of DSM-III, referring, in the latter analysis, to "psychiatry as an agent of normalization, state control, and multicultural oppression" as well as to its implication in the "pharmaceutical industry boondoggle" (109).

And yet, Lewis argues, bad science and bad rhetoric aren't even the worst problems. The ugliest part of the DSM-III story is "the people involved," those who practiced what Lewis calls "bad politics" (109). This story is a shocking array of subterfuges and exclusions, with the role of chief villain going to Robert Spitzer, chair of the task force that created DSM-III. Lewis reports that the committee assembled by Spitzer during late 1974 and early 1975 consisted of five psychiatrists who formed an "'invisible college' of like-minded researchers" (112) and "carefully eliminated any people with alternative perspectives," including clinicians (114). The task force quickly made major changes to the manual, including its new emphasis on medicalization and classification, and then, for five years, "covered its tracks" by engaging in a long process of "field trials" that, Lewis maintains, "effectively covered over" the fact that a very small group had already made most of the major ideological and procedural changes (114). The DSM-III, Lewis points out, claims that the field trials involved over 12,000 patients evaluated by about 550 clinicians, and lists hundreds of "contributors" (114). But those involved in the field trials "'tested' the manual according to the rules, norms, and priorities of the initial [five-member] task force" (115). In other words, these "contributors" were "testing" a model that had *already* been radically shifted; they were not involved in the ideological, rhetorical, and clinical shift itself.

From that point, Lewis's story of "bad politics" grows even more disturbing, citing exclusion of psychologists, social workers, and researchers who attempted to bring feminist perspectives to DSM-III. "[P]retty much anyone who was not a privileged, white, male, academic psychiatrist," Lewis concludes, was "systematically snubbed, ignored, denigrated, and dismissed" (115). Looking briefly at DSM-IV and anticipating DSM-5, Lewis argues that we can continue to expect more of the same, with the manual making some changes to content but retaining its "basic scientistic frame and its fundamental power relations" (119). *Moving Beyond Prozac* offers more than this scathing critique, however. In its final chapter, the book turns to an extensive and detailed plan for ways that psychiatry might be refigured to become "a theorized postpsychiatry" (17), a profession that is less coercive and more democratic, one that includes not only all its practitioners but also its "patients" as important and powerful voices. Unfortunately, as Lewis concedes in the book's epilogue, such a revolution "will not occur soon" (165).

The criticisms of DSM presented here are only the tip of the proverbial iceberg. I selected them because their attention to rhetoric and discourse analysis makes them especially salient to my own project, but the total number of DSM criticisms must number in the hundreds, perhaps even in the thousands. And yet, although decades of work have exposed not only the rhetorical nature of psychiatry, but also the dubious agendas of the rhetors who compose its key texts, most teachers and scholars tend to accept psychiatric rhetoric on its own terms: as an objective, benign, and stable authority. References to mental phenomena in academic discourse—"rational" argument, "critical" thinking, "emotional" pedagogies—often use psychiatric discourse as a touchstone, presuming both its authority and its benevolence. As a result, our practices reflect its biases, so that the mad subject in academic discourse is repeatedly diagnosed, "healed," ostracized, fetishized, or expelled.

The Rational (or Critical) Man Speaking Well

In a deeply influential 1982 *College English* article, James A. Berlin offered a taxonomy of pedagogies with reference to the rhetorics of reason. Although his article addresses itself to writing teachers, I believe it can be usefully applied to pedagogies of all kinds, for its subject is not merely writing in the technical sense, but rhetoric in the broader sense of higher education: that is, knowledge manifested through communicative delivery. Berlin's taxonomy identifies four kinds of pedagogies: Neo-Aristotelian (Classicist), Current-Traditional (Positivist), Neo-Platonist (Expressivist), and New Rhetoric. Berlin argues that the first three approaches, each in a different way, understand language as a way to access essential truths. He summarizes their beliefs:

> Classical Rhetoric considers truth to be located in the rational operation of the mind, Positivist Rhetoric in the correct perception of sense impressions, and Neo-Platonic Rhetoric within the individual, attainable only through an internal apprehension. In each case knowledge is a commodity situated in a permanent location, a repository to which the individual goes to be enlightened. (773–74)

As this quotation indicates, Berlin is worried about the prospect of a pedagogy that views knowledge as a "commodity" located in a static place where an individual student can go "to be enlightened" (774). How to break away from that reliance on essential knowledge? The answer, Berlin maintains, is to be a New Rhetorician, one who understands language as the dynamic constructor of the "dialectical interplay between the individual and the world" (774). In other words, an individual does not perceive the world (or himself) and then report those perceptions through language; rather, the language an individual uses constructs his world and himself.

Although current-traditional and positivist approaches still hold great sway in postsecondary education, what Berlin calls the New Rhetorical approach has also gained in influence, especially in practices labeled "critical pedagogy" (discussed in more detail below). I am—under Berlin's taxonomy—a New Rhetorician myself. But I am troubled that Berlin's view of academic discourses seems to keep one point solid: rationality. Although Berlin does not use this term to describe New Rhetoric, his entire theory hinges on the notion that all minds work in basically the same way, albeit with different experiences and points of view. For example:

> In teaching writing . . . we are teaching a way of experiencing the world, a way of *ordering and making sense* of it. As I have shown, subtly informing our statements about invention, arrangement, and even style are assumptions about the nature of reality. (776; emphasis added)

In extolling his method, Berlin takes for granted that the individual rhetor will *be able to* make sense of her world for an audience. Although Berlin attempts to make room for diverse perspectives, by accounting for the social construction of different rhetors' "assumptions about the nature of reality," I argue that this theory nevertheless overlooks the dilemma of "ordering and making sense" faced by rhetors whose worlds may be not simply marked by, but composed of, ways of knowing fundamentally invested in dis/order and non/sense. To illustrate the dilemma Berlin's theory may present to rhetors with mental disabilities, I turn to the dance piece *Invisible in Disabled Country,* written and performed by Kathy Mancuso.

In this piece, Mancuso combines a series of floor-based movements with a dialogue between two interlocutors, both of which she voices while dancing. The first voice is an oppressive questioner, one who demands knowledge. "*Where have you been?*" it says. "*Tell me your story. Account for yourself. What are your symptoms? What are your signs?*" The second voice resists the questioner, crying out at one point, "Sometimes I think the problem is you!" and, at the close of the performance, demanding, "Why do *you* get to ask all the questions?" The moment on which I want to focus is one in which the first voice asks, "*What is your disability, anyway?*" In response, Mancuso, embodying the strengthening resistance of the second voice, rolls onto her back, legs in the air, and shouts directly into her backside: "If I could tell you, it wouldn't be there!"

Katherine Mancuso performs *Invisible in Disabled Country.* Still frame of videotaped performance courtesy of Katherine Mancuso and Lori Teague.

I've taken the time to illustrate this performance-based moment because I believe it, with its combination of movement and dialogue, offers a powerful retort to Berlin's suggestion that any rhetor ought to be able to "order" and "make sense" of her experience for an audience. *Invisible in Disabled Country* suggests that attempting to voice the "truth" of mental disability creates a paradox that is the very opposite of "talking out one's ass." If talking out one's ass means producing fluent, inauthentic rhetoric, then talking *into* one's ass might mean producing rhetoric whose very authenticity destroys its fluency—perhaps even its ability to be voiced at all. Applying this argument to Berlin's notion of rhetoric, I suggest that although Berlin does acknowledge that the truths sought by the New Rhetorical approach should be "the product of individuals calling on the full range of their humanity" (777), he misses the fact that those with mental disabilities are always already defined as nonhuman, by dint of their failure to *make sense.* In other words, he has not considered the possibility that some subjects might lack rhetoricity.

Following the social turn of the 1960s, administrators and teachers of academic discourses began to replace "reason" and "rationality" with "criticality," or "critical thinking," as their highest aim; however, the presumption of a rational subject remained stable. This presumption has received quite a bit of criticism, often from authors taking a feminist or poststructuralist viewpoint. An early critique is Elizabeth Ellsworth's now-classic 1989 article "Why Doesn't This Feel Empowering? Working Through the Repressive Myths of Critical Pedagogy." In this piece, Ellsworth takes critical pedagogy to task on a number of issues, including its belief that "the foundation for classroom interaction is reason" (304). This belief plays out in many ways, including exhortation of students to engage in learning through "sharing" and "dialogue" (310). Ellsworth explains why "sharing" and "dialogue" are more problematic than critical pedagogy generally assumes them to be:

> Dialogue in its conventional sense is impossible in the culture at large because at this historical moment, power relations between raced, classed, and gendered students and teachers are unjust. . . . Conventional notions of dialogue and democracy assume rationalized, individualized subjects capable of agreeing on universalizable "fundamental moral principles" and "quality of human life" that become self-evident when subjects cease to be self-interested and particularistic about group rights. (316)[8]

Ellsworth's point here is that reason itself—at least at the present social and historical moment—is an oppressive construct, played out through seemingly benign imperatives such as "sharing" and "dialogue." The notion that any rhetor, including a student or a professor, can engage in dialogue about oppression presumes that all rhetors share a universal and "reasonable" basis for that dialogue. But, as Ellsworth emphasizes, "all voices in the classroom are not and cannot carry equal legitimacy, safety, and power in dialogue" (317). Nor do all rhetors bring an equal (or rather, equivalent) sense of what concerns are "reasonable," what are "rational" and "appropriate" ways to voice ideas—in short, what sort of human to be in the classroom. Knowledge in academic discourse, Ellsworth argues, should be recognized as "contradictory, partial, and irreducible" (321), but at the time of her article's publication, twenty years ago, the default presumption was that each rhetor would come from a shared rational standpoint.

Does such a presumption still hold? Well, yes and no. While *theories* that challenge rationality in academic discourse abound, everyday *practice* tends to adhere to the presupposition of the rational student (or teacher). In other words, we (the neuroatypical) are still required to pantomime our way through our work, embodying—or enminding—as best we can the "good man speaking well."[9]

A relatively early challenge to the rational subject of academic discourse came from Lester Faigley's *Fragments of Rationality* in 1992. Faigley expresses a concern similar to Ellsworth's: that the "process movement" of writing pedagogy in the 1960s and 1970s was "domesticated" in the 1980s through the continued coupling of rhetoric to rationality and "the preservation of the belief that the student writer is a rational, autonomous individual" (225). Faigley argues that postmodernism might be the key to decoupling rhetoric from rationality, suggesting that we might, instead, take up a view of the writer as an "ethical subject." Ethical subjectivity, Faigley maintains, is an "obligation of rhetoric":

> It is accepting the responsibility for judgment. It is a pausing to reflect on the limits of understanding. It is respect for diversity and unassimilated otherness. It is finding the spaces to listen. (239)

Faigley's notion of the ethical subject offers an alternative to the (presumably) rational, dialoguing/sharing student in the classroom. His suggestion—one that has been considerably elaborated in the last fifteen years—is that networked classrooms and other forms of digital rhetoric might be key to fostering the presence of the ethical, rather than the rational, subject. Yet his exhortation is also fairly vague. It's one thing to call for attention to "limits of understanding" and "unassimilated otherness" (239); it's quite another to attempt to enact this sort of attention in a classroom. The pragmatics of Faigley's "ethical" pedagogy remained for other teacher/scholars to articulate fully.

Two such articulations have come from Amy Lee (*Composing Critical Pedagogies*, 2000) and Krista Ratcliffe (*Rhetorical Listening*, 2005). I've chosen these two texts because both are concerned with everyday classroom practice; both take up the challenge from Ellsworth and Faigley to account for the learning subject through theories other than rational autonomy; and both emphasize "listening" as a key feature of postmodernist critical pedagogy. Each text comes from an important, but distinct, theoretical basis: Lee grounds her argument in the educational theories of critical pedagogy propounded by Freire, Henry Giroux, Peter McLaren, and Jennifer Gore, while Ratcliffe draws upon a wider but largely philosophical or rhetorical spectrum of authorities, announcing that her study "is indebted to [James] Phelan and [Andrea] Lunsford, to [Victor] Vitanza and [Michelle] Ballif, to [Martin] Heidegger, [Jacqueline Jones] Royster, [Alice] Rayner, and [Toni] Morrison" (27). And, most importantly for my project, both studies earnestly attempt to engage difference in academic discourse, paying a great deal of attention to "listening" as a rhetorical strategy. But in doing so, both continue to presume that rhetorical subjects will *be able to* speak from their own experiences, will *be able to*—returning to Berlin's phrase—"make sense." I am heartened and also troubled by this presumption. I must ask: If a student (or teacher) lacks rhetoricity, what happens to this vaunted process of *listening*? Is it possible to listen to the mad subject?

Lee's *Composing Critical Pedagogies* centers upon a theory of "revisioning," which Lee describes as an ongoing process of gaining sociopolitical awareness, "recognizing that one's mind is made up along an array of choices and *why* it is made up this way" (181). Bringing together strategies from process and critical pedagogies, Lee argues that approaches such as peer response and personal narrative can be used as a means to heighten students' awareness of their sociopolitical positions (80). She summarizes her goals as "engaging students in a consideration of their 'selves' and their texts as constructions, foregrounding how they can, to some degree, author those constructions, and a recognition of discourse's role in 'shaping' those constructions" (246). In short, her pedagogy is grounded in the "faith" (93) that the self must be seen in relation to the larger world, to others, to language. This is a self fundamentally grounded in community and interchange.

A passage in *Composing Critical Pedagogies* that exemplifies that faith is Lee's description of a heated exchange in her classroom that she names the "Rap on Rap" (241). This exchange, taking place face-to-face, involved Lee and six students. One student (Jason) argued that rap had no link to violence, and the other five students (Magdalana, Joseph, Albertina, Patrick, and Karen F.) argued that the issue was more complex (241–45). Jason, whom Lee describes a "white American from Long Island" (242), repeatedly interrupted the other students and caused tension in the discussion, despite Lee's having "shot him effectively silencing glance[s]" (245). Afterward, Lee was told by the other students that they felt she had "let him win" and that Jason had failed to "respect" her as the teacher (245). In a later "revisioning" of the "Rap on Rap" (256), Lee suggests that Jason's position as a middle-class white male permitted him to view his position as "seamless"—that is, not fragmented, nor contested, nor irrational (259). Others participating in this discussion, including Karen F., were forced to contend with their own subjectivities precisely because those subjectivities were "Othered" in the classroom, were both apparent and contested. Reflecting on the "Rap on Rap," Lee says she was "unsettled" by her students' criticism of having "let" Jason "win," and that a strategy of listening might provide an alternative to what she saw at the time as a dualistic struggle between her own position and Jason's:

> Magdalena's criticism unsettled me. Should I have enforced more structure onto the conversation? Should I have imposed an interpretation as *the* "truth" at the end of the discussion? The problem is, that at the time the discussion took place, I was conflating these two positions. Rather than considering an array of choices or of roles, I only envisioned two: *either* I could impose order and therefore impose a "truth" *or* I could choose not to intervene directly and hope my own refusal to be interrupted was teaching him [Jason] something. However, I could have imposed structure, evoked my authority as teacher-facilitator, without simultaneously silencing the debate. I could have advocated reciprocity in speaking and listening to one another, without advocating a particular "right" answer. As Magdalena pointed out, I had failed them, not because I did not speak up for her side, but because I didn't require that *everyone* present participate as active listeners while she and the others were speaking. (263)

Through her "revisioning" of this classroom event, Lee arrives at a position that suggests *listening* is as important to critical consciousness as is speaking from one's position. In doing so, she adds a crucial consideration to theories of critical pedagogy: the issue is not simply speaking one's truth, but also receiving others'.

The notion of listening as critical strategy is further developed in Ratcliffe's *Rhetorical Listening,* which offers an extended theory of rhetorical listening, arguing that it involves four primary "moves":

1. Promoting an *understanding* of self and other
2. Proceeding within an *accountability* logic

3. Locating identifications across *commonalities* and *differences*
4. Analyzing *claims* as well as the *cultural logics* within which these claims function. (26)

Like Lee's, Ratcliffe's study focuses on race as a key construct through which rhetorics of listening play out in the classroom.[10] Arguing against the prevalent myths of gender-blindness and race-blindness (5) in classrooms, Ratcliffe suggests that instead, teachers should strive to "lay all gender and race 'cards' on the table in hopes [of] negotiating the existing (mis)perceptions about them and their intersections" (135). This is a thread of rhetorical listening that Ratcliffe names *pedagogical listening* (146), and entails strategies that involve explicit study of constructs such as whiteness, as well as how these constructs intersect with local situations—that is, "our daily lives" (151). Analyzing works by four students with whom Ratcliffe has practiced her strategies for pedagogical listening, Ratcliffe concludes that these essays "represent what students are capable of producing when they listen to how discourses of whiteness are performed by themselves and/or others" (170). Like Lee's study, Ratcliffe's ends on a hopeful note: rhetorical listening offers the possibility of "greater understanding" and "more ethical rhetorical conduct" (171).

I applaud both Lee's and Ratcliffe's efforts to explore concrete possibilities for a postrational classroom, and both studies have strongly affected my own teaching. Yet I am still left with my primary question: What happens to the rhetor who *cannot be* "listened" to—because ze is not present, or fails to participate in discussions, or fails to "make sense" on a neurotypical scale? Have we truly moved beyond the premise of the rational subject freely taking part in the "dialogue" of academic discourse? Have we really found a way to transcend the "good man speaking well"? Or, perhaps, do we now simply have lots of good gender men, women, and genderqueers, located in diverse positions of race, class, sexuality, and mobility/sensory ability, who still must *speak well* in order to access this new pedagogy of listening? If we seriously regarded mentally disabled subjects in the classroom (and in other arenas where the power/knowledges of academic discourses are exchanged), what would happen to our concepts of diversity and difference?

In his 2006 article "Transcending Normativity," David L. Wallace tackles this dilemma, noting the ways that academic discourse—even when it earnestly tries to engage human difference—is governed by a "presumption of normativity" (503). His own awareness of difference, he says, involves

> continual reminder[s] that my ability to make a substantive accounting for difference—particularly systemic differences such as race, gender, class, sexual identity, religion/spirituality, and physical or mental/emotional abledness—depends not only on the recognition that my perspective is always limited by my experiences, and thus can never be taken for normative, but also that I must take initiative in educating myself if I hope to understand difference and speak about it responsibly. (503)

In this call, Wallace makes several important moves. Two coincide with moves made by Ellsworth, Lee, and Ratcliffe: First, he notes that one's experience will necessarily limit one's perspective, so that no one holds a truly normative position; and second, he emphasizes the importance of "continual reminder[s]," which he later amplifies to mean ongoing practice. In other words, mere awareness is not enough. Even as academic writings resound with calls for attention to difference, Wallace argues, our actual practices rarely enact this attention. It is this sort of specific attention to practice that, I believe, makes studies like Lee's and Ratcliffe's so valuable. However, Wallace also makes a third move, which is not shared by most other proponents of critical pedagogy: he asserts that recognition of differences including disability may involve mental as well as physical conditions. Although Wallace doesn't elaborate on the complications that attend inclusion of mentally disabled students (and instructors) in academic discourse, he does at least place this concern on the map.

If we shift our perspective to another angle, however, mental disability has been on the map of academic discourse for quite a while, through studies that address topics including emotion, affect, and (occasionally) trauma. And although critical pedagogy is notorious for eschewing emotion in the form of "sentimental," "personal," or "expressivist" writing (see, for instance, Bartholomae's "Writing With Teachers"), research in critical pedagogies quite often addresses the issue of emotion in academic discourse. This is because critical pedagogy takes as a given that teachers ought to address issues of power, identity, and ideology in the classroom, issues that are always already emotionally charged. The emotions that get discussed in critical pedagogy tend to be ones like anger, frustration, and defensiveness: that is, the sort of reactions one might expect when asking students to reexamine their investments in structures of power and privilege.

The Emotional Turn in Academic Discourse

Critical pedagogy, as C. Mark Hurlbert and Michael Blitz declare in their collection *Composition and Resistance,* "causes, perhaps requires, an uncomfortable state of mind" (43). This theme of affect or emotionality runs through much scholarship on critical pedagogy: Lee says she was "unsettled" by her students' responses to the "Rap on Rap" (263); Ratcliffe characterizes white women's responses to public debates on race as "defensive" and "guilt[y]" (90–91); Sally Chandler suggests that critical pedagogy may inevitably cause "fear that manifests as resistance" (60); and Timothy Barnett, putting it most bluntly, maintains that "we cannot hope for material change to occur for individuals or society if we do not make space in our classrooms for students . . . to ethically and productively use emotions such as pain, anger, and guilt" (359). Such scholarship often extols the potential of emotion to decenter the autonomous (rational) subject, or, as Hurlbert and Blitz suggest, to take "a loss of composure" (1) as educational opportunity. In this way, contemporary educators, especially those invested in critical pedagogy, may be said to *welcome* emotion in the classroom, despite their reputation to the contrary.

The wave of interest in emotion reaches well beyond those working specifically on critical pedagogy. Teaching is a profession that involves what sociologists have called "emotional labor," first defined by Arlie Hochschild as the "management of feeling to create a publicly observable facial and bodily display" (7). While Hochschild's study was of workers in service industries, including flight attendants and bill collectors, researchers have since built upon her theory to argue that emotional labor is also required of professionals including teachers and doctors—anyone whose labor involves "displaying organizationally sanctioned emotions by those whose jobs require interaction with clients or customers and for whom these interactions are an important component of their work" (Wharton 160). Teachers and scholars in disciplines ranging from the sciences (Zembylas) to the social sciences (Roberts and Smith) to the humanities (Brennan) cite emotional labor as an important factor in pedagogy, while others have extended the theory to apply to administrative as well as pedagogical work (Jacobs and Micciche, section 3). Related theories include "felt sense" (Gendlin, Perl) and the "ethics of care" (Gilligan, Noddings). While this wave of research, which we might call the *emotional turn* in academic discourse, is welcome, too often it leaves in place key assumptions that prevent actually *listening* to mentally disabled subjects, in Ratcliffe's sense of rhetorical listening.

In this section, I identify and provide examples of three habits that characterize pedagogical scholars' approaches to emotion in academic culture. First, such discussions usually presume an able-minded subject. "Emotion" is typically discussed as something experienced by mentally "normal" students and teachers, to such a degree that writers may include an explicit statement that they are *not* addressing the cases of those with mental disabilities. Second, teachers who do venture into the realm of examining the non-normal cases, such as students who write about trauma, nearly always include a disclaimer of some kind, to the effect that teachers are not and should not function as therapists. While I don't feel that the disclaimer itself is necessarily insidious (it's often necessary, from a practical point of view), the firmness with which it is usually made, and the lack of attention to *why* it must be made, are important to notice. Third, when researchers (most often teachers) do give extended attention to neuroatypical or mentally disabled subjects (most often students), these students are usually treated as "Other," that is, as special cases who should be written about—even diagnosed—by scholars writing from a "normal" perspective. Such studies often adhere, either tacitly or implicitly, to a medical model of disability that assumes that doctors and psychiatrists are benign authorities and that diagnosis is a deterministic tool offering predictable insights into students' ways of composing.

HABIT 1: *Emotional but Not Crazy.* Studies of emotion often draw a line, either tacitly or explicitly, between the "normal" and the pathological. For example, Stephanie Shields's 2005 study of the politics of emotion takes a sociopolitical and rhetorical approach, arguing for greater attention to gender politics in the ways that emotions are interpreted by audiences, as well as a reconsideration of the oversimplified "reason-emotion dichotomy" (5). Yet, like many other researchers, she circumscribes her attention to exclude those whose emotions would be labeled pathological, specifying that her concern is "the range of emotion experience and expression characteristic of everyday life experiences rather than traumatic experiences or those dramatically out of the ordinary: life at the office rather than life on *Jerry Springer*" (9). While this statement is presented as simply operational—a quick clarification of what Shields's article will cover and what it will not—note the division it sets up: emotions that are "traumatic" or "dramatically out of the ordinary" are not those of everyday life. This neatly categorizes those for whom "out of the ordinary" emotions *are* part of everyday life out of rhetorical existence. The remark about Jerry Springer further belittles those with "out of the ordinary" emotions, suggesting that if one's emotions do not fall within this presumed range of "ordinary," one must therefore exist in the realm of lurid, shrieking talk-show expression.

This habit of adhering to a presumably clean line between the "normal" and the pathological shows up frequently in studies of emotion in the classroom. For instance, Sally Chandler's 2007 study of "fear of tutoring" announces, "This analysis does not equate 'fear of tutoring' with trauma; student fears are not the same as near-death experiences, illness, and loss of loved ones. The feelings evoked by these very different events are not the same as feelings surrounding student writing" (61). Another example occurred at the 2009 Conference on College Composition and Communication, where Christy Zink gave an insightful presentation on the experience of teaching through grief (in her case, due to traumatic personal experiences and the loss of a parent), arguing that experiences of grief and loss are "too rarely represented" in research on writing pedagogy, and that there is a lack of institutional support for faculty who may be coping with grief and loss. Unlike Shields and Chandler, Zink suggests that "dramatic" emotion *is* a part of everyday experience, pointing out that the grief of a loved one's death is perhaps "the most common human experience." And yet, in an extemporaneous comment as she read her paper, Zink drew the same bright line: looking up from her paper, she told the audience that the disclosure of her personal losses had felt "very uncomfortable and awkward," after which she immediately assured us, "I'm not crazy."

As these examples show, in our published works as well as our more offhand comments, even among those who believe that emotion in the classroom should be taken seriously, a presumed divide still exists between the "normal" emotions that most students experience and the "very different" (Chandler 61) emotions that attend pathologized mental situations such as trauma or being "crazy." I don't mean to argue that these teacher-scholars' work isn't valuable; I appreciate their courage in exploring these topics at all, particularly since research into classroom emotion is often considered naive and unscholarly (Richmond 69–71; Ryden 85; Micciche 48–49). However, I argue that, given the frequency of such remarks, we need to pay attention to their ideological function. The DSM, and medical discourse in general, are not the only entities governing the operation of mental disabilities in university culture. We, academics, are also governing ourselves.

HABIT 2: *A Teacher but Not a Therapist.* Another way we govern ourselves is to announce to our audiences that we are not therapists.[11] This habit probably stems in part from our awareness that attitudes toward the study of emotion in pedagogical discourse are overall fairly negative; thus, we seek to distance ourselves from anticipated accusations of being "soft," unscholarly, or taking a prurient interest in our students' personal lives. (Prurience—or what I call fetishization—does actually become a problem sometimes, as I discuss in the next subsection, "Diagnose and Heal"; however, avowals of our lack of therapeutic training do not seem an appropriate antidote.) The following selection of examples are all drawn from teachers of writing, though it should be noted that teachers in a wide range of disciplines receive "emotional" writings from students and are concerned with the operation of emotions in the classroom.

- "Writing professionals are, of course, acutely aware of the dangers of merging the processes of therapy and writing instruction. Writing instructors are not therapists" (MacCurdy 161).
- "Jeff [the instructor] did not analyze or interpret Jon's [the student's] diaries, thus avoiding the role of therapist" (Berman and Schiff 304).
- "We do not take such findings [on the therapeutic effects of writing and trauma] as warrants for using testimony in writing classes as a form of therapy" (Goggin and Goggin 48).
- "We're not psychologists, but we are teachers. We can respond as teachers—that is, I never try to analyze or counsel, only talk" ("We Have Common Cause" 207).
- "I cannot presume to counsel or provide therapy for my students. It's not my job, I'm not qualified, and I'm probably more upset than they are [about the 9/11 attacks]" ("We Have Common Cause" 225).

As these assertions indicate, professors seem to feel great unease about being accused of fancying ourselves therapists. I sympathize with the desire to make such distinctions, for professors are routinely reminded by our bosses not to try to "counsel" students, but to refer the students to more "appropriate" authorities—usually the university health center. And I'm not arguing that we *should* attempt to counsel our students, for whether or not we are "qualified," the prospect is unworkable on a practical level: we could be disciplined, fired, or sued.

However, I *am* arguing that, first, we ought to notice the level of anxiety that attends our efforts to keep the teaching/therapy divide intact; and second, we should delve more deeply into the sort of responses we *can* offer. As Michelle Payne points out, a teacher's abilities in analysis and critical questioning might be more useful than commonly imagined:

> In worrying about where the lines are between being a therapist and being a writing teacher, we can forget that students can bring the same kinds of writing strategies to an essay on a painful experience that they can to other essay subjects. . . . This fear is based on a belief that emotional and intellectual responses can't coexist or inform each other, that emotions are tainted by intellectual ideas. . . . I think it is important that we, as writing teachers, stop seeing emotion, pain, and trauma as threatening, anti-intellectual, and solipsistic, and instead begin to ask how we might, like therapists, feminist theorists, and philosophers, begin to recognize them as ways of knowing, not signs of dangerous pedagogies or teachers who are acting as therapists. (30)

Payne's book, *Bodily Discourses,* focuses on just this project: opening possibilities for ways that we might respond as teachers to "emotional" topics and writings in the classroom. Despite the large body of work on emotionality in the classroom, Payne's critique of the teacher/therapist divide is unusual. However strongly our theories might welcome emotion in to the classroom, in practice, as Payne demonstrates, we still treat emotionality and intellectuality as adversaries. Therefore, if we (teachers) feel strongly compelled to assert that we are not therapists, we ought to question *why* that compulsion is so strong, and why we feel that it would be dangerous to explore the links between teaching and therapy. Who has told us it is so dangerous? What ideologies are supported by maintaining that divide so fiercely?

One such ideology, I argue, is adherence to medical discourse as the ultimate authority on disability in the classroom. Positioning students (and ourselves) as mentally "normal," even while acknowledging the importance of emotion, is a tactic used to govern mental disability in the classroom. Another tactic is to treat emotional experiences, such as trauma, as shared rather than marginalizing experiences. This is the case with Shane Borrowman's collection *Trauma and the Teaching of Writing,* which focuses on emotional and pedagogical responses in the classroom "during moments of shared national trauma and tragedy," with particular attention to September 11, 2001 (4). I want to add that Borrowman's collection is thought-provoking, timely, and much-needed; in other words, I have no argument with what it does. Instead, I offer it as an example of what pedagogical research generally does *not* do, that is, give serious and respectful attention to trauma (or other forms of mental distress) as a marginalizing, rather than a collective, experience. Thus, while *Trauma and the Teaching of Writing* offers important insights, it also reinforces the notion that everyone in academe is mentally "normal" until something "happens to" us. This in turn reinforces the assumption that mental disability exists in a separate realm from school-as-usual.

Ironically, persons with mental disabilities that involve severe anxiety, flashbacks, panic attacks, or other forms of mental distress may experience a paradoxical sense of relief at times of "shared" trauma. Consider this description offered by Geneen Roth, a survivor of childhood abuse and writer on eating disorders, of her state of mind following the 1989 earthquake in her hometown of Santa Cruz, California:

> The cleaving earth had turned us into children who could not depend on our families, the ground we walked on, for safety. We were frightened, anxious, irrational. Sleep was impossible. Psychologists call it post-traumatic stress disorder, said it could last six weeks or six months. But it was so familiar to me, this irrationality, this insistent need to protect myself from the possibility of disaster at any moment, that I felt as if I'd been living with post-traumatic stress disorder all my life, and that finally, everyone I knew, met on the street, talked to in a store—the entire community of Santa Cruz—mirrored the child's world I knew. (219)

Roth's experience illustrates the topsy-turvy feeling of encountering what Borrowman calls "shared moments of horror" (5) from a neuroatypical position. While the sense of horror is, well, horrible, there may also be a feeling of relief at finally no longer being the only person around who shakes unpredictably, loses words, can't sleep, can't get it together.

I don't wish to suggest that we can draw a clean line between personal and cultural traumas. As many writers have shown, traumas on a national, cultural, or historical scale are deeply caught up with the unfolding of individuals' material lives. In addition, to make such a distinction would only reinforce a positivist and medicalized notion of mental disability, one that focuses on causes, chemicals, and cures, without sufficient attention to the more complex psychosocial forces at work. But I do suggest that *Trauma and the Teaching of Writing* points the way toward an important question: If academics have an ethical responsibility to respond to occasions of "shared moments of horror" (5), as Borrowman suggests, then what is our responsibility to the *unshared* experience of mental disability as felt and known by neuroatypical subjects? What is our ethical obligation then?

HABIT 3: *Diagnose and Heal.* Although the great majority of work that addresses emotion in the classroom presumes that all persons involved will be mentally "normal," some teachers and scholars do take up the question of the mentally disabled subject. Unfortunately, such works often treat mentally disabled subjects (almost always students) as "Other," that is, as special cases who should be written about—even diagnosed—by teacher-scholars writing from a "normal" perspective. These studies often adhere, either tacitly or implicitly, to an individualistic and medical model of disability. They also tend to adhere to an overcoming narrative in which the "broken" minds of disabled writers may be "healed" through rhetoric. This leads to pat conclusions that substitute rhetoric-as-cure for the more complex problems and questions we might pose instead. Two examples of these tendencies are Jacqueline Rinaldi's "Rhetoric and Healing: Revising Narratives about Disability," published in 1996, and Ann Jurecic's "Neurodiversity," published in 2007.

Rinaldi's article concerns writers with multiple sclerosis (MS). I include it in this study of mental disability because Rinaldi places great emphasis on the mental states of her participants: their "anxiety and depression" (822), their feelings of "failure" and "anger" (823), and the "therapeutic value" of writing to counteract these troubling mental states (831). Rinaldi and her colleague Ann Spector organized a ten-week writing seminar for persons with MS, in which seven persons enrolled, three men and four women ranging in age from twenty-eight to sixty-three. Their goal was to "design a rhetoric workshop grounded in an interactive pedagogy that would encourage the participants to write about their disability in ways they would find therapeutic" (821). Rinaldi does not say anything about her own or Spector's disability identification, thus implicitly marking them as "normal"; here again, we see Nagel's "view from nowhere" and Haraway's "god-trick" (189).[12] Although Rinaldi acknowledges that her participants' distress arose from their location in an ableist culture "that privileges strength, beauty, and health over frailty, deformity, and illness" (821), her own perspective seems firmly rooted in that same ableist stance. For example:

> Since MS strikes most adults during their most productive years—between twenty and fifty—its impact can be as psychologically devastating as it is physically debilitating. Before becoming entirely crippled, MSers may limp, stumble, and drop things; often, they need help with the simplest tasks—tying a shoelace, unscrewing a jar lid, putting out the garbage.

This description is filled with assumptions that reflect a deficit understanding of disability. The notion that one should be most "productive" between ages twenty and fifty, for instance, is based upon a normative model of adult development (not to mention the assumption that "productivity" is key to human fulfillment). Emphasizing the "debilitating" and "crippl[ing]" nature of MS, Rinaldi suggests that tasks people with MS find difficult are actually "the simplest" of tasks. However, these tasks are "simple" only on a normative scale. More subtly, word choices like "strikes" imply that MS is a catastrophic event, akin to being struck by lightning. Rinaldi's troubling language choices persist throughout the article. For example, she notes that when group members wrote about their experiences, "many wrote about feeble hands, hobbling legs, and shuffling feet" (824). Reading these paraphrases, I found myself wondering—are these the participants' word choices, or is this a perspective Rinaldi is placing upon their writing? Although some direct quotations from participants do appear in the article, I could find few that seemed to directly echo Rinaldi's perspective, although one participant, Glenn, did write that he was delighted to "be productive" when he found a job as a telephone solicitor.

Overall, Rinaldi's article offers the case of her and Spector's writing seminar as an overcoming narrative, an occasion through which its disabled participants could "transcend the confines of their illness" (830). Near the close of "Rhetoric and Healing," she argues that the experience for participants was "wholly renewing," even going so far as to say that "Though writing and revising narratives of disability could not restore the crippled bodies of these writers, the insights gleaned from the heuristics of writing did seem to have therapeutic value for those grappling with the darker issues of chronic illness" (830–31). Although I do not doubt Rinaldi's desire to address the topic of disability and healing with respect, the "healing" she promotes is largely a journey of individual overcoming. Participants, according to "Rhetoric and Healing," went through "transformational stages" and "realigned their internal mirrors" (830). And although Rinaldi notes that several participants published their work (see Liebensohn), the focus here is not on challenging socially constructed presumptions about illness, but rather on coping individually with the "darker issues" of individual psyches and lives. Rinaldi's "overcoming" stance extends to her reading of psychotherapy: noting that "psychotherapists rely extensively on rhetoric" (832), she takes this as evidence of its healing potential, ignoring the abundant history of psychoanalytic rhetoric as a force that has incarcerated, physically harmed, isolated, and dehumanized persons labeled as mentally ill.

Published about a decade later, Ann Jurecic's "Neurodiversity" takes a stance that appears more aware of disability studies and its radical approach to disabled subjects. The title of her article indicates that she has some knowledge of the language used by persons on the spectrum, although her definition of autism is drawn straight from DSM-IV (421). However, the central project of her article, which is to analyze the work of one student, Gregory, is based upon a rather astounding announcement: although Gregory "remains undiagnosed and is perhaps still unaware of his Asperger's" (428), Jurecic has decided that he does have Asperger's and proceeds to diagnose and analyze his writing according to this assumption.[13] She bases her diagnosis on a range of observations:

> As if to help me answer that question [of what will happen to students with Asperger's when they arrive at university], Gregory appeared in my class. From the first day, his difference was obvious. He participated enthusiastically, but his voice seemed too loud and insistent, and his comments focused narrowly on his own idiosyncratic concerns, revealing a rigidly mechanical way of thinking about writing. He began the course by obsessively reading and rereading an MLA style manual and asking scores of detailed questions about correct citation form. He repeatedly requested explicit instructions on how to write each paper and fix each problem. Given this behavior and other quirks—a tendency to rock in his

> chair, an inability to understand humor, problems with attention and small-group work—I suspected that Gregory has Asperger's Syndrome. (424–25)

Jurecic then went on a kind of diagnostic treasure hunt, consulting a neurologist and parents of autistic children, "all of whom agreed that any student with such behavior . . . must be on the spectrum" (425). She also contacted one of Gregory's high-school English teachers, apparently without Gregory's knowledge, who agreed with the suspected diagnosis. Throughout the article, Jurecic sticks with her presumed diagnosis, saying that "when I examine the particular characteristics of [Gregory's] writing that reveal his ways of thinking—I see both his unique mental capacities *and* the impairments of his Asperger's" (439).

In their response to Jurecic's article, Cynthia Lewiecki-Wilson and Jay Dolmage point out a problem with Jurecic's impulses: namely, they "lay bare the essentially ableist desire" to diagnose before adjusting her assumptions and teaching practices (316). This desire reveals the extent of the teacher's adherence to a medical and deterministic model of disability—and, in fact, of teaching in general. What if, as Lewiecki-Wilson and Dolmage suggest, instead of "the usual paradigm of the [unmarked] teacher worrying about the disabled student," we "focus on the disabling aspect of some teaching" (316)? This is not as sexy as "discovering" Asperger's in a single student, but it would have a more beneficial effect on more students—regardless of their disability identifications (or diagnoses). Importantly, Jurecic's goal is allied with the goals of DS: she repeatedly mentions Gregory's intelligence, argues that her methods for teaching him do not provide a template for teaching all students on the spectrum, and states that teaching methods will need to change. However, as Lewiecki-Wilson and Dolmage point out, Jurecic's underlying presumption of the importance of Gregory's diagnosis, and her disrespectful way of arriving at it, undermine her DS agenda.

Another commenter on "Neurodiversity" is Paul Heilker, who notes that all the interlocutors in this discussion "are guilty here of speaking for, about, and through the people on the spectrum rather than with them" (320). In response to his astute point, I want to introduce another voice into this discussion, that of Melanie Yergeau, who has written insightfully about the increasing prevalence of the "autism anecdote" in pedagogical scholarship:

> *Cue the anecdote.* You're teaching a first-year writing course. One of your students consistently speaks in a loud, booming voice, often interrupting other students. He barely makes eye contact. He frequently stays after class, asking off-topic questions, all the while wringing his hands and rocking the whole of his body back and forth. His writing lacks transition, you tell him, and it also tends to focus on minute details that would bore most readers. Several weeks into the term, he discloses his diagnosis of autism spectrum disorder (ASD). A Temple Grandin book and a WebMD article later, you feel you've got a grasp on this ASD thing. . . .
>
> I speak of these autism anecdotes not because I *enjoy* them, but because I have heard and read them far too frequently, have myself been featured in them far too frequently. . . . As things currently stand, we, as teacher-scholars, aim to cure autistics (and their writing) rather than value them and what they have to say—as well as how they say it. Simply put, this approach needs to change. ("Narrating Telepresence")

I listened to (that is, I read; Yergeau provided a script) this paper, which I heard/read at the 2009 CCCC, with some discomfort. For I too have told the "autism anecdote," have made assumptions about my students based on their affect and behavior, have prided myself on my marvelous awareness and open mind. In fact, chapter 2 of this book begins with such an anecdote—one less thrilled by the diagnostic chase than Jurecic's, I hope, but part of the genre nevertheless. What I take from Yergeau's analysis is that we must resist facile conclusions about our students based upon their diagnosed, self-identified, *or* suspected neuroatypicalities, and focus instead on ways that their writing and ways of knowing might change and inform our practices. This is a familiar argument, but one that apparently cannot be repeated often enough. It brings us back to the concept of rhetorical listening, and to my question: Is it possible to "listen" to the mad subject? What might such listening entail? How will it function? *What do I do on Monday morning?*

Rectifying the omission/demonization/fetishization/infantilization of mental disability in academic discourse is no "add-and-stir" problem,[14] for it strikes at the core of the presumption of most educational theories: *by definition* this subject may be neither rational nor "critical" in a normative sense. The rest of this book is concerned with just that: what to do on Monday morning. And not only in the classroom, but at a faculty meeting. At a conference. When you open the paper and learn that another "whack job" has committed another school shooting (Ehrenreich 163). When you notice—or do not notice—the negative spaces of academe, the absence of scholars who cannot access this privileged world because they fail to make sense in the approved ways. And the rest of this book also includes abundant examples of what can happen when, against the odds, those with mental disabilities find ways to speak, write, dance, and otherwise communicate against the grain of able-mindedness.

There are things we can do. Let's do them.

CHAPTER 2

Ways to Move

Presence, Participation, and Resistance in Kairotic Space

Goddamn it, how hard is it to write a 10 page academic paper on comparative race relations during the post–World War II rupture when I'm having an episode! Call up my mother, scream, cry, cuss out my roommate, kick over the table, turn back three months of sober, anti-violent, depression-coping skills and cut into the fiber of my body with stainless-steel scissors, tear down the house.

—*Wendy Marie Thompson,*
"Her Reckoning: A Young Interdisciplinary Academic Dissects the Exact Nature of Her Disease"

No significant differences or interaction effects [regarding attendance] were found for students' special needs.

—*Nitsa Davidovitch and Dan Soen,*
"Class Attendance and Students' Evaluation of Their College Instructors"

Several years ago, a colleague told me about a student in her Introduction to Women's Studies class who was behaving in a way that puzzled and annoyed my colleague. The student spoke out at odd moments, making remarks that didn't seem to relate to the discussion topic at hand. As the semester went on, her behavior become more unconventional. One day she brought a large bowl of ice cream to class.

"She just sat there, eating it!" my colleague told me, half laughing. "I don't even know where she got it! It was this big ceramic bowl! We were all staring at her, and then she said, 'Does anyone want some? It's really good.'"

It was hard to know what to say. Finally I said, "That's weird."

We paused. "She brought *ice cream,*" my colleague said.

My colleague and I struggled to know what to say because this student's behavior had taken us outside of our conventional understanding of what should go on in a classroom. Not only was she not following the tacit script for classroom participation, she wasn't even following the tacit script for classroom resistance. She wasn't sullen, or silent, or combative. She spoke up readily, but her remarks didn't follow a pattern my colleague could follow. She attended class, but she brought a bowl of ice cream. Almost at the end of the semester, the student brought my colleague a form from the school's Disability Services office: she had been diagnosed with a learning disability that also impacted her social interactions. She wasn't requesting any specific accommodations; her case manager had said to bring the form, so she was bringing it.

This account is similar to a genre that Melanie Yergeau identifies as the "autism anecdote," discussed in more detail in chapter 1. Although the student in question is not labeled autistic, the similarity to the anecdotes described by Yergeau is clear. In relating it, I am hoping to call attention not to the student herself, who does not have a direct voice in the account, but to the institutionally affiliated persons and structures that contemplate, label, and diagnose her: my colleague's and my uncomfortable laughter and unsureness of what to do; our unspoken assumption that classroom conduct should follow particular norms; and the hazy role played by Disability Services. My point here—and a forecast of the argument in this chapter—is that the student is not "the problem," although she was cast in that role by the institutional authorities around her, including myself.

The Scene of Academic Discourse: Kairotic Space

This anecdote, and my rereading of it years later, highlights a number of the problems that access to academic discourse may present to students with mental disabilities. First, there is the issue of formal accommodations. We are accustomed to thinking of classroom accommodations in terms of measurable steps that help "level the playing field": note-takers; extra time on exams; captions on videos; lecture slides posted online; Braille and large-print handouts; the presence of a sign interpreter. But what accommodations can be offered for the student who is earnestly participating, but in ways that do not fall into the (usually rationalist) pattern of classroom discussions and activities? Although the notion of a classroom "discussion" implies that it is open to all perspectives, this setting is in fact controlled by rigid expectations: students taking part in a "discussion" are expected to demonstrate their knowledge of the topic at hand, raise relevant questions, and establish themselves as significant, but not overly dominant, voices in a crowd of at least fifteen—and usually many more—other persons. Further complicating the transaction is the fact that different teachers have different expectations for the "script" of a classroom discussion. One teacher might want straightforward paraphrasing of the reading; another might want provocative questions; yet another might want connections drawn between today's material and last week's. These expectations may or may not be communicated directly.

Classroom discussions are one example of a type of discursive setting that I call *kairotic space*. These are the less formal, often unnoticed, areas of academe where knowledge is produced and power is exchanged. A classroom discussion is a kairotic space, as is an individual conference with one's professor. Academic conferences are rife with kairotic spaces, including the question-and-answer sessions after panels, impromptu "elevator meetings," and gatherings at restaurants and bars on the periphery of formal conference events. Other examples from students' experiences might include peer-response workshops, study groups, interviews for on-campus jobs, or departmental parties or gatherings to which they are invited.

"Kairos" is a concept from classical rhetoric usually translated as "the opportune or appropriate time"; however, kairos really goes further than this. Cynthia Miecznikowski Sheard suggests that it incorporates multiple elements of context, including not only time but other factors including physical space and attitudes, none of which, Sheard argues, can be meaningfully separated (306). As this implies, kairos carries ethical and contextual as well as temporal implications, a point that has also been discussed by scholars including Michael Harker and James Kinneavy.

In a similar vein, although not referring to kairos directly, Jeffrey T. Grabill offers a concept he calls "infrastructure." Grabill's work is important here because he emphasizes the centrality of *access* to infrastructure, which many writings on kairos do not. Drawing on work by Susan Leigh Star and Karen Ruhleder, Grabill defines infrastructure as follows:

> [I]nfrastructure means something more than a static, installed base. For Star and Ruhleder (1996), "infrastructure is something that emerges for people in practice, connected to activities and structures" (p. 112). In other words, just as a tool is not an artifact

> with "pre-given attributes frozen in time" (p. 112) but rather given meaning as a tool by specific users working on particular problems in specific situations, so too does the meaning and value of an infrastructure emerge. To ignore infrastructure, then, is to miss key moments when its meaning and value become stabilized (if even for a moment), and therefore to miss moments when possibilities and identities are established. (464)

Thus, a classroom's infrastructure comprises not only its tables and chairs, its technologies, and its participants, but also the beliefs, discourses, attitudes, and interchanges that take place there. Grabill's notion of infrastructure and my notion of kairotic space share this concern: when considering the spaces of academe, we must observe—and hopefully intervene in—the unfolding of power relations by means of "studying the unstudied" (Grabill 465). In this case, (some of) the unstudied are students and faculty members with mental disabilities.

I define a *kairotic space* as one characterized by all or most of these criteria:

1. Real-time unfolding of events
2. Impromptu communication that is required or encouraged
3. In-person contact
4. A strong social element
5. High stakes

I specify "all or most of these criteria" to indicate that the boundaries of such spaces are neither rigid nor objectively determined. So, for instance, an online discussion, a professor-student conference taking place via instant message, or a job interview held by telephone, could all qualify as kairotic spaces despite the lack of in-person contact. But an informal study session between two students who have been friends for years and who experience minimal risk in studying together might not. The key element is the *pairing of spontaneity with high levels of professional/academic impact.* Attention to relations of power is of great importance in understanding kairotic space, as is recognition that different participants in kairotic spaces will perceive those relations differently.

Consider the common instance of a professor and a student—perhaps her thesis advisee—having lunch together. Although the professor might feel very comfortable in such a space, and assume that the event is just a friendly lunch (even a treat for the student), it is likely that the student will feel at least a bit on display, called upon to behave appropriately and to perform academically (although subtly) as well. Now imagine that this student experiences severe anxiety. He finds it difficult to meet his advisor's eyes at appropriate intervals, and for appropriate lengths of time; in trying to attend to the eye-contact issue, he finds himself missing much of what she is saying. She asks him a question about his research, and he tries to explain the theories he has been considering, but cannot remember any of the researchers' names. (Zorro? No, that's not it. The name is something like Zorro, but if he says that, he will be laughed at, perhaps thought stupid.) In the middle of all this, a waiter arrives to take his order; he has not had time to peruse the menu, and in any case would need at least five silent minutes to absorb its densely printed verbal information. He says, "Do you have any salads?" The waiter responds, "Yes, they're all there on the menu," and then begins to list them rapidly, in a monotone. Suddenly, the student remembers the name of the theorist and blurts it out: "Zola!" His advisor and the waiter both look at him with puzzlement. He knows he is not making a good impression.

In their study of academic conferences, McCarthy and colleagues (2004) have observed the inequities of interchanges in such spaces:

> [O]pportunities for "give and take" tend to be unevenly distributed among the conference attendees, depending on one's status in the community, level of participation in the formal conference program, and more subtle issues such as one's native language and level of extroversion. (39)

Of course, we can and should add "and disability status" to the list of issues that McCarthy and his cowriters have identified, since—as is common knowledge among persons with disabilities—our attempts to access kairotic spaces are often fraught. This fraughtness has much to do with time and how it is perceived by different persons. *Crip time,* a term from disability culture, refers to a flexible approach to normative time frames (Gill; Zola). At a conference, adhering to crip time might mean permitting more than fifteen minutes between sessions; it might mean recognizing that people will arrive at various intervals, and designing sessions accordingly; and it might also mean recognizing that audience members are processing language at various rates and adjusting the pace of conversation. It is this notion of *flexibility* (not just "extra" time) that unites kairos and crip time. Even more than academic conferences, classrooms tend to be run under strict time constraints. Students are expected to arrive on time, absorb information at a particular speed, and perform spontaneously in restricted time frames (as in discussions or peer-response groups). It is often assumed that smaller or more discussion-oriented settings constitute better learning environments for all students. For example, Alison Roberts and Keri Iyall Smith, studying teaching in sociology classes, straightforwardly presume that small discussion groups "create a safe space" for students (294). However, if we consider the position of the mentally disabled student in such a context, we can guess that this environment might feel anything but safe.

Despite their importance, kairotic spaces tend to be understudied. One reason for this is that it's difficult to collect data in them (Ventola, Shalom, and Thompson 361). Another, more compelling reason is that their impact tends to be underestimated by those who move through them with relative ease. The importance of kairotic space will be more obvious to a person who—for example—can hear only scraps of a conversation held among a group sitting at a table, or who needs more than a few seconds to process a question asked of her in a classroom discussion.

In the chapter "Divided Curriculum" from *Claiming Disability,* Simi Linton argues that higher-education curricula tend to split between applied fields and liberal arts, with "disability" usually shunted into the applied fields and treated as a medicalized "problem" requiring remediation. However, Linton also notes that with the growth of disability studies, the gap is narrowing and disciplinary divides are blurring. One example is the *International Journal of Inclusive Education,* many of whose writers take an explicitly DS stance while addressing familiar "special education" questions, including participation. Individual researchers, such as Joan Ostrove, Constance Pledger, and Patricia Silver, work from a DS perspective within disciplines that have traditionally taken a more individualized and medicalized view. And even within psychiatric fields, researchers have begun to call for supported education and to note the inadequacy of accommodations provided for students with mental disabilities (Collins and Mowbray).

In studies of classrooms, kairotic exchanges have been theorized from the perspectives of gender, race, class, and specific disabilities including blindness, deafness, and mobility impairments. In addition, some researchers have theorized the complex interactions of the classroom without reference to identity markers, focusing instead on the differences in perception between professors and students. I propose that we can learn from these studies' conclusions, noting their typical failure to account for the specific issues facing students and professors with mental disabilities, but also drawing upon the strategies they suggest to redesign a more inclusive classroom infrastructure.[1] In order to do so, I will examine the classroom with reference to topoi including presence, participation, and resistance. Following calls in DS methodology for "studying up," or investigating the paradigms and practices of those in dominant positions (Fine; Oliver; Price, "Disability Studies Methodology"), I examine work by teachers and researchers on these phenomena. I intersperse analyses of published research with accounts from my own classroom experiences and writings by students with mental disabilities.

Presence and Absence

> Attendance should be one of the easiest variables for students to control.
>
> —*Steven E. Gump,* "The Cost of Cutting Class"

In *Speech and Phenomena: And Other Essays on Husserl's Theory of Signs,* Jacques Derrida argues that presence is not the phenomenological notion of a coherent body, object, or sign existing in a coherent moment, but rather a diffuse series of repetitions whose imaginary original referent is endlessly deferred. The phenomenological understanding of presence (specifically Husserl's), Derrida argues, presumes "the systematic interdependence of the concepts of sense, ideality, objectivity, truth, intuition, perception, and expression" (99). Although Derrida's theory has been widely applied in areas such as literary analysis and gender studies, most pedagogical research continues to value a stable, rationalist notion of presence, both in the ways that texts are produced and in expectations for participation in kairotic spaces such as the classroom. "Presence" is usually taken as empirically obvious, and as an a priori good. When its questionable epistemological status is mentioned at all, the purpose is often to brush it aside, as in this passage from Gordon Harvey's "Presence in the Essay":

> [W]e should probably find a different, more general word for "the personal" in essays. I suggest "presence," since this is the concept

> we invoke when we feel life in writing, when we feel an individual invested in a subject and freely directing the essay—not surrendering control to a discipline's conventions, or to a party line, or to easy sentiments and structures, or to stock phrases. It's unfortunate that "presence" is the name that Derridean detectives have given to their evil Moriarty; but we needn't use the phrase as they do, to mean some truth or self existing wholly apart from writing. We can use it to mean simply a certain feeling in the reader, subjective but discussable, caused by something in the writing. (650)

Harvey's nod to the problematics of presence, however dismissive, is useful because it clarifies his essay's own position: not just in favor of presence, but in favor of a *rationalist* discourse of presence, one that "freely directs" discourse and is not "surrendering control" to other voices. This "free," individual writer is "invested" in the work, and her investment is signaled by her ability to provoke "a certain feeling in the reader." Such a perspective forthrightly commingles *presence* with the vexed concepts of the individual, freedom, and control.

When presence appears more literally on the scene of academic discourses—that is, when it is used to refer to whether or not students physically attend classes[2]—the conflation of presence, goodness, freedom, control, and individuality is used to construct pedagogies that presume that, first, presence is the sine qua non of learning in higher education, and second, that the "choice" of whether or not to be present belongs to the individual student. Studies of classroom attendance generally agree that presence is correlated with higher grades. From that finding, researchers often move automatically to the conclusion that students therefore "should" attend classes since that factor is one they can "control" (as in the quotation from Gump). When this research is examined from a DS viewpoint, however, disturbing omissions arise: some studies ignore the fact that disabled students face barriers to attendance; others make vague gestures such as including "special needs" as a background factor, but fail to consider disability in any detail; yet others use methods which in themselves presume that certain disability-linked traits, such as "neuroticism," are inimical to academic achievement.

Most common is the first type of approach—that which simply ignores the possibility that any sort of disability, let alone mental disability, may play a role in students' presence in class. Typical of this approach is Marvin Druger's "Being There: A Perspective on Class Attendance," published in the *Journal of College Science Teaching*. Druger states that " 'being there' is the essence of learning and maturing, and this is something that we need to reinforce in our teaching" (351). Notably, Druger equates presence ("being there") with "experiencing" a class:

> If students are not in classes regularly, they miss the experience. Even if the instructor is a terrible lecturer, students learn from the experience. We tend to forget information, but we don't easily forget experiences . . . [if] students don't participate, they will miss the experiences, and nobody can ever adequately explain to them what they missed. (350–51)

From the perspective of mental disability, the problems with this argument are readily apparent. First, simply sitting in class does not mean that the attendee is "experiencing" the class. Students with difficulty concentrating, who are falling asleep due to anxiety- or depression-induced insomnia, or who struggle to follow the "logical" structure or typical speed of most lectures are indeed experiencing something, but not what Druger means by "the experience." Second, this view presumes that all learners learn in the same way: among people. While this sort of learning may be effective for most learners, Druger takes *most* to be *all.* A student with social anxiety, or one on the autism spectrum, for example, might get a great deal more out of a learning process that does *not* involve close contact or interaction with others.

I learned this latter point, somewhat to my chagrin, with a student—I'll call him Jeff—whom I tutored through the Disability Services office at UMass-Amherst. I was Jeff's writing tutor for over a year, and during the first few months I struggled to involve him in various collaborative and dialogue-based exercises that I considered synonymous with learning to write better. We tried brainstorming, listing, sketching, dialoguing, walking around campus, even phone calls—a huge array of activities that I thought would unlock his latent ability (and, I assumed, his *need*) to write in recursive, building-over-time drafts. Jeff kept telling me that these methods "didn't work" for him, although he patiently tried them all. His method of drafting was to think by himself for a long time, and then to write a complete essay—beginning with the first word and ending with the final citation on his "Works Cited" page. As a writing teacher steeped in process-oriented pedagogies, I was horrified by this approach. I would go through Jeff's drafts with him and make various suggestions.

Each time, Jeff would revise exactly as I suggested, and exactly to the extent I suggested—no more, and no less. Finally, I was forced to concede that what I had assumed to be true of all writers was not true for this writer. His drafting process was indeed a process; it just wasn't one that I could easily observe and participate in, since most of it took place via thought rather than physical action, and when he was alone. He was earning fair grades on his writing, and I finally admitted—to myself and to him—that I was pushing him to try other strategies not because his writing "needed" it in terms of the way it was valued by his teachers, but only in terms of how *I* valued his process. Shortly thereafter, we shifted our focus to a different subject area, one that required more review and "quizzing," which better suited his actual needs as a learner in college.

What I want to emphasize about this story is not just my own slowness to learn how Jeff learned—although that's important—but that Jeff continued to try to apply my methods long after he realized (and had told me) that they just weren't working for him. As his tutor, and an employee of Disability Services, I was an authority, and I exercised that authority by pushing him toward noneffective styles of drafting for quite a while. Pretty much the only authority Jeff could have exercised in that situation would have been to choose to stop attending sessions—that is, to remove his presence from the kairotic scene of our tutoring sessions. I'm thankful he did not, for it permitted me to learn what I needed to, and also (finally) to become a more effective tutor for him. Jeff exhibited great motivation in continuing to attend sessions led by his chipper, "process"-obsessed tutor. If he had not been so motivated, he would have risked being labeled with one of the terms typically used to describe students who are not accessing academic discourses in approved ways: resistant, having a "bad attitude," or—had his patience run out—simply absent. And hence, not motivated.

Motivation is a term that comes up often in studies of student attendance, and frequently, the presumption made about motivation is that it is closely correlated with students' presence or absence in the classroom. For example, Randy Moore's study of students in an introductory biology course for nonmajors argues that

> attendance is directly related to motivation because it requires a personal effort that relates directly to the course and learning. Students who are motivated enough to attend class consistently are also probably motivated enough to study outside of class, read and

> study the course textbook, turn in assignments on time, and attend help sessions. Together, these activities greatly increase students' time-on-task and, as a result, increase learning and improve grades. (370)

To further reinforce this presumed causal relationship, Moore provides its corollary in the next paragraph: students "not motivated enough to attend class regularly" will "seldom" be motivated enough to perform other activities such as studying, reading, and attending help sessions, which "produces less learning and lower grades" (370). I don't disagree that nonattendance may produce lower grades, since teachers routinely penalize absences; however, I'm troubled by the quick slide Moore makes from attendance to out-of-class studying behaviors to "increase[d] learning." In fact, a highly motivated student may often miss class; may spend a huge amount of "time-on-task" yet not retain what he has studied, or not be able to perform his knowledge in approved-of ways; and may find that his learning "increases" when he is alone but falls apart when he works in a small group or a crowded lecture hall. To be clear, I am not arguing that we should ignore the importance of attendance, nor throw out the notion that academic "achievement" is, to at least some degree, possible to assess. I am arguing that most of our research and practice forms quick assumptions about the interdependence of presence, motivation, achievement, and learning—each of which is vastly complicated in itself, let alone in combination.

What about studies that do take a more nuanced view of the attendance phenomenon? Some researchers have considered differences in gender, race, "special needs," or personality type in their studies. The "special needs" approach is taken by Nitsa Davidovitch and Dan Soen, whose study was conducted in Israel. However, the authors do not explain what they mean by "special needs," nor how this term was identified to students on the questionnaires used. Perhaps it is not surprising, then, that "no significant differences or interaction effects were found for students' special needs." Although "special needs" was identified as a demographic category (along with area of study, gender, and age) and was not the focus of the study, still it is disappointing that so little attention is paid to this concept.

Studies that use personality inventories do pay explicit attention to disability—specifically, mental disability—because most personality inventories are structured in ways that both mark and pathologize mental disability. This is the case with the Five-Factor Personality Inventory, also called the "Big Five" and, more recently, the NEO PI-R, developed by Paul T. Costa Jr. and Robert R. McCrae. Woodfield, Jessop, and McMillan report that this tool is "dominant" in the field of personality psychology (2), and it comes up quite often in educational research (it will reappear in the section on "Participation," below). The five factors are Extraversion, Agreeableness, Conscientiousness, Neuroticism, and Openness to Experience. Each factor is grouped with a number of attributes that define it further: for example, facets of agreeableness include "generous, kind, sympathetic," while facets of neuroticism include "anxious, self-pitying, unstable" (McCrae and John, n.p.). Unsurprisingly, such studies find that neuroticism tends to correlate with lower attendance rates as well as lower academic achievement in general. As Caspi and colleagues put it, "Neuroticism is the opposite of emotional stability, a dimension which generally predicts university success . . . emotionally stable students perform better than neurotic students" (133). (Ironically, *neurotic* is a highly dated term, and fell out of general psychiatric use in 1994, with the advent of DSM-IV [Aho 245]. Yet it persists in educational models that direct current research and practice.)

Although my temptation is to brush off instruments like the NEO PI-R, understanding that their agendas are vastly different from a DS agenda, it's worth examining with more care the *various* ways that educational use of this instrument fails students, for it is frequently applied in university settings.[3] My concerns about using the NEO PI-R to make decisions in educational contexts are these: First, the broad category of "neuroticism" collapses together all kinds of mental disabilities, missing important features of difference (Morey and Zanarini). Second, defining "neuroticism" by means of "self-pity" reifies the myth of disabled persons as self-pitying and narcissistic.[4] Third, I am concerned about the implications of using five orthogonal (nonoverlapping) categories that define traits such as anxiety against traits such as being "enthusiastic," "appreciative," "generous," or "forgiving" (McCrae and John, n.p.). While the factors are meant to delineate *dimensions* of personality—thus, one respondent to the instrument questionnaire will probably exhibit some degree of all five factors—it is an inescapable fact that, according to this type of measurement, anxiety is defined as *different from,* occupying a different lexical space than (for example), generosity. Fourth, for all their careful measurement and observation, educational users of this model have little to say about *how* we might make attendance less of a barrier for our more anxious, neurotic, self-pitying students. Woodfield, Jessop, and McMillan call for "the identification of what universities can do to improve the attendance records of all its students, but particularly those groups most vulnerable to absences" (19–20)—and yet this vague call is not followed up with any concrete suggestions, nor have universities themselves widely taken it up. In fact, the impulse seems to be moving in the opposite direction: personality tests are becoming more and more popular, not as grounds for intervention and support, but as predictors of academic success, with some educators even suggesting that they could be used as admission criteria (Harrison et al.; Conard).

Where and when do students' voices enter the debate on attendance? Some researchers do investigate students' points of view, more often by means of questionnaires than interviews or other more narrative methods. One of the most carefully constructed of these is the 2001 study by Paul Friedman, Fred Rodriguez, and Joe McComb, which included an initial phase through which students' own reasons for being absent from class were collected (twenty-three distinct reasons were identified) and then administered a detailed questionnaire that incorporated these reasons. Friedman, Rodriguez, and McComb did not ask about disability status when assembling student profiles but, perhaps as a result of constructing a questionnaire based upon student perspectives, the "Reasons for Absence" list includes a number of items that implicitly reference disability. Among the reasons listed on the questionnaire (including "Other") are these:

> I was sick.
> Emergency arose—I met an urgent, unexpected need.
> I wanted to take a break when class was meeting.
> The class was hard to reach (e.g., far from where I live or work, parking is inconvenient).
> The teacher digresses, is repetitious, confusing, or goes too quickly, so I don't learn much when I attend class.
> The teacher's speech or handwriting is not intelligible.
> The teacher is rude or doesn't like me.
> I didn't want to participate in a scheduled activity.
> I dislike (an)other student(s) in that class. (127)

While any of these reasons could apply to nondisabled students (and Friedman et al. seem to assume all their participants are nondisabled), note the space this questionnaire makes for the possibility that a class might not be a useful learning environment for cognitive or emotional reasons, as well as the possibility that illness, need for rest, or sudden unanticipated barriers might be important factors as well. This is a welcome change from teacher-centered studies of attendance that make facile assumptions about absent students' attitudes, lack of motivation, and failure to spend "time on task." Friedman, Rodriguez, and McComb make the familiar point that attendance is highly correlated with academic achievement; however, they also emphasize the importance of the factors "The teacher notices or cares that I am there" and "I like participating in this class" (129). Rather than presuming that students must attend class and that absent students are deficient, Friedman, Rodriguez, and McComb begin to make substantial suggestions for ways that kairotic spaces themselves, not students, might be remediated.

Testimonials from students on presence as a feature of undergraduate education, beyond aggregated survey responses, are hard to find. One of the few available is "Drawn Out of Dejection" by Timile Brown, published in *Disability Studies Quarterly.* (I should note that I taught Timile in several classes, and was her independent-study instructor as she composed this essay; my experiences working with her are discussed in more detail in the section on participation.) She writes:

> I was a freshman in college, and I wanted some help. I wanted to know why I was feeling this way. Why I couldn't get out of bed in the morning. Why I cried for no reason some days, out of nowhere. Why I couldn't cry at times when it made sense to cry. Why I felt sick all of the time when I didn't have a cold or the flu. Why I couldn't concentrate. Why it made me physically ill when I thought of having to sit in the classroom around other people. Why? What is wrong with me?

As this passage illustrates, what teachers often assume to be "poor motivation" may in fact be a more complex situation: a student who, for a variety of reasons, cannot get to class—perhaps cannot get out of bed. When Brown did make it to class, as the essay later narrates, the experience could be agonizing:

> Dr. Mantage was a great teacher, and I wanted to give him my undivided attention. He deserved that. But I just couldn't. My mind had a mind of its own. It wouldn't let me concentrate. I missed the lesson on Marcus Garvey! What is it that he did? He . . .
>
> Now my heart is pounding. It's getting warm in here. Why am I so tired all of a sudden? It's as if something is touching me. I can feel it drawing the energy from my limbs. My head hurts. Now a migraine is coming. I hate it when I get those. We have to write a paper on Marcus Garvey by next class. It's not a big paper, but if I don't learn the lesson in class, I won't understand the reading and then I can't write the paper, and if my migraine gets worse I'll see spots in my eyes and then I won't be able to read at all . . . Panic. The room is spinning. Ringing. Loud ringing in my ear. What is that? Does anyone else hear that? Oh no, I can't breathe. Take a deep breath, Timile. Maybe you're just having an asthma attack. You just got a little worked up and it triggered your asthma. You are okay. No, I'm not. It's getting worse. That pain in my chest. Maybe I'm having a heart attack. But I can't. I'm only 18. I hope no one is watching me. Please God, don't let anyone see me like this. Please let me make it to the end of class. Where's my phone? What time is it? Only two minutes left in class. Oh, no! I missed the whole lesson. Where was I? How did I miss 48 minutes? What day is it? Gasping for air. I have to go! I have to go! I speed-walk back to my dorm room. Terrified that there is a witness. . . .
>
> My mom called them my hankty moods. When I would isolate myself in my room, away from everyone else, or when I didn't feel like talking to anyone, I was being hankty. But hankty wasn't cute or funny here. Not in college.

What Brown's mother called "hankty," college instructors and administrators have other terms for: lazy, unmotivated, low-achieving, or—to borrow one of the neuroticism descriptors from the "Big Five"—self-pitying. Why do we so rarely hear from students about how it *feels* to miss classes? Certainly, there is plenty of teacher lore about the elaborate excuses we sometimes receive, usually couched as jokes. But why do we have so little understanding, either in the methodological form presented by Friedman, Rodriguez, and McComb or in the narrative form presented by Brown, of what presence and absence really mean in the classroom, their weight, their significance, their consequences? And how might we move beyond the circular logic of "attendance = high grades = students must attend class" toward more inclusive ways of understanding *presence* in education?

In "On Autistic Presence," Stuart Murray argues that persons on the autism spectrum confound traditional notions of what it means to "have presence," and that their narratives can "form a conception of autism that extends beyond the ways in which the condition is labelled in medical and other institutional contexts" (4). One such institutional context, of course, is that of school: the conventional narrative of the autistic student constructs her as the "hand flapping, self-stimulating, echolalic young child displaying no interest in others and obsessed with rituals" (Murray 2). Murray argues that the presence of persons on the autism spectrum confounds such narratives and "stops the condition [of] being only subject to the workings of metaphor and fascination" (9). In written narrative, which is the focus of Murray's study, I believe this to be true. It is potentially true in the narratives constructed by our presence in kairotic space as well; however, in kairotic space, persons with mental disabilities are especially vulnerable to being *over*written by dominant narratives. The moments are fleeting, the timing is precise and quick, the cues for appropriate behavior both rigid and subtle. In the next section, I turn to the question of what happens when persons with mental disabilities are written by teachers and researchers—and when they write their own narratives—in kairotic classroom space.

Participation and Discussion

One key issue to recognize is that the classroom is *not* a safe space.

—*Peter N. Goggin and Maureen Daly Goggin,* "Presence in Absence: Discourses and Teaching (In, On, and About) Trauma"

Participation[5] in the classroom (and attendant spaces, such as office hours) has been affiliated with many ideals, including engagement, attitude, citizenship, and leadership—to name just a few. Studies of participation range widely: some assume that all students and instructors come from similar cultural or experiential backgrounds, while others are carefully attuned to difference. Some take an explicitly rhetorical stance, while others assume that pedagogies can be objectively and universally applied. A vast literature exists in disability-oriented pedagogical journals such as *The Journal of Special Education;* however, this literature tends to view "participation" as an issue of whether students are getting to class and completing their work successfully, rather than how they are *experiencing and navigating* kairotic spaces such as classroom discussions. Conversely, a fairly substantive literature on classroom participation appears in more general journals, such as *College Teaching,* but these studies usually ignore disability altogether, addressing kairotic exchanges in terms of other markers such as race and class—when such markers are considered at all. Among what I have termed *mental disabilities,* the disabilities most often considered in higher education research are learning and cognitive differences; psychiatric disabilities are addressed much less often.

It's not difficult to find articles proclaiming that students should not "disrupt" the classroom. An example of this point of view comes from Lloyd J. Feldmann's "Classroom Civility is Another of Our Instructor Responsibilities," which states unequivocally that "incivility" in classrooms is a rampant problem and must be eradicated. Feldmann defines incivility as "any action that interferes with a harmonious and cooperative learning atmosphere in the classroom," and classifies it in terms of four categories: "annoyances," such as arriving late or answering one's phone during class; "classroom terrorism"[6] such as going off-topic or holding "private conversations" during class discussions; "intimidation," such as threatening to give negative teacher evaluations; and "involv[ing] or threaten[ing] violence" (137–38). Clearly, some of Feldmann's objections are justifiable and important; threatening violence, for example, is a serious problem (and, not incidentally, is experienced disproportionately by those of minoritized identities). However, I want to call attention to the fact that what an instructor experiences as an "annoyance" or "rudeness" *might in fact be a student participating* in a way that performs, or attempts to accommodate, her own mental disability. For example, a late arrival could mean the student is lazy and thoughtless, but could also mean the student has any one of a number of disabilities that interfere with navigation. Whispering to a classmate or passing notes may be efforts to "catch up" on discussion that is progressing too fast to follow; they might also signal that a student cannot speak in front of the group but deeply wishes to express some idea. Even that bête noire of college instructors, the dreaded cell phone, might represent not "incivility" but any one of a number of strategies to enhance participation, including an attempt to diffuse the stress of sitting quietly in a classroom in the first place.

Not surprisingly, Feldmann's argument that classrooms must be "civil" hews closely to the rationalist imperative that tacitly governs so much of academic discourse. In addition to advising instructors to "take action immediately" to quell incivilities, Feldmann specifies the importance of *omitting emotion* from such exchanges:

> We [instructors] must always remain calm, analytical, and unemotional. Unless carefully planned, expressed emotion tends to make any situation worse. . . . The cardinal rule here is to keep your cool. (139)

My problem here is less with Feldmann's insistence that instructors be always "unemotional," which is obviously rather silly, but rather with its presumption that "incivility" is not *always already* about emotion. Returning to Andrea Nicki's point, it is one thing to struggle with emotional upheavals in kairotic space, which everyone does, and quite another to have a disability that is *composed of* lack of calm or difficulty apprehending socially sanctioned levels of intensity. Feldmann's one reference to the possibility that an instructor might not enjoy his privileges of being a "big white older male" (and apparently one with easy access to calm and objectivity) is to urge "non-BWOM" instructors to work hard to "overcome" these limitations (139).

Less strident than Feldmann's, but retaining the presumption that classrooms will be filled with rational subjects, is Robert Brooke's study "Underlife in the Writing Classroom." This study was one of the earliest to recognize that what instructors assume is disruptive behavior—non-participation, or even anti-participation—could in fact be a form of active participation, albeit with a different agenda. Brooke defines underlife as

> those behaviors which undercut the roles expected of participants in a situation—the ways an employee, for example, shows she is not just an employee, but has a more complex personality outside that role. . . . [B]oth students and teachers undercut the traditional roles of the American educational system in order to substitute more complex identities in their place. (141)

In the classroom Brooke studied, students engaged in "private conversations" during discussions (145), made comments on people's roles in the classroom, and engaged in nonsanctioned activities such as reading the student newspaper or writing journals while they were supposed to be taking notes on discussions. Brooke's analysis, which draws on Goffman's *Stigma* and *Asylums* as well as literature in writing instruction, demonstrates that these "disruptions" can have a positive role: they seek to "provide the other participants in the classroom with a sense that one has other things to do, other interests, that one is a much richer personality than can be shown in this context" (148). Naturally, these positive efforts may not enhance the instructor's agenda; however, they are not simply destructive impulses.

An important distinction between Brooke's reading of underlife and mine is that Brooke treats all such activities as coming from equally situated participants, without regard to differing levels of access. For example, he does not consider the possibility that such unscripted behaviors could stem from lack of ability to follow social cues; from anxiety, confusion, or exhaustion; or from difficulty adhering to the prescribed pace of classroom activities. However, I believe we can and should extend the notion of underlife to include these situations, and recognize that students with mental disabilities may disrupt conventional agendas of participation not out of laziness or malice, nor even rebelliousness, but through sincere efforts *to* participate in ways that reflect their own abilities and needs.

The notions of participation (as well as presence) have been deeply inflected over the last twenty years by the rise of kairotic spaces that do away with literal, fleshly presence—classes held entirely online, or supplementary spaces to conventional classrooms including blogs, discussion boards, and online course-management systems. Digitally mediated spaces are important not only because they have become almost ubiquitous in higher education, but also because their development is closely entwined with disability in education. Online courses are often touted as ways to accommodate mobility, sensory, and other kinds of impairments—sometimes including impairments of the mind. Indeed, it would seem that online spaces offer great promise for those with mental disabilities, since they diffuse kairotic space and enable it to flex in unexpected directions—in other words, they are capable of "cripping" it. However, digital technologies are not simply new-and-improved modes of access: the impression that they will "confer unalloyed benefits upon people with disabilities" presumes that disability is a "static, biologically originating deficit of a given individual, as opposed to a contingent phenomenon that is constituted through social structures and discourses" (Goggin and Newall 263). Moreover, as Jason Palmeri has shown, pedagogical applications of digital technologies tend to reify a static divide between "dis" and "abled," with some technologies regarded as "assistive" and others as "normal" (58).

As a result, studies that explore participation in online kairotic spaces often replicate rationalist notions of this concept. This is the case in a 2005 article by E. Michael Nussbaum and colleagues, which examined the effect of "note starters," or specific prompts such as "My argument is . . . " or "I need to understand . . ." on online discussions. Presuming that "productive argumentative discourse should involve some level of student disagreement" (116), Nussbaum and his coauthors studied this pedagogical strategy as it affected differing personality types, which they measured using the "Big Five" inventory. The authors focused on assertiveness (a subfactor of extraversion), openness to ideas (one of the big five) and anxiety (a subfactor of neuroticism), hypothesizing that those traits would be particularly relevant (117–18). They found that the note starters did increase disagreement for students exhibiting all three types of traits; however, "students who were anxious benefited less from note starters" (125). The subfactor of anxiety, in fact, proved complex enough that Nussbaum and his coauthors to treat it at length in their discussion:

> Anxious students might be somewhat afraid of how other students might react if challenged. . . . [T]he findings suggest that note starters do help initiate arguments but may do little to alleviate "face" concerns, especially for anxious students. In retrospect, this finding makes sense. Note starters may prompt students to take opposing viewpoints, but a student may still be anxious about making a foolish argument or making others look foolish. (128–29)

To their credit, Nussbaum and colleagues argue that because of this finding, "other steps may need to be taken to make [note starters] more effective for students high in anxiety" (129). However, they miss a key problem in their understanding of classroom participation: their adherence to the rationalist belief that conflict is a—if not *the*—key ingredient for "productive" participation in kairotic space.[7] If the rationalist assumptions of ableist pedagogies are simply imported into online discussion spaces, then we may expect that their barriers for students with mental disabilities will not be greatly alleviated.

I'm aware that the barriers of kairotic spaces might seem trivial to those who have little trouble navigating them. Are you too shy, too sensitive, too garrulous, too undisciplined, too nervous? Just get over it! I've now worked for disability services offices at two schools, and have worked with disabled students at four, and I am frequently surprised by how hard it is to refute the presumption that, because mental disabilities are not consistently and easily apparent, they must not exist, or must not be that big a deal. A passage from Brown's "Drawn Out of Dejection" illustrates this presumption:

> "I find that pretty hard to believe," she [a member of the support staff] said to me. . . . Why would she say that to me? I'm not a liar. Do I look like a liar? Maybe I do. I told her that I hadn't been able to get out of bed the last two weeks. I didn't feel well. I told her that I even went to the doctor several times. But they'd always tell me that they didn't know what it was. And she said to me, "I find that pretty hard to believe." . . . Those words chime into my thoughts at random, even years later. Those words make me cry, even years later. Those words make me feel worthless, even years later. I didn't reach out for help again for three years.

In the full section of which this passage is a part, Brown strikes a number of themes pertinent to mental disabilities in academe: immobility, dread of entering classroom spaces, unpredictability of symptoms, and difficulty concentrating. Most important, perhaps, is her reaction to being disbelieved: she withdrew from the services that were ostensibly in place to support her and "didn't reach out for help again" for almost the entirety of her college career.

As Timile's instructor in several classes, and also her advisor for a year, I knew her quite well, but she was a second-semester senior before I learned of her depression.[8] She came to class often enough to pass; and, although she was quiet in discussions, she gave ample evidence of having studied the material through other channels, such as quick-writes and essays. In fact, as her retrospective essay in *Disability Studies Quarterly* specifies, she had adopted a deliberate strategy to compensate for her difficulty participating: "I would just ace all of my tests and papers." She was passing in more ways than one, and she was doing so precisely because she had been told that her disability was not credible.[9] To place this account in terms of participation, Timile was putting tremendous effort into her participation; however, the picture presented to her professors, including me, was generally that of silence—metaphorical when she was absent, literal when she came to class.

In the last decade, some work on academic discourse has managed to move beyond the notion that argument must equal disagreement, and that silence equals nonparticipation. Two important works on silence are Mary M. Reda's *Between Speaking and Silence: A Study of Quiet Students* and Cheryl Glenn's *Unspoken: A Rhetoric of Silence.* Glenn acknowledges that sometimes students are silent because they *have been* silenced; at other times, silence may operate as a powerful rhetorical strategy. She argues, "Both the spoken and the unspoken can resist domination; both the spoken and the unspoken can invite consideration. . . . Silence [can be] a rhetorical art of empowered action" (156). In addition, a qualitative study by Paul Michalec and Hilary Burg found that when silence/listening was included as an explicitly valued means of participation in class discussions, students identified this factor as a valuable learning resource (320). This research opens space for deeper consideration of mental disability in the classroom when one of its manifestations is silence: perhaps we can view such silences as forms of discourse in themselves.

More intractable, however, are the "uncivil" forms of participation that do not remain silent, but vocally or behaviorally interrupt the conventional script of classroom discourse. Teachers often call such forms of participation "resistant."

Resistance

To vastly oversimplify the matter (for a moment), theorists of resistance in education tend to divide resistance into two kinds: bad and good. "Bad" resistance is like Feldmann's notion of incivility: it seeks to impede the flow of knowledge. "Good" resistance is a creative form of disruption: it seeks to interrupt dominant agendas and question authorities in ways that enhance the flow of knowledge. Sometimes instructors will view resistance against general hegemonic norms as "good" while also attempting to prevent resistances against the norms established in their own classrooms. At other times, however, and particularly within the tradition of critical pedagogy, instructors will view resistance more flexibly, and seek to include disruption of their own classroom-based agendas as part of the learning process. An example of this latter approach is that taken by Cecilia Rodríguez Milanés, who describes her efforts to construct "a dialogic pedagogy" (116) through means such as cowritten grading contracts, classroom votes on policy matters, and asking students to help choose course texts. However, as Milanés emphasizes throughout the article, this pedagogy was difficult to implement for a number of reasons, including students' own resistance to the unfamiliar approach.

Milanés's story exemplifies three types of classroom resistance outlined by Elizabeth Flynn, who describes the types as follows:

> [T]he first involves planned and positive action in opposition to resistance, which I will call "strategic resistance"; the second involves resistance that deliberately disrupts liberatory practices, which I will call "counter-strategic resistance"; and the third involves resistance that is a spontaneous and emotional reaction that may have multiple and conflicting motivations and effects, which I will call "reactive resistance." (18)

Quite often, when practitioners write about "resistance," they mean only the first of the three types named by Flynn. Their goals tend to be lofty, the names of their pedagogies inspiring, and their reaction to students' discomfort in "feminist" or "liberatory" classrooms impatient. I am more interested in the work of teachers who recognize the subtle interchanges between the various kinds of resistance. Milanés is one; another, discussed below, is Michelle Payne, in *Bodily Discourses: When Students Write about Abuse and Eating Disorders*. I am also interested in privileging students' own accounts of classroom resistance, because the great majority of work on this topic is written from the instructor's standpoint, and often relies on descriptions of students such as "they looked at me blankly" or "I could see the hostility in their eyes" without any counterpoint from students as to what might be behind those putatively blank or hostile looks. My aim here is to show that our accounts of classroom resistance will be enriched if we recognize the role—tacit or explicit—that mental disability plays in them, and also that an accessible classroom neither forecloses emotion nor is overrun by it, but makes constructive and creative space for it.

While many writers on pedagogies of resistance prefer to leave emotion out of the equation, Flynn argues that reactive (spontaneous, emotionally charged) resistance "in its positive manifestations is necessary for successful teaching" (33). She also points out that her definition of reactive resistance is similar to the definition of "outburst" offered by Kathleen Dixon and William Archibald in their introduction to *Outbursts in Academe: Multiculturalism and Other Sources of Conflict*. However, the meaning of "outburst" actually goes further than Flynn's "reactive resistance," because Dixon and Archibald recognize that an outburst is subject to multiple interpretations, not only by different participants in the scene, but also by one participant over time. In other words, it is a kairotic event.

> An *outburst* is a response to a conflict that expresses a person's orientation to that conflict and to the social and political conditions that underlie it. . . . Outbursts are not reducible to mere expressions of "resistance" to "oppression." An emotional display made in a classroom or at a conference might feel good at the moment, feel bad later, advance one's cause, and set it back simultaneously. Furthermore, one person's outburst may create the conditions for another person's silence. (Dixon and Archibald xi)

This recognition of the apparitional, shape-shifting nature of an outburst is important because it acknowledges the often-forgotten point that, in kairotic spaces, the "meaning" of an emotion or reaction is never stable. Moreover, people with mental disabilities will often find themselves on the losing end of such interpretations, either by being told that their outbursts are inappropriate, overly emotional, or simply nonsensical; or—on the other hand—by responding to highly emotional situations with panic, decompensation, or shutting down.

The latter concern is one I couldn't shake as I read Milanés's article, because it relies heavily on the assumption that consensus and negotiation are discussion-based events. My rereading is not intended to discredit Milanés's pedagogy, which in fact does include practices that may be helpful to students with mental disabilities (such as holding intense conversations individually rather than in groups, or seeking feedback both orally and in writing), but to point out how the classroom she describes might inhibit full participation for students with mental disabilities. I'm thinking of one of the stories her article tells, a moment that Dixon and Archibald would call an outburst. I quote the story at some length here, with the intention of rereading it within the framework of disability studies.

[T]here were about a half dozen students that liked to chat with each other but not with the whole circle. They tended to congregate near the door for an easy exit. . . . Every couple of days I would interrupt their private conversations and call attention to their rudeness, noting that other class members had listened to their input during the discussion. Anyway, on this particular day, as the rest of the class moved the desks into a circle, a few students gathered around me to hand in late papers or incomplete assignments. These few, their faces displaying grave concern, wanted to give me excuses before turning their papers in. As a class we had come to consensus on what were legitimate excuses, and what I was hearing didn't sound like any of those. I asked these students to see me after class, but I was bothered. Hadn't the contract, the one we wrote together, clearly outlined the guidelines and due dates for papers? I was antsy about getting to work, and so I asked someone to begin the discussion with a go-around, where everyone in the circle speaks to a sentence/passage or whatever. The half dozen conversationalists were having a grand old time on one side of the room, and then one young woman from the other side flippantly said, "Start with me—I didn't read it so go on to the next person." There were chuckles and then a lull—even the talkers' attention was seized. Here it was, I thought, they're testing me.

Somehow, the people who had crowded around me with late papers and lame [*sic*] excuses, the disregard for the contract (which stipulated that all reading was required before coming to class), the chattering, the smirks—it all came to a head and I felt compelled to talk at the class . . . [Milanés's ellipsis]. Okay, so I yelled at them. There. I shocked myself. I took out a copy of the contract, waved it at them, and reread out loud some of the requirements, reminding them that they had authored this contract. I asked them why they had put me in this position, this position of authority (my neck veins were bulging by then). I told them again that I didn't like that position and that I was trying to be democratic not authoritarian. I was angry, and after about five minutes of scolding them for not being more responsible, I shut my mouth. Guilt began to pulse at my temples. There was silence. I like to think that some of them hung their heads in shame, for that was exactly what I was doing. After some awkward moments and nervous coughing, one of the students began the discussion, the work of the day. (122–23)

Milanés's account is unusual because it offers close description of a classroom moment during which no one, including herself, behaved in a composed manner. For this, I admire it. I also admire Milanés's response to the event, which was to talk to students in a more informal setting, afterward, to discuss what had happened, and to get feedback from a colleague as well. The article later reflects on this and other outbursts in the classroom: "So I yelled. They [students] yelled at each other from time to time when discussing something or other, but I found that in both classes tolerance reigned. That is not to say that hostility never reared its ugly head, but when it did, we talked it out, talked around it, negotiated the disagreement at hand, and moved past it" (123). I suspect that teacher-researchers (me among them) have a habit of glossing moments of classroom conflict to portray ourselves as having at least a little—sometimes a lot—more composure than we really did. But it is precisely because Milanés has provided this richness of detail (shaped and authored though, of course, it is) that we can reread for the interstices in her story where mental disability tacitly enters, or is excluded from, the "negotiated" outcome.

To reread, then: First, why might those half-dozen students have been sitting together? While one interpretation is that they were forming a sort of gang and willfully using the power of numbers to oppose Milanés's agenda ("the work of the day"), we can use Brooke's concept of underlife to recognize that their habit of clustering, their "private conversations" and "rudeness," were forms of underlife. Further, we can consider the possibility that the clustering and private conversations are ways of coping with the confines of the classroom, a space in which one must exhibit at all times focus, attentiveness, and engagement with the sanctioned topic. Now, this is not to say that the cluster of students were whispering about that day's reading (they probably weren't), nor that all or any of them had mental disabilities (a possibility, but not a probability). It is, however, to point out that the hallmarks of approved participation in most classroom spaces, even those which earnestly strive to be democratic and to welcome all, sets up a space of nearly relentless focus, composure, turn-taking, and rational exchange—and that failure to participate in these strict ways is often labeled "resistant."

Second, why were the excuses for the late work "lame"? Milanés's anger stems from the fact that the excuses did not adhere to the contract the class had coauthored: "I took out a copy of the contract, waved it at them, and reread out loud some of the requirements, reminding them that they had authored this contract." But what happens to notions of consensus and collaboration when considered from the perspective of mental disability? Were all members of the class able to apprehend the speed, social nuances, and communicative styles made available throughout this process? Did any of them feel too much anxiety, or too much pressure from social stigma, to include a concern such as "I can't sleep because of my nightmares / depression / mania, and so my work might be late sometimes—but I can't tell you when or why it might happen"? Who was absent, either materially or mentally, during the negotiations? Even in the most dedicated efforts to create consensus and a cooperative learning environment, the very structures that shape academic discourse remain rationalist.

Michelle Payne's case study of a student named Ann, who was abused by her father and her boyfriend, helps fill in some of the gaps I've pointed out here. In her writings and in interviews, Ann practices various forms of resistance to rationalist classroom discourse. Payne introduces Ann's work:

> On August 30, 1994, eighteen-year-old Ann handed her Freshman English instructor, Katherine, her response to the first writing assignment of the year: Write an essay about something that has affected the person you are today. Ann had not met with Katherine in conference yet; in fact, the class had only met a few times. The writing she handed in described the night of Ann's junior prom when her boyfriend became so angry with her that he tackled her, punching her in the lower back as she hit the ground. As Ann describes him, her boyfriend tried to manipulate her into staying with him by threatening suicide, later telling her "that it didn't matter if he turned out to be a wife batterer, that [she] wouldn't stay with him long enough to see it happen anyway." After the attack, Ann became anorexic, losing over thirty pounds, exercising twice a day. (81)

Payne reprints the full essay, along with Katherine's comments, and argues that Ann's choice of when and how to disclose her abuse and eating disorder reflects a strong sense of agency, even to the way sentences are constructed: "There are points where her boyfriend has no agency, and Ann casts herself in the object position" (87). Payne also points out that Ann begins the essay by placing herself in the position of author, choosing what and how to disclose. From Ann's essay:

> As I sat in my first session of Freshman English class earlier on this clear fall day wondering what I could write about that has affected the person I am today but that wasn't so personal I'd have a crisis writing about [it], and was still a significant event, I had kind of a difficult time. Finally, I decided to write about a point in my life when I wasn't very happy with the person I was and how I managed to make it through that difficult time. (83)

Although it would be easy to shrug off Ann's framing of her essay as a story of overcoming, I believe that the use of such "commonplaces" (Bartholomae 137, qtd. in Payne) can also signal a gesture toward claiming power on the part of a student/author.[10] Another gesture is Ann's choice to describe an incident of abuse in detail: "I hadn't gone very far [away from his car] when I heard the footfalls of my boyfriend sprinting after me. I had just begun to turn around when he plowed me into the ground, prom dress and all. Not only had he ran me over full force, but he drove his fist into my back while he was at it" (84). Like Timile Brown, Ann uses concrete detail and narrative style to reconstruct a kairotic space in a way that allows her to shape, consider, and intervene in it.

When Payne observed Ann's behavior in face-to-face situations, she learned that Ann's rhetorical strategies formed an intriguing mixture of compliance *and* resistance, of silence *and* outburst. In person, Payne reports, Ann was a quiet person: "she rarely spoke in class, and during our interviews she seemed shy and hesitant, a demeanor that became increasingly more at odds with the persona I read in some of her later writings" (88–89). Recalling Milanés's account, we can imagine that Ann might be an unlikely candidate to speak up during classroom negotiation of a course contract. In fact, Payne provides an extended transcript of one classroom discussion during which "students' frustrations or annoyance seethed below the surface" (102), and during which Ann did not speak at all. However, she felt strong resistance, as the response she later wrote showed:

> Ann did not speak during this class discussion, and the response essay she wrote later describes how furious she became as more students argued why the messages and situatedness of rap music could be ignored. . . . [Ann's essay said] "I was overcome by pure frustration. I knew I should have said something in class and wanted to, but I was past frustration. I was mad. I'm not sure why I got so angry, but I even had the little tremors and hot cheeks of true anger." (108, 111)

The multilayered design of Payne's methodology allows her to access the (apparent) paradoxes that may arise when trauma, abuse, anger, and conflict enter the classroom: sometimes quiet students are practicing resistance too, and not just resistance to classroom authority, but to larger social injustices as well. As Payne suggests, "By analogy, [Ann] is arguing to have her own anger (at her father, her boyfriend) mean something beyond immaturity, selfishness, and *irrationality*" (111; emphasis added). In the carefully observed context of Payne's case study, then, a response that might be quickly labeled "neurotic" by the "Big Five" inventory, or "inappropriate" by a less thoughtful educator or researcher, takes on a different kind of coherence.

Even in classrooms like Katherine's, which offered multiple avenues for students to practice resistance, or Milanés's, which worked to incorporate resistance into an inclusive pedagogy, negotiating resistance remains difficult. Student essays that engage mental disability will often be read, as Payne acknowledges, as "weepy" and confessional (1). And, as Milanés acknowledges, there is no way to completely overturn the structural assumptions that there must be some "work of the day," that students must demonstrate adequate engagement with that work, and that the teacher will assign a value to their work: "the university sees to that" (118). However, I emphasize that the situation is *difficult* but not *impossible*. At heart I am more of a reformist than a revolutionary—or rather, the kind of revolutionary I am seeks to create change while not destroying lives, for it is the very persons who are most disenfranchised by academic discourses (those who are nonwhite, working-class, disabled, and/or queer, for instance) who have the most to lose when teachers spout lofty radical goals but provide little of use in day-to-day survival. I'm a fan of the concept of microrebellion, which I see as different from merely "working within the system" or "using the master's tools." Microrebellions, as I understand them, get beyond the inside/outside notions of systems and houses to recognize that academic discourse is always already composed through and by the deviant. We—the "mad, bad and sad" (Snelgrove)—are in the academy already, few and stigmatized and silenced as we may be. As Brueggemann and colleagues write, "We are sitting beside you. No, we *are* you" (369). We can take concrete action. The final section of this chapter is dedicated to describing how such actions might unfold.

A Way to Move: Redesigning the Kairotic Space of the Classroom

> College professors should be aware that simply posting office hours on their door and sitting in the office during those hours does not provide adequate opportunities for interaction. Professors need to be aware of students' personality differences and their effects upon students' behaviors.
>
> —*Ibtesam Halawah,* "The Impact of Student-Faculty Information Interpersonal Relationships on Intellectual and Personal Development"

My suggestions for ways to redesign the classroom's kairotic spaces to make them more accessible for persons with mental disabilities are grounded in the principles of universal instructional design (UID; also called universal design for learning [UDL], or simply universal design). The "universal" part of the moniker expresses an aim rather than an accomplished fact: Universal design sets as its ideal a learning environment that is accessible to all learning styles, abilities, and personalities, but acknowledges that such efforts must always be partial and engaged in a process of continual revision. (Some, including Jason Palmeri, refer instead to "participatory design.") "Design" is understood broadly, indicating not just material criteria (such as large-print handouts or extended time on tests) but attitudes[11] as well. Patricia Silver, Andrew Bourke, and K. C. Strehorn explain the purpose and value of universal design:

> If this approach becomes part of the institution's instructional methodologies, students with disabilities in higher education will no longer need to rely as heavily on support systems that are secondary to the primary instructional programs. In the typical service delivery program, modifications in an instructor's approaches or assessment procedures for students with disabilities require that students identify themselves as disabled, request specific accom-

> modations, and wait for these specific adjustments to be implemented—a process that often takes weeks to complete. This traditional case-by-case instructional approach is quite conservative when compared to UID, which places accessibility issues as an integral component of all instructional planning. (47)

As Silver, Bourke, and Strehorn indicate, one important value of universal design is that it dilutes the intensity and necessity of "disclosure" at the beginning of the semester: all students are seen as diversely situated learners, and the classroom is set up with this assumption in mind. However, it's important to note, as Silver and colleagues do, that support services will remain necessary so long as the ideal of universal design is not reached—and, as more than a decade of serious applications of universal design has shown (their article was published in 1998), this ideal is more an ongoing series of adjustments than a goal to be reached.

This view of universal design as a "way to move" rather than a fixed set of practices is also taken by Jay Dolmage (24). Dolmage notes that many resources available on universal design can make it seem like a set of concrete (and burdensome) activities that must be added to the classroom. However, Dolmage argues, universal design is best understood through intentional verbs that can be applied in various ways—for example, those drawn from Ohio State's faculty tip sheet on universal design, which emphasizes "permit," "listen," "update," "guide," "clarify," "review," and "allow" (qtd. in Dolmage 24). Dolmage explains further:

> Registered as action, [UD] is a way to move. In some ways, it is also a worldview. UD is not a tailoring of the environment to marginal groups; it is a form of hope, a manner of trying. (24)

Understanding and acknowledging that universal design must be responsive as well as prepared, flexible as well as accommodating, brings up an inevitable question: Won't this still mean that our students must disclose their disabilities, discuss their needs, help us understand their ways of learning? Yes, they will. However—and this is the key difference between universally designed instruction and conventional "remediation"—under the principles of universal design, *all* students are encouraged to consider, share, and assist with the implementation of this information. Universal design is not for a few "special" students, but rather a way to move forward with all our learners (and ourselves) in as accessible a way as possible.

But here's another problem: haven't I been arguing, throughout this chapter, that students with mental disabilities are among those who may be least able to "share" such information in discussions, conferences, or even on paper? How can we implement universal design principles without relying on the same rationalist assumptions that have shaped classroom "participation" for a hundred (or a thousand) years? My answer is both a suggestion and a disclaimer: We can open as many different channels of communication as possible, in hopes that at least one will be accessible enough for a given student to use it, and trust that our own attitudes will have much to with student response. As Ibtesam Halawah's investigation into student-faculty relationships shows, students' perception of faculty's concern for and commitment to their learning has a strong impact on their academic success. Too, we must accept that universal design is not one specific procedure, nor a recipe for success, but rather, as Dolmage emphasizes, "a form of hope" (24). I am a teacher, and I have no magic to offer, beyond the magic of persons working hard to understand one another and learn together—which, I believe, is magic enough.

Before launching into my suggestions, I must also offer a disclaimer, or rather a series of them: Beeping cell phones in the classroom do annoy me. Even worse, *I* have been known to send text-messages during classes. (I also chew gum sometimes.) Students whispering to each other during discussions make me anxious, occasionally irritated. All of my syllabi include attendance policies, and one class—a creative-writing workshop—permits very few absences. I use a lot of printed handouts that surely are less accessible for some of my students than others. In short, I am no paragon, and my own classroom approaches are continually under revision. (After writing this chapter, I'm feeling particularly uncomfortable about the idea of attaching grade penalties to absences.) The best I can offer is not perfection, nor even frequent success, but consistent effort. This list reflects some of my efforts—those I practice myself, and those that I have learned from, as a person with mental disabilities, when I navigate kairotic classroom space.

1. FOCUS ON WHAT'S FEASIBLE.

I realize that some of my ideas, listed below, might sound absurd to a teacher who is accustomed to face-to-face office hours, does not have access to chat or text-messaging, or would be overwhelmed by trying to navigate multiple online spaces simultaneously. These suggestions are meant to be used as a kind of tasting menu rather than a course-by-course meal. Each suggestion should be modified or ignored based upon a teacher's own context, abilities, and style. For my own frenetic, visual/verbal ways of learning—not to mention my anxiety during face-to-face interactions—holding two or three conversations via chat is considerably more effective and energy-efficient than holding one oral/aural conference in person. But of course, your mileage will vary. The point is not to do just what I do, but to assess each particular instructional context and consider ways that the avenues of communication can stretch and flex. And set limits: you are not establishing yourself as a constantly available answer machine, but rather as someone who can respond in different ways at different times—within your own abilities.

2. MAP THE CLASS EXPLICITLY.

Syllabus statement.

College teachers in the United States are required by law to include a "disability statement" on their syllabi. This statement is often written in second person and presumes that responsibility for accommodation lies with the student: for instance, "If you have a documented disability, you should register with the Office of Disability Services to obtain reasonable accommodations." While working within legal and institutional guidelines, we can change or add to the required language in order to emphasize the universality of learning differences and our openness to negotiating these. For example, in addition to the language I am required to include, I have added the following sentences to the statement on my syllabi: *I assume that all of us have different ways of learning, and that the organization of any course will accommodate each student differently. For example, you may prefer to process information by speaking and listening, so that some of the handouts I provide may be difficult to absorb. Please communicate with me as soon as you can about your individual learning needs and how this course can best accommodate them.* If your school's required statement includes outdated language such as "special needs," address this issue with the person or office that mandates the language.

Beginning-of-class remarks.

Spend some time on the accommodation statement when you review the syllabus with your class. I generally include a few interactive syllabus exercises—for example, it is the first document we annotate (see appendix

A) in my classes—so that students have multiple chances to interact with it. My practice is to read aloud and then elaborate on my syllabus's accommodation statement, giving examples of my own needs as a learner in order to emphasize that such needs are not a question of needing "more" support, but needing different kinds of support. One of the first things I tell students is that I have difficulty processing aural information; therefore, a question I can't respond to immediately should be written in a note, communicated via email, or they should make sure I write it down.

Since I began actually speaking about accommodation rather than just pointing to that section of the syllabus, I have noticed an increase in the number of students who discuss their learning needs with me early in the semester—some of which involve documented disabilities, some not. The most memorable of these instances occurred during a recent semester in a first-year composition class. Having delivered my opening-day speech about learning styles, communication, and access, I was approached after class by a student whom I had already mentally marked as a "potential problem." (Not a reaction I'm proud of, but in the spirit of Milanés's account, I believe it is important to describe and question our less-composed teacherly moments, because they are valuable learning opportunities.) I'd noticed this student staring out the window for much of the class, hanging her head back, and closing her eyes for long intervals. After class, she approached me and explained that she had a disability that made it very hard for her to stay awake for any extended period of time. I am guessing that the content and structure of our first class may have opened an avenue for this student to raise the issue, since I subsequently learned that she had not approached her other instructors that semester until a couple of weeks later, when she had her forms from the Office of Disability Services in hand. Finding accommodations for her particular learning needs was difficult for me, and sometimes we struggled, especially when navigating situations like small-group workshops. However, it was immensely easier on both of us than it would have been if I hadn't known about her tiredness from the very beginning of class. Important to notice here is the shifting location of *problem:* my observations of the student during our first class led me to the assumption that she would be a "problem," but after she spoke to me, I realized that my *perception* of her actions was in fact a problem. Once we had that conversation, we were able to shift focus to the actual problem at hand, which was how she could best access our classroom.[12]

Description of your class's kairotic spaces.
It is traditional to state explicitly what students must do in terms of completing reading, papers, and exams; however, it is much rarer for an instructor to offer explicit information about an upcoming class's kairotic spaces. A model for establishing "norms for class discussion," based upon the Courage to Teach (CTT) model, is offered by Michalec and Burg in "Transforming Discussions from Collegiate to Collegial." According to Michalec and Burg, the students in their study found value in receiving explicit information about the "norms" that would govern class discussions (318).

Questions that may be useful for instructors to consider or discuss with their students include these: Will information be shared primarily via lectures? Will lectures be supplemented with online notes or slides? Will the class be discussion-based—and what does "discussion" mean in your classroom? Will students be giving presentations—and again, what does "presentation" mean in your classroom's context? How much group work is involved? How firm or flexible will deadlines be? If you can give students a clear sense, within the first week, of how the class will unfold kairotically, students will have more time to either transfer to a different class or communicate their concerns to you. Many barriers will still exist, of course: sometimes students cannot change their schedules because of their jobs, majors, childcare needs, and so on; sometimes a concept you think you have explained clearly will be murky to one or more students. Again, the key is not to solve all problems but to deepen and broaden the channels of possible access.

Explaining participation in our own classrooms may require some reflection for teachers, for until we are forced to do so, we often treat participation like Justice Stewart's famous (and later recanted) definition of obscenity: we assume we know it when we see it. Be as direct as possible. What behaviors indicate to you that students are participating? What are your pet peeves? What alternative modes of communication would you like to try, and how can your students help you implement them? What are your own abilities and limitations in kairotic spaces? The more often I have these conversations with students, the more I learn about myself: for example, I tend to place high value on questions students ask of each other; I prefer not to speak much during oral/aural discussions, instead offering a "wrap-up" comment to recap main points and guide students toward the next reading or activity; and (again because of my own aural-processing difficulties) "side conversations" distract me a great deal. I have found that when I provide clear goals for a discussion (about which more below), and acknowledge my own limitations, the conversation progresses much more easily than when I simply open up the floor and assume students already know what I expect.

The role of presence.

If presence is a necessary component of the class, be direct about that. I teach one class for which I accept very few absences: a workshop in creative nonfiction that meets once per week. The class as I have designed it is primarily composed of students' kairotic exchanges; in other words, most of the course content is built by the workshop members as the semester goes on. I emphasize this aspect of the class at the beginning of the semester, and explain why this is the policy. In part because of my concerns about "presence" as they intersect with class attendance, I have also begun offering the class as an independent study.

When possible, make use of nonphysical classroom spaces. Because I teach in a computer classroom, I tend to alternate between oral/aural and online modes of discussion; within online spaces, I alternate between synchronous and asynchronous formats. Maria J. Lavooy and Michael H. Newlin found, in a study of web-based learning over seven semesters, that students consistently selected courses, whether "live" or online, that enabled some form of synchronous interaction. Taking part in a synchronous discussion that does not require one to "jump into" an oral/aural conversation can benefit all students, particularly those for whom the timing and social pressures of face-to-face situations are difficult to navigate. I have used course-management software and also free "blog" spaces (WordPress and LiveJournal) to construct spaces that enable both synchronous and asynchronous discussions.

3. PROVIDE DIRECT INSTRUCTION FOR PARTICIPATION.

Annotation.

Like Anne Fitzsimmons, I view annotation as an "ethical practice," in that it is a component of kairotic space that enables students to move from being passive receivers of texts to active interveners in texts. The first document we annotate in my classes is the course syllabus (appendix A); I also provide direct instruction on what I mean by *annotation* (appendix B). Drawing upon Fitzsimmons's guidelines, I use a broad definition of annotation so that a course reading, a policy document, a peer's draft, or the classroom itself can each be construed as a text in which a student's annotations can intervene. (Fitzsimmons asks students to annotate her class each day by writing her a note at the end of the period.) Annotations often provide the basis for discussions, whether oral/aural, online, small-group or large-group; they also provide opportunities for me to check students' understanding, as when I begin a discussion by asking where they wrote "?" or "I don't get it" in their annotations and focusing on those areas. Finally, I encourage students to develop their own styles of annotation. Most choose to follow the model I provide, which involves handwriting notes in the margins of a document; however, others, for reasons ranging from learning style to ability to economic concerns (needing to resell books), have chosen to use Post-its, color-coding, typed notes on a separate page, or tape-recorded voice notes.

"Annotation" in my view includes not just "new ideas," but also thoughtful paraphrasing. In their study of oral discussion in an inclusive middle-school classroom, Cynthia Okolo, Ralph P. Ferretti, and Charles A. MacArthur found that one successful strategy was "revoicing," or paraphrasing what someone else had just said (161). This strategy has several advantages: it models rhetorical listening; it affirms the speaker's words without using evaluative language; and, if requested directly, it can also provide an avenue for a more "quiet" student to enter the discussion, since in some cases it may be less stressful to paraphrase another's words than to come up with an "original" comment. Oral paraphrases can be facilitated via heuristics like the "note starters" described by Nussbaum and coauthors: for example, "I hear so-and-so saying that . . . Another part of the text that supports her point is . . ."

Valuing quiet, enabling voice.

Establish systems to take pressure off "quiet" students. When I have a sense that discussions are getting off-balance—with three or four students commenting often and other members of the class remaining quiet—I sometimes set up a "calling around" discussion, in which each participant responds to some question or idea, then calls on the next person of her choice, until each member has added a thought to the conversation. This practice can offer a space for students—like Ann—who would like to establish a presence in oral discussions but can't find the right kairotic moment to enter.

Another alternative avenue of participation is to ask for volunteers to take notes on a particular discussion, then post them for the class to access; in some cases, students who have difficulty entering spontaneous oral exchange are skilled at listening and "translating" information. Yet another way is to ask each student to do a bit of writing at the end of a discussion, to share on paper something he did not say but wanted to say; such writings can go into a student's folder of "private reflections," shared with peers, or turned in for the instructor's comment. (Note: if you sometimes collect writings, but sometimes do not, always let students know before they begin whether the task at hand will be private, sharing-optional, or sharing-required.)

Yet another feedback strategy, offered by Matt Tincani, is that of "response cards" during lectures. Tincani suggests that, at different points during a lecture, students can use preprinted cards or write their own with brief responses to questions (generally yes/no or one-word); all cards are held up simultaneously (130). This allows each student to experience a brief interaction with the material without putting an individual student on the spot. Instructors can respond to cards in various ways—as quick comprehension checks, prompts for small-group discussions, or material for later follow-up questions from students. Graham and coauthors describe a similar system using electronic handheld devices or "clickers." Clickers are now common in larger classroom settings, particularly in the social and natural sciences.

4. EXPERIMENT WITH MULTIPLE CHANNELS OF FEEDBACK.

Requesting feedback.
Establish a system of regular feedback, using multiple modes, to ask students about their learning processes in your class. Examples include impromptu writes, text messages, individual conferences, online chat spaces, or letters. Whenever possible, organize the system so that students' diverse communication styles and possible difficulty "sharing" information are given room. Vary between written, oral, sketched, and diagrammed; private, small-group, and class-wide; anonymous and identified. Assume that some students may need to be asked for feedback several times before they are ready to take you up on the suggestion; and, if you use impromptu writing as a mode of communication, build in a way to stretch the time available (for example, invite students to finish their writings later and bring them to the next class). Keep the basis of the system simple and direct; for example, while varying modes of communication, select a few consistent prompts, such as "I've learned . . . I'm struggling with . . . I want to ask . . ." For those instructors now won-

dering whether I ever sleep, I should add that I give myself permission to respond very lightly to these communications. Except in cases when it seems that a student needs more attention, I limit myself to one short sentence, or even just a word or two, of response each. Depending on the size of a class, my energy level, and my perception of the class's need, I make these feedback requests between twice and five times a semester, although, of course students are invited to offer them as often as they like.,

Providing feedback.
Offer frequent feedback on how well the class as a whole is responding to your concern for participation. Let students know that you notice when strong moves are made in discussion or peer response. Correspondingly, give feedback when students' ways of participating are not meeting your expectations (although, of course, never single out a student in front of peers for negative feedback). I've told a whole class before, for example, that I was disappointed by their written feedback for each other on a particular peer-response exercise. This kind of concern can stand alone, or can also be paired with a "let's redesign this" exercise, in which students provide ideas for redesigning a component of the class. (For an extended study on incorporating student feedback into course design, see Catherine Luna's "Learning from Diverse Learners: (Re)writing Academic Literacies and Learning Disabilities in College.")

Multimodal communication.
Varying the mode and style of communication enables access for a wider range of students. Patricia Dunn's study *Talking Sketching Moving: Multiple Literacies in the Teaching of Writing* points out that composition has historically been heavily dependent upon "word-based pedagogies" (15) and that in U.S. educational contexts generally, intelligence tends to be conflated with use of language, as opposed to other modes including oral dialogue, movement, or drawing. Although Dunn's study focuses on the writing classroom in particular, her ideas can easily be applied to other disciplines:

> Focusing so narrowly on only one way of knowing [linguistic] not only squanders the thinking power of those who flee such a system as soon as they can, but a linguistic pedagogy also limits the insights even conventionally "good students" (good writers) may have if challenged to think outside their intellectual comfort zones. (26)

Like Dolmage, Dunn regards universal design in the classroom as a "way to move" (Dolmage 24), that is, as a flexible and ongoing series of adjustments and experiments adhering to an underlying belief in access. In this section I offer a range of examples from my own and others' classrooms that illustrate different ways we have found to move.

For example, I hold office hours both in person and via real-time computer chat. During my office hours, I open a chat program and log in with the username I've designated for teaching purposes. When no one is physically present at my office hours, I can carry on two or—depending on the conversations' intensity and complexity—even three conversations at a time. If I need to just chat with one student at a time, or a student arrives in my office, I'll ask the others to wait, operating on a "first come, first served" basis. Typically, it's more convenient for students to "wait" online, so that they can pursue other activities, than to stand or sit in a bored line outside my office.

Mixing up the mode and style of communication heightens the chances that a student will find at least one mode that works for her. And, based on my own experience, she is then more likely to continue to use it. In one case, a student who text-messaged me a couple of times in response to direct suggestions then continued to "check in" periodically via text message—in one case, offering an extended response to a reading on a day that she was too ill to get out of bed. However, contrary to popular opinion, I am not deluged with text messages (and this is at a school where students, as a group, tend to be extremely communicative with professors and most instructors' office hours are filled nearly all the time).[13] In my experience, students' communication styles are diverse enough that I rarely experience an overload in any one location or mode. Teachers in different contexts will, of course, have to make decisions about what is appropriate for their particular situations; my suggestion here is simply to try out alternative channels of communication and see what works.

In addition to classroom communication, multimodality can be practiced through exercises and assignments. Essays can be "written" using sound and image in a digital format; a mathematical proof or chemical principle can be rendered as a short story (or vice versa);[14] exams can be designed as collaborative as well as individual exercises. Dunn's *Talking Sketching Moving* provides a wealth of such strategies.[15] For example, she describes an exercise using "rhetorical proof cards," which she makes up in packs that student groups "play with" together (60). Each card, prepared by the instructor, includes a note that might be included in a hypothetical argument (e.g., on capital punishment): the information on a card might be a quotation, a fact, or an "emotional news story" (60–61). Working in small groups, students shuffle, discuss, and reassemble the cards in different configurations to construct an agreed-upon argument. Dunn explains that "the act of physically moving these cards around and a discussion of the effects of doing so makes the abstract job of organizing an effective argument into a visual, oral, and kinesthetic task to which students with a variety of talents can contribute" (63). Such an exercise could also be carried out individually or in pairs.

A related exercise, familiar to many writing teachers, is the one I call "Cut and Paste," in which the writer cuts up an in-progress draft and shuffles the pieces around. Theoretically, this could be accomplished on a computer screen, but may be more beneficial for kinetic and other kinds of learners if carried out physically and in a larger space. As she shuffles the pieces, the writer may choose to take notes, add or delete ideas, engage in conversations with peers, add color-coding, or perform other revisions.

Time should be set aside at the end of exercise (which has no definite moment of conclusion) so that students can number the portions of their essay, write a note to themselves, staple pieces together, or otherwise remind themselves of what they want to "keep" from the session. Like Dunn's, this exercise can be carried out individually or in groups.

5. INCORPORATE MENTAL DISABILITY INTO APPROACHES TO DISABILITY.

Disability studies has been incorporated into a vast range of undergraduate and graduate courses; however, as with DS research, references to mental disability—let alone focused examination of it—are still rare in our courses on disability in history, literature, law, art, cultural studies, and science. (This broad generalization excludes courses in psychology that focus on mental disability as a component of human "abnormality.") Exceptions do exist, of course, and I believe that the growing acknowledgment of madness in academic discourse will result in more courses that "knit" (Garland-Thomson, "Integrating" 16) mental disability into our approaches to teaching disability studies.

The independent study I conducted with Timile Brown, described above, is one example. This course, titled Writing and Depression, exam-

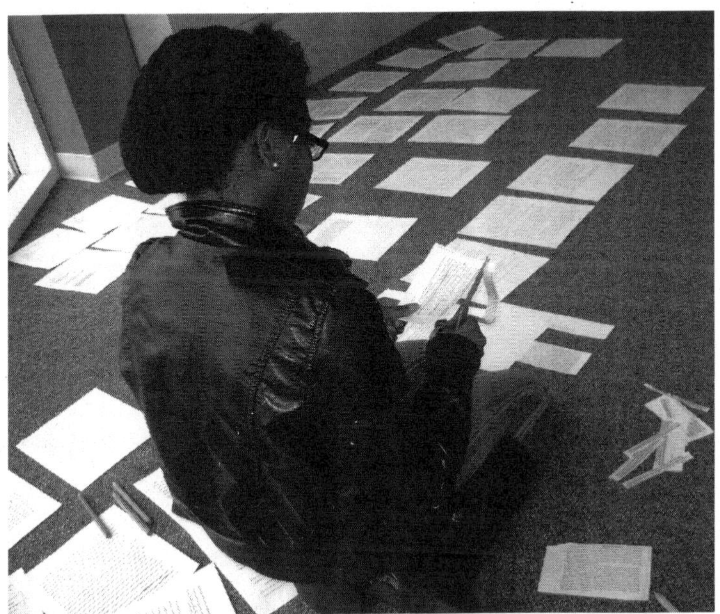

A student lays out a large number of cut-up pieces of an essay. Photograph by author.

A student arranges and reconsiders the cut-up pieces of an essay. Photograph by author.

ined depression from standpoints including feminist, clinical, psychoanalytic, and autobiographical. Another example is the course Madness, Medicine and Mythology taught by Geoffrey Reaume, which he describes in the article "Mad People's History." Reaume emphasizes that the central consideration of such classes is that they offer not just "a history of ideas about madness . . . [but] serious inclusion of the people whose stories make up this history" (171). Other courses, such as Susan Burch's Madness in American Literature, are beginning to dot the curriculum. As yet, however, we are far from widespread inclusion of mental disability as a significant component of DS pedagogy.

6. MAKE USE OF "SAFE HOUSES."

In her now famous *Profession* article "Arts of the Contact Zone," Mary Louise Pratt calls for recognition of what she calls "contact zones" in the classroom. Probably the most often-quoted line from this article is her definition of contact zones: "social spaces where cultures meet, clash, and grapple with each other, often in contexts of highly asymmetrical relations of power, such as colonialism, slavery, or their aftermaths as they are lived out in many parts of the world today" (34). Pratt's idea has given rise to voluminous articles that take it up in various ways, and even a whole pedagogical approach termed "contact zone pedagogy." Less often mentioned is Pratt's concern about her theory's potentially painful impact upon students. Pratt argues for what she calls "safe houses," that is, "social and intellectual spaces where groups can constitute themselves as horizontal, homogeneous, sovereign communities with high degrees of trust, shared understandings, temporary protection from legacies of oppression" (40). Pratt suggests that such spaces might include "ethnic or women's studies" (40). Now, it is obvious that no group, no matter how similarly identified, will necessarily be safe for all participants; I tend to think in terms of "safer" spaces rather than "safe" ones. However, Pratt's point is important, and applies to instructors as well as students. Safer kairotic spaces could take many forms, including gatherings of friends, sessions of private writing, or—as is suggested by Jane Thierfeld-Brown, who works with students with Asperger's syndrome—"safe rooms" on her college's campus for students to visit if they need a break from the constant stimulation of more public space (Farrell). (The annual conference of the Society for Disability Studies establishes a "quiet room" for a similar purpose.) "Safe(r) houses" will take as many forms as their users;

they are one form of the ongoing adaptation required by universal design.

7. UNDERSTAND THAT YOU WILL NOT BE ABLE TO FULLY MEET EVERY STUDENT'S STYLE AND NEEDS.

As teachers committed to creating more accessible kairotic spaces for those with mental disabilities, we are not "solving problems"; we are finding ways to move. If we view universal design as a process of "solving problems," we run the risk of feeling angry and frustrated at students who will not *be* solved (a closed-ended project akin to "cure"). And we must understand that our efforts are only one part of the larger design. To presume that one can achieve a perfect classroom design that will turn out perfect learning outcomes is not only unrealistic, it is demeaning to our students. We must try, think, query, flex, observe, listen, and try again. And when we are too tired, we must be willing to let it go for a while. Access is not going to happen overnight.

I want to close with another anecdote, this one about a close friend of mine, who recently finished a master's degree in molecular biology. As she planned her final year of course work, she ran into a problem: her last required course was being taught by a professor whom she knew to run discussion-based seminars. My friend is severely hearing-impaired, and uses speechreading but not sign language for communication. Her ideal class would be lecture-based, preferably led by a speaker who uses a microphone and detailed slides. In groups of three or four, she can generally follow about half to three-quarters of the conversation; in larger groups, her comprehension drops to about one-tenth of what is said. If she sits near the back of a classroom (set up in rows), she will miss nearly everything the instructor says; if she sits near the front, she has a better chance of comprehending the instructor but will miss everything said by persons sitting behind her.

I encouraged her to take the course anyway: it was her last requirement, it was a topic that excited her, and the university was required by law to provide adequate accommodations. "If you can't get CART [computer-aided real-time translation]," I said, "at least you can get a note-taker. You could sit next to the note-taker and follow the gist of the conversation through what they write. Or you could get a small mike that people pass from hand to hand—it hooks up to a receiver that you wear. One of my friends in grad school used that."[16] I was full of suggestions.

However, this was not what my friend wanted. She didn't want an accommodation; she wanted a class whose *ordinary* workings accommodated her hearing and her learning style. To be honest, I felt a little frustrated with her refusal to explore the possibilities of accommodations. However, I took away from the conversation a deepened understanding of how nonmechanical "accommodations" really are. True accommodations are not *added on* to a classroom environment; they are *built into* its infrastructure, with flexibility and ongoing revision part of its very foundation. I cannot anticipate the needs and styles of every student who will walk into my next classroom. Nor can I become a fundamentally different kind of teacher than I am: I will never be much for lecturing; I will always incorporate small- and large-group discussions; I will rarely be at my best during a long procession of individual conferences; and my own modes of communication will probably continue to be heavily visual and verbal. What I *can* do is explicitly name universal design as one of the ongoing goals of my classrooms, and be aware that meeting this goal requires regular input and advice from my students. And I can also acknowledge that not every student will want to be a part of this dialogue, that some will choose not to engage in it for their own reasons, and respect that. Accommodations are not charitable offerings; they are spaces we open to the best of our abilities, and revise, and revise again.

CHAPTER 3

The Essential Functions of the Position

Collegiality and Productivity

> As a senior manager said to me recently, "We got the toilets right, what more do you want?" While we remove some of the physical barriers we actually haven't changed the underlying attitudes.
>
> —*Christopher Newell,* "Flourishing Rhetorically: Disability, Diversity and Equal Disappointment Opportunity"

> Across the board, the candidate with the best interpersonal skills—all else being equal—is offered the job.
>
> —*Walter Broughton and William Conlogue,* "What Search Committees Want"

In the summer of 2005, I had just completed the first year of my first tenure-track academic job. I still read the "Careers" section in the *Chronicle of Higher Education,* in part to enjoy a sense of relief at actually being employed (with health insurance!), and in part out of a sneaking fear that I might be back on the market anytime. It was in this frame of mind that I encountered a column written by "Ms. Mentor" (Emily Toth), titled "Can I Dazzle Them With My Energy?" On this day, she was responding to a question about a new buzzword that seemed to be cropping up in many postings for academic jobs: "energetic." "It looks like an attempt to insert age discrimination into hiring," the questioner, "Linda," wrote. Ms. Mentor responded that not only did the term *energetic* raise questions about age, but also regionality, ethnicity, and disability. In fact, to my excitement, she discussed disability in some detail in her response. But as I read, my reaction slid from interest to dismay to open-mouthed disbelief. The first section of the response, which addresses life on campus for professors with disabilities, reads:

> Here Ms. Mentor must salute courageous professors with disabilities who have made themselves as dynamic as the nondisabled—through dramatic gestures and well-trained voices, as well as PowerPoint and all its cousins. Professors have hired students to be their ears and their eyes—and thereby taught all students that being deaf or blind does not affect the brain. Teachers with "invisible disabilities" have endured chronic pain without publicly wincing; many have been considered "antisocial" for going home early, because they must rest to stay out of the hospital.
>
> Ms. Mentor knows one professor who heroically, and secretly, performed kidney dialysis for herself in her office, lights off and door locked, during lunch hours. Her students, who loved her wry sense of humor, never knew until she got tenure and "came out."

I found the references to courage and heroics disturbing, though not surprising; here was the familiar overcoming narrative, rehearsed yet again. But the image of a professor "secretly" performing dialysis on herself, "lights off and door locked," felt particularly upsetting. Why did her secrecy receive special praise? And after she got tenure, what changed that enabled her to "come out"? Did she now perform dialysis in her office with the lights *on*? Why did Ms. Mentor's remark that the professor's students "never knew"—until, of course, she was tenured—sound so approving?

This point of view, which imagines disablement as a personal deficit that must be "heroically" and "secretly" borne, strikes at all persons with disabilities. But singled out for particular disadvantage in Ms. Mentor's response are those whose disabilities affect the mind. In the section quoted above, she notes that "being deaf or blind does not affect the brain," implying that academic fitness requires an "unaffected" brain. In a later passage, the presumption of able-mindedness becomes more explicit:

> Once at the interview stage—whether on the telephone, at a conference, or on a campus—all candidates are equal, and it's their job to outdo each other.
>
> At an interview, Linda will have to project energy by talking quickly and clearly, moving briskly, looking keenly alert, and re-

> sponding vivaciously. . . . An energetic candidate sits up straight, makes eye contact, and, when asked a question, is more apt to begin her answer with "Oh, . . ." (which leads to "Oh yes! I'd like to!") rather than with "Well, . . ." (which leads to "I'm not sure" or "I'm not so eager").

From a DS point of view, we can discern a number of problems with this ideal candidate description. Anyone who has used a TTY, for example, knows that this form of communication is unlikely to be considered "equal" to normative oral/aural telephone conversation. And any number of disabilities would make it difficult, if not impossible, to "sit up straight" and "move briskly." If we add mental disability to our consideration, virtually every trait described by Ms. Mentor, including the importance of eye contact, becomes problematic. The fact is, not only are all job candidates not equal in kairotic space, but kairotic spaces such as interviews may single out and punish with particular force traits associated with mental disability. To put it simply, some of us are more charming online. Or over a long period of time. Or while lying down, or while our hands are occupied with a stim device. What we say might be fascinating, but our voices might tremble or be slurred; we might need to stare out the window, or tap on the table, while saying them. We might shake visibly, sweat profusely, or make remarks that seem off-topic. In short, the problems facing students required to "actively participate" in classes, discussed in the previous chapter, haunt professors as well. Students' and professors' participation may take place in different domains, but the rules of conduct in such domains are similarly narrowly proscribed.

There are also important differences between students' and professors' positions in kairotic space, because academe is a workplace as well as a place of study. This chapter focuses on the problems of academic discourse in professional academic arenas. The central question I address is this: What are the "essential functions" (Americans with Disabilities Act) of academic employment—specifically, employment as a faculty member? How are those functions defined, evaluated, and rewarded? What happens to faculty members with mental disabilities in this system? And finally, how might recognition and accommodation of faculty members with mental disabilities enrich academic discourse? What might "universal design" come to mean if it is applied in professional kairotic space?

To address these questions, I begin with a review of the ADA's precise language regarding the "essential functions" of work as a faculty member, as well as the discouraging history of ways that these "essential functions" have been defined in case law. Two topoi of particular importance in interpreting (attempted) implementation of the ADA are *productivity* and *collegiality*. Both these features, generally acknowledged as key aspects of a faculty member's job, are often defined in ways that foreclose participation in academic discourse by persons with mental disabilities, as when uncollegial behavior is collapsed with "neurosis" (Bloom 210), or when "difficult" faculty members are identified as being "isolated," "paranoid," or having "mental illness" (Wells 32). In order to explore the material ways that these prejudices play out in kairotic professional space, I then analyze two different rhetorical situations, each of which is highly kairotic in its design, and each of which is important—if not required—for successful academic employment: the job interview (including both initial interviews and campus visits) and the academic conference. In closing, I offer concrete suggestions for ways that the academic profession might be redesigned to provide an environment that is more inclusive of those with mental disabilities, and more successful—perhaps even more *productive* and *collegial*—for all.

The Americans with Disabilities Act and Mental Disability

On September 25, 2008, President George W. Bush signed into law an amendment to the ADA that broadens the definition of "qualified individual with a disability," and also limits what may be considered "mitigating" measures, such as use of medication or hearing aids (H.R. 3195 / S. 3406).[1] In addition, the amendment specifies that courts may not consider whether a disability is "episodic, in remission or latent" when determining whether it qualifies. All three of these issues have been particularly problematic for persons attempting to bring suit under the ADA, as is discussed in more detail below. At this writing, it is unclear what impact the amendment will have on judicial decisions. In an audio conference following the amendment's passing, L. Scott Lissner, ADA coordinator at the Ohio State University, stated that he believed changes would come "relatively quickly"—but added that "relatively quickly," in the context of the federal government, can be a slow process. The following section examines definitions and case law as they have emerged from the original version of the ADA, since it is that version that determined employees' fates from 1992 to 2008.

In the ADA as it was passed in 1990, subchapter I ("Employment") offers a number of definitions, including that of a "qualified individual with a disability":

> The term "qualified individual with a disability" means an individual with a disability who, with or without reasonable accommodation, *can perform the essential functions of the employment position* that such individual holds or desires. For the purposes of this subchapter, consideration shall be given to the employer's judgment as to what functions of a job are essential, and if an employer has prepared a written description before advertising or interviewing applicants for the job, this description shall be considered evidence of the essential functions of the job. (Emphasis added)

Unsurprisingly, questions and litigation about applications of this definition have often turned upon the phrase "essential functions of the employment position." For some jobs, those essential functions are easily defined. However, in academe, what constitutes an essential function for a faculty member is much more contested. Most people agree on the conventional triad teaching-scholarship-service, but some would add a fourth requirement—collegiality—and others do not agree on what constitute appropriate forms or quantities of teaching, scholarship, or service.

To place this quandary in rhetorical terms, two important stasis questions arise when we think about the "essential functions" of employment as a faculty member. The first question is *What is the nature of the thing?* In other words, what in fact *are* the essential functions of work as a faculty member? Must they always include teaching, service, and scholarship, or can a faculty position consist of a different mix of activities? And is collegiality an aspect of teaching, service, and scholarship, or is it a fourth criterion that should be assessed separately? The second question is *What is the quality of the thing?* In other words, how good is the faculty member's performance of teaching, scholarship, service (and perhaps collegiality)? How shall that goodness be determined?

In the next subsection of the "Employment" subchapter, the ADA defines reasonable accommodation. According to this definition, "reasonable accommodation" may include

> (A) making existing facilities used by employees readily accessible to and usable by individuals with disabilities; and

> (B) job restructuring, part-time or modified work schedules, reassignment to a vacant position, acquisition or modification of equipment or devices, appropriate adjustment or modifications of examinations, training materials or policies, the provision of qualified readers or interpreters, and other similar accommodations for individuals with disabilities.

In this definition, as the text lays out just what *reasonable accommodation* means, we can perceive the clash between its directives and the "essential functions" of work as a faculty member. For example, if a "modified work schedule" is provided for a faculty member, what precisely will that mean? Lighter teaching loads are infused with academic structures of power and prestige: a load of two courses per semester, as opposed to four, is not merely a numerical, but also a value-laden difference, often reflecting positions with vastly different prestige, security, and pay. Or what if a "modified work schedule" means a longer tenure clock? Again, such a measure is not simply a quantitative difference in time, but a qualitative shift of the competitive structure of tenure clocks, in which junior faculty are expected to produce *x* amount of scholarship in *y* amount of time. This atmosphere has given rise to the academic truism "publish or perish." Although in some cases tenure clocks can be adjusted, the usual expectation is that a faculty member will be productive not only in particular quantities but at a particular speed.[2]

If we revisit the discussion of "crip time" from chapter 2, we can perceive yet more pressures that the ADA's examples of "reasonable" accommodation place upon the academic infrastructure. Just as students with mental disabilities may struggle to meet conventional requirements for "presence" in the classroom, so too may professors with disabilities. For example, what if a professor who has agoraphobia or panic disorder must miss classes on an unpredictable basis? Does the burden lie upon him to find a substitute, no matter how short the notice or distressing the situation that gave rise to the absence in the first place? If he does find a substitute, is that an adequate replacement for the work expected of him? What if he cannot be physically present, but periodically holds classes online? Can we still say that his teaching is good? Good enough? That it can be called *teaching* at all? Shifting focus from the classroom to the conference, what about a professor who cannot function in crowds? Or when speaking in front of groups? Could one of her accommodations be nonparticipation in academic conferences—or participation in ways that omit "speaking" roles? And if she did use this accommodation, would that mean her performance as a scholar would be merely *different* or actually *worse* than that of her peers?

These questions have been debated in the courts. And so far, the record of ADA implementation in higher education has not been encouraging. In a 2003 issue of the *Journal of Law and Education,* Suzanne Abram published a review of ADA case law that involved faculty members. Abram paints a bleak picture:

> By far, the majority of college and university instructors who sue under the ADA lose their cases. Worse yet, they lose them at the summary judgment stage. Since the standard for summary judgment is the absence of any genuine issue of material fact, or the inability of a reasonable jury to find for the plaintiff, it is particularly ominous that disabled faculty lose their cases at this early stage in the litigation, without obtaining the opportunity to put their cases before a jury.

The daunting number attached to that majority, Abram specifies, is about 93 percent. Why is this number so high? One of the main problems, she goes on to explain, is the razor-thin balance that ADA plaintiffs must maintain between being disabled "enough," under the ADA, to require accommodations but not so disabled that they cannot perform the "essential functions" of the position or that accommodations would place an "undue hardship" (ADA) on the employer. Abram clarifies:

> The [ADA] actions often fail because the faculty members cannot walk the fine line between being disabled enough and being too disabled. A disabled professor must construct his complaint so that he is demonstrably able to perform the essential functions of his position with reasonable accommodation and yet not so disabled that he is unable to perform his duties with accommodation. In the majority of cases, the plaintiff professors seem unable to place themselves within this narrow range.

Another knotty issue is that of receiving benefits. If an individual has received benefits from the Social Security Administration (SSA) or other organization, some courts have found that this alone disqualifies them from being "able" to work. This view, as a number of analysts have pointed out, ignores the possibility of accommodations that can make work feasible, as well as the likelihood that a disabled person's condition will fluctuate over time (Diller 71; Longmore 236–37). To summarize this gloomy stream of evidence, although the ADA was constructed on a civil rights model, and was intended to bring about broad change, the very broadness of its language has made way for ongoing discrimination in judicial decisions.

Plaintiffs bringing cases based on their mental disabilities have often been excluded from protection under the ADA. The "narrow range" (Abram) that plaintiffs must fall within is inflected, in these cases, by the issue of medication. Although the Equal Employment Opportunity Commission states that disability should be defined without consideration of "medicines," several judgments in 1999 and following found that an individual's qualification for status as disabled should be assessed in a "corrected," that is, medicated state. In a 2001 article in *Psychiatric Services,* John Petrila and Thomas Brink analyzed the implications of that first landmark case (*Sutton v. United Airlines*) and others that followed it:

> [A]n individual might still [despite medication] experience significant and disabling stress in some situations—for example, in a work environment—that could substantially limit major life activities. If the correction of mental illness is reduced simply to the effects of medication, an individual could be considered to be no longer disabled—because symptoms are controlled—and therefore not protected by the ADA, even when that individual is still in a tenuous situation in terms of long-term recovery. (629)

Suggesting that a person's mental disability effectively disappears with the application of medication is as absurd as suggesting that his hearing disability has disappeared because he uses hearing aids (another presumption that has been upheld by courts considering ADA cases). And, as Petrila and Brink point out, although medication may alleviate some of the most impairing features of mental disabilities, it can also cause side effects that carry new impairments, such as memory loss, blurred vision, or extreme fatigue. Finally, if the argument is framed in terms that assume that medication offers a "correction of mental illness" (Petrila and Brink 629), this traps the mad person in a discourse that assumes the necessity of "recovering," in psychiatric terms, from the supposed "illness." But many consumers/survivors/ex-patients of the psychiatric system do not identify as having disabilities and see no need for medication (or other "treatments") as a response to their neuroatypicality (L. Morrison 112).

In addition to the judicial fondness for the notion that persons with mental disabilities have access to magical pills that erase our disabilities, the courts also show a propensity for discrimination based upon the commonsense belief that mental illness is closely allied with violent behavior.[3] In "Psychiatric Disabilities, the ADA, and the New Workplace Violence Account," Vicki A. Laden and Gregory Schwartz describe the emergence of the "workplace violence account," which imagines a "pathogenic worker, lurking unnoticed in the workplace, poised to explode in lethal violence against his supervisors or coworkers" (189). This account claims that workplace violence is "epidemic" and is largely committed by mad persons (194–95). Despite legislative statements against the presumption that madness is causally linked to violent behavior, Laden and Schwartz argue, judicial decisions tend to adhere to this commonsense myth:

> When a popular account is at odds in crucial respects with a prescribed judicial duty, it can be expected that judicial responses will be modulated by the popular account, particularly where, in this area, the popular account has a strong valance and taps into a wellspring of fears . . . [T]he scientific approach to risk advanced by the ADA has frequently been subordinated to a less rigorous approach characterized by overgeneralization, stereotyping, and other forms of heuristic thinking. (203)

Laden and Schwartz analyze several cases that illustrate the operation of the workplace violence account in judicial decisions. In addition to presuming that workers with psychiatric disabilities pose a threat, the authors demonstrate, requests for accommodations for psychiatric disabilities "are routinely deemed per se unreasonable by reviewing courts" (207). Such accommodations include working at home, being transferred away from certain coworkers or supervisors, or modification of standards for behavior (207). In short, not only are workers with mental disabilities likely to be considered a threat, and thus unqualified for employment, but their requests for accommodations are likely to be deemed "unreasonable."

Even when violence does not overtly enter the equation, faculty members with mental disabilities attempting to bring suit under the ADA face special barriers. For example, Abram describes the 1996 case of *Horton v.*

Board of Trustees of Community College District No. 508. In this case, the professor claimed to have an "unspecified nervous disorder" and missed time from teaching. The court ruled that since the "essential functions" of a community college professor's job are "to prepare, attend, and teach classes," and his disorder caused him to miss class, he did not qualify (Abram). Here we see the problem of presence, explored in terms of students' experience in chapter 2, affecting faculty members as well. If presence is considered an essential function of an academic position, and presence is defined in terms of one's fleshly appearance in a classroom, then many faculty members with mental disabilities are de facto not qualified for their jobs.

This brings me to a question that has been troubling me for years, as long as I have been seriously thinking about access, the ADA, and faculty with mental disabilities. Is it possible that fluency in kairotic space *is* an essential function of an academic job? Is it true that a faculty member who is unable—perhaps occasionally, perhaps often—to make predictable, material appearances in kairotic space, or who is unable to operate smoothly in such spaces, is unqualified? Are we ready to say that people with severe depression, or schizophrenia, or agoraphobia, cannot be professors? I want to say no; I want to imagine an academic workplace where accommodations for mental disability *are* feasible, where we can bring our differences to work in ways that enrich our students, our colleagues, and ourselves. But I know that this imagined world will require enormous, paradigm-shifting changes to some of academe's most dearly held tenets. In the next sections, I examine two of these tenets, *productivity* and *collegiality*, in the specific context of two kairotic spaces: the job interview and the conference. As a person who has cried with the frustration of being unable to leave my house, who has cringed with the knowledge that my remarks during conference sessions have seemed puzzling or even offensive, who has told my students that some days I might have to communicate with them via instant message or email rather than cope with the exhaustion of face-to-face conferences,[4] I know that the answers to this question will not be easy.

Productivity and Collegiality

The "essential functions" of a faculty member's job vary from position to position. In some, particularly for contingent faculty, teaching is the primary or sole emphasis, whereas in a conventional tenure-track position, the employee must perform in at least three major areas: teaching, scholarship, and service. Obtaining and keeping a tenure-track job, and eventually achieving tenure, may be of particular importance for faculty members with disabilities, not only because these jobs carry higher prestige and pay, but also because they are more likely to include health benefits. Having worked as a lecturer for several years after I earned a terminal master's degree (an M.F.A.), I decided in 1998 to try for a Ph.D. and a tenure-track job almost solely because of the issues of health insurance and stability. Because I have what is often termed a "preexisting condition" (an autoimmune disease), I could not afford to go more than ninety days without insurance, because future insurance could be denied simply on the basis of my "condition."[5] A lecturer job at the University of Michigan did include health insurance; however, the coverage disappeared each summer and had to be reinstated each September.[6] Also, as many adjunct positions do, mine came with an expiration date—no more renewals after four years. I found, somewhat to my surprise, that I liked engaging in scholarship and service as much as I did teaching, but that was certainly not my primary motivation in attempting to get onto the tenure track. I mention this to illustrate the particular pressures that are placed upon persons with disabilities in the academic profession. Loss of health insurance may be not simply dangerous, but disastrous; and the costs, both monetary and physical, of attempting to hold (a) job(s) including a heavy teaching load, travel between institutions, and little institutional support, may be not merely draining but prohibitive.

A faculty member's performance of the required proportions of teaching, research, and service are often referred to as her "productivity." However, productivity is inflected by another factor, which may or may not be made explicit: collegiality. In some cases, collegiality is cited as a means to achieving productivity; in others, collegiality is considered a literal measure of productivity, and included as a fourth criterion during tenure and promotional reviews. In 1999, the American Association of University Professors published a policy statement titled "On Collegiality as a Criterion for Faculty Evaluation." This statement speaks strongly against the use of collegiality as a discrete category in faculty evaluations:

> [C]ollegiality is not a distinct capacity to be assessed independently of the traditional triumvirate of teaching, scholarship and service. It is rather a quality whose value is expressed in the successful execution of these three functions. . . . The elevation of collegiality

> into a separate and discrete standard is not only inconsistent with the long-term vigor and health of academic institutions and dangerous to academic freedom, it is also unnecessary. (39–40)

AAUP's policy statement defines collegiality as the "successful execution" of one's tasks in teaching, research, and service so as to distinguish it from expectations that faculty members display traits including "enthusiasm" or "excessive deference" (39). It also notes that requirements for collegiality can be used to mask discrimination on the basis of factors such as race, gender, or class. This is a concern reiterated by many writers on collegiality, including Heather Dubrow, who notes the danger that collegiality can become "an excuse, code, for prejudices of various sorts" ("Collegiality: A Roundtable" 111).

However, when viewed in terms of mental disability, the problematic nature of collegiality runs deeper than straightforward discrimination against "the misfit and the eccentric" ("Collegiality: A Roundtable" 230). The notion of *collegiality* itself is regularly *defined against* mental disability. For example, Lynn Z. Bloom's essay "Collegiality, the Game" notes that satirical novels about academic culture abound with characters who fail at being collegial, "whether from stupidity, ineptitude, bureaucratic entanglements, paranoia or neurosis" (210). While Bloom probably did not mean to insult persons with paranoia or neuroses, her list of uncollegial traits suggests that the latter two qualities are as likely to hamper one's collegial efforts as "stupidity" and "ineptitude." *Paranoid* also appears in Susan Wells's "Notes on Handling Difficult Faculty Members"; her list of "difficult" traits is "isolated, unfriendly, uncooperative, inactive in research, explosive, paranoid, or the subject of many student complaints" (32). Unlike Bloom, Wells does discuss mental disability directly, but the impulse is similarly to separate faculty members with these disabilities from the "normal" crowd. Wells's essay begins with a section titled "Assumptions of This Workshop" (as the material was originally presented during the 2007 ADE Summer Seminar South). These are the assumptions:

> We aren't therapists (or saints) and cannot solve serious personal troubles. And we need skilled professional help if our colleagues' problems include addiction, mental illness, or violent behavior. But we are entrusted with the public life of our departments; we can and should enforce collegial norms there. Mentoring, supporting

> productive teachers or researchers, and troubleshooting for faculty members in crisis are all more important than managing difficult faculty members. (32)

In the main, I concur with the points made in this essay, and appreciate Wells's emphasis on mentoring and support. But the rhetorical move that troubles me here is the familiar educational refrain of "we aren't therapists," as well as the clustering of "addiction, mental illness, or violent behavior." The assumption appears to be that a faculty member who has the "problem" of mental illness is not part of the collegial group Wells means to address in the rest of her essay. Those faculty members require "skilled professional help."[7] What Wells means to say, I expect, is that a faculty member's addiction or mental illness may require support outside that which can be provided by a department chair or administrator. What her statement achieves, however, is a division between those who should receive support within academe and those who should be sent to outside, medicalized forms of support.[8] Implicit in this statement is an either/or distinction: the addicted, the mentally ill, and the violent over there; the merely "difficult" and reachable through mentoring and academic support over here.

Mental disability enters the picture again in the 2006 issue of *Profession,* which published a cluster of articles on collegiality. This time, mental health is held up not as a requirement for collegiality, but as its outcome: Jeffrey Theis avers, "Collegiality, as a counterbalance to our overemphasis on individualism, can yield many benefits. Certainly mental health is the clearest reward" (88). As with Wells's remark, I am troubled less by Theis's overall point than by its presumption that collegiality and mental disability—unhealth, as it were—have an incommensurable relationship.

Several of the authors in the *Profession* cluster agree with the AAUP's stance against using collegiality as a requirement distinct from teaching, scholarship, and service, as well as its argument that collegiality should not be measured in terms of personal affection, deferential behavior, or agreement. However, they also concur—as I do—that this requirement is not going to go away, at least in implicit form, and the best strategy is not to try to eliminate it, but to define it more clearly and ethically. Philip Lewis suggests that we might define collegiality as having two forms, practical and structural, and explains each:

> [Practical collegiality is] a relationship of mutual respect and support among faculty members in an academic unit . . . [and] means that differences of opinion or outlook can coexist in a productive tension, that people who disagree with one another or who dissent from the majority view are still behooved to collaborate in the ongoing work of their unit's team of educators. . . . Structural collegiality is the relationship of colleagues who agree to agree, who value the collective authority they hold and exercise in concert, who believe their mode of interaction conforms to a model that should pervade the academic organization from top to bottom and provide for the homology of the institutional order . . . [and] is woven into the fabric of administrative discourse as a presumption of negotiated correlation. (76, 79)

Lewis's notion of structural collegiality is distinctly DS in outlook, and particularly important for faculty members with mental disabilities, because it calls for more democratic systems of communication that make room for difference, as well as turning its focus upon structural rather than individual problems. It has much in common with the recently popular phrase "shared governance," which presumes that faculty are stakeholders in a common enterprise and emphasizes the importance of collaboration, negotiation, and wider distribution of power and information (Guy-Sheftall).

No matter how we slice it, collegiality is a *social* phenomenon, manifesting through interpersonal relationships. Many writers who attempt to give advice on fostering collegiality name social events as a means to do so. Dubrow suggests that colleagues should "eat together" (58); Wells recommends "social events" (33) generally; Susan B. Taylor mentions potlucks ("Collegiality: Statements" 96); Jamie Dessart notes that department meetings should include "some social time" ("Collegiality: Statements" 97); and Timothy Dow Adams reports that his department "sponsored a prom" ("Collegiality: Statements" 98). It is this aspect that I want to examine in terms of the kairotic spaces of job interviews and academic conferences. Both of these spaces are deeply inflected by their relationships with productivity and collegiality. And both are highly social spaces. Much of the "work" that takes place during conferences and interviews is social: it includes meals, hallway or elevator conversations, and pre- or postevent small talk (which is not usually "small" at all). In the following sections, I read each of these high-stakes academic spaces in terms of the foregoing discussion of productivity and collegiality, noting both difficulties these spaces can raise for persons with mental disabilities and ways that mindful design of kairotic space can increase their accessibility.

The Job Search

The academic job search, or "going on the market," is a stressful prospect for any candidate. Although all stages of the process are arduous—including selecting schools; assembling applications; asking for recommendations; organizing and delivering materials; laying out the money for paper, postage, transcript fees, and (often) clothing; and arranging travel and accommodation—I focus here on the stages that are most likely to require participation in kairotic space: initial interviews and campus visits. As Sarah F. Rose argues, these are two parts of the job search at which disabled candidates are likely to encounter "challenges." Rose offers an overview of these events:

> If you are selected for a conference interview, you may hear just two or three days before the conference starts—which obviously poses challenges for both financially-strapped graduate students and candidates who need accessible hotel rooms. . . . After interviews comes the campus visit—a one- to two-day affair during which you will be under the microscope at all times. Generally, you'll need to teach a class, give a "job talk" about your research, and meet with faculty, students, and deans, all while remaining charming, professional, and calm.

Rose's story is told from her own perspective as a person with "moderate hearing loss but normal speech," and she is careful to acknowledge that disabilities of various kinds will inflect the process in various ways. With this in mind, I want to add a few points to her astute description. First, a last-minute interview offer is challenging not only in the ways she names, but can also become an insuperable barrier for a mentally disabled person who must carefully plan his appearances in kairotic space. Such planning may include needing more than a few days to absorb and retain information about the campus and the faculty in question; preparing extensively to get on a plane or even simply to leave the house; or scheduling around periods when one's functioning may be particularly impaired, such as deep depressions or intervals of medication adjustments. Being "under the microscope" can create stress that goes beyond uncomfortable to unbearable. And, of course, appearing "charming" (in a conventional sense) and "calm" is quite a trick if one is short of breath, unable to make eye contact, stimming, struggling to process aural/oral information, and/or unable to attach faces to names. A study by Charles Avinger, Edith Croake, and Jean Kearns Miller describes a faculty member with Asperger's, Clarice, who emphasizes the difference between her experience in kairotic settings from that of "normal" faculty members. In Clarice's experience, the authors argue, "'Be yourself' doesn't mean 'Be yourself.' It means, rather, to respond within a more or less codified and limited range of experiences" (208–9). A direct quotation from Clarice places it in starker terms: "A meeting can be a disaster for someone on the spectrum" (211).

Given all this, should a job candidate facing an interview discuss his or her access needs with the search committee? Rose's experience was that her interviewers were "extremely gracious in dealing with accommodations." Unfortunately—as she also notes—this may be the exception rather than the rule. The grim history of ADA lawsuits brought by professors with disabilities, discussed in the previous section, indicates that employers do not rise enthusiastically to the challenge of access, nor do the courts support plaintiffs' efforts to gain access through legal channels. There is little current research on how well mental disabilities are accommodated outside the context of ADA suits; however, what research does exist seems to indicate that employees fear asking for accommodation, and when they do ask, report being further stigmatized (Goldberg, Killeen, and O'Day). In fact, employers may avoid hiring people with mental disabilities in the first place (Starnes, cited in Goldberg, Killeen, and O'Day). This creates what Goldberg, Killeen, and O'Day call a "disclosure conundrum": to obtain accommodation, a person with a mental disability must disclose; but the act of disclosure itself may bring about stigmatization and retaliation.

Larger-scale studies from various disciplines confirm the anecdotal evidence that fluency in kairotic space is a key factor in job candidates' success. A 1998 survey of ninety-eight search committee chairs in psychology found that a candidate's performance during interviews and colloquia, as well as her "personality," were among the most important factors considered in the later stages of job searches (Sheehan, McDevitt, and Ross

10). Once a candidate had gotten to the interview stage, "performance at interview with search committee" was rated as the most important factor, with "performance" in other kairotic spaces such as colloquia and teaching demonstrations rated second and fifth, respectively (9–10). "Candidate's ability to get along with other faculty" was rated sixth, and "Candidate's personality" ninth (10). To offer some context for these ratings, criteria that were rated as less important than "get[ing] along" and "personality" during the interview—that is, outside the top ten—included book authorship, graduate GPA and transcripts, awards for research, service experience, and grant writing (9–10). Thus, the real-time performance of a candidate in kairotic space was found to be more important than activities that might more easily be carried out in "crip time," including writing, service, and obtaining grants.

Sheehan, McDevitt, and Ross also inquired about "errors" made by candidates (10); the top two responses in this category both involve performance in kairotic space. The most commonly cited error was conducting a poor colloquium; the second most common was a failure in "interpersonal interactions" (10). Such errors of interpersonal interactions were described by respondents in terms including "abrasive or insulting," "generally obnoxious," and "not a team player" (10). Having sat on search committees before, I admit that I would be unlikely to endorse a candidate who seemed insulting, obnoxious, or "sexist" (another failure of "interpersonal" skill mentioned by respondents). But I also wonder just what sorts of behaviors were deemed so obnoxious. Further details are not available in this study.

In 2000, Walter Broughton and William Conlogue conducted a study of 368 English departments that offers more texture to the judgments about interpersonal skills as they are evaluated by search committees. Two of their research questions have particular significance for candidates with mental disabilities: "How significant are interpersonal skills?" and "What egregious errors kill a candidacy?" (40). As in the study by Sheehan, McDevitt, and Ross, Broughton and Conlogue found that "interpersonal skills" were a major factor: this criterion was deemed decisive by 28 percent of respondents, and in response to a question about what factors "negatively affected" candidates' chances, "poor interpersonal skills" was rated third, just behind poor teaching and poor research (48). (It is worth noting that "ignorance of the institution," which might seem to be displayed by a person with difficulties recalling information or processing it orally/aurally, was rated fourth.) Broughton and Conlogue relate several specific comments made on their open-ended questionnaire that described candidates' poor interpersonal skills:

> "Behavior perceived as insulting, dismissive."
> "During one of the interview questions, she threw up her arms and said, 'Jesus.'"
> "One candidate was overly argumentative, even belligerent, during the interview with the search committee."
> "One campus visitor ignored many important people and failed to thank those who helped him." (48)

As in the survey of psychology departments by Sheehan, McDevitt, and Ross, these comments appear out of context, and are therefore difficult to interpret fully. Perhaps the "insulting, dismissive" candidate and the one who "ignored many important people" are just jerks. Perhaps the "outlandish coif" (48) worn by one candidate indeed portended an outlandish, uncollegial working style. My aim here is not to suggest who deserves accommodation and who does not, but to inject some provocative questions into the ossified tradition of kairotic job interviews. Isn't it the case that persons with Asperger's, or anxiety, or schizophrenia, may unintentionally come across as dismissive, even insulting? Isn't it possible that short-term memory impairments might impede a candidate's ability to extend thanks, display knowledge of unfamiliar schools, and pay attention in approved ways? Are we comfortable treating these difficulties as deal-breakers in candidates' search for academic employment? What sort of academic culture are we creating if the job candidates we accept are *only* those who successfully avoid outbursts, memory lapses, or "outlandish coif[s]"? Can we imagine a collegiality that embraces mistakes and grows stronger through the ways we address those mistakes? Isn't that what we tell our students about *learning*?

Conferences

I will never forget my first SDS conference, because it was the first time I felt something close to adequate accommodation at a conference. My partner accompanied me, and served as ad hoc personal assistant, helping me navigate through the hotel (which was itself relatively small, on one level, and much more navigable than a multistory Hilton gigantus), taking notes during panels, and accompanying me on social occasions. I was offered a stim device (a "koosh ball") when I registered. And there was a quiet room where I could go to get away from the incessant buzz of conversation and the thousands of roving eyes.[9]

It wasn't Eden. For instance, one afternoon, when I repaired to the "quiet room," I found that two other conference-goers had decided to use the space for a spoken meeting. However, the response to this incident exemplified what Annette Harris Powell calls "access-as-practice": that is, an approach to access that assumes that accessibility is a rhetorical event, and as such must be responsive to particular and dynamic situations. In that case, I went to the SDS organizer at the registration desk and explained that the quiet room was not quiet. She went to the room, asked the two conversationalists to move elsewhere, and I gratefully lay down on one of the two cots provided. Significantly, the organizer I approached intervened without question or hesitation—that is, there was no "Why can't you ask them yourself?" Overall, the attitude was one that presumed accommodation might be needed at any moment, in unpredictable ways, and the large number of assistants available indicated that access-as-practice was a consistent concern.[10]

A conventional conference is not like that. It usually takes place in a hotel or convention center, with each session or meeting scheduled in a mysterious location such as "Rose Ballroom IV-A." Crowds throng the halls between events, lines for food and coffee are long, and elevators are jammed. At any moment, you may run into someone you knew ten years ago, met ten minutes ago, or whom you've never met but with whom you have had sharp professional exchanges in journals. Fluorescent light dominates, noise carries between the thin temporary walls between suites, carpets and upholstery are treated with toxic chemicals, and bathrooms may or may not be accessible. Information is usually delivered orally/aurally—often without the use of microphones—and alternative formats such as scripts, sign interpretation, or computer-aided real-time transcription (CART) are usually either unavailable or difficult to arrange. Also, many of the most power- and information-laden exchanges do not take place in a conference's official spaces, but in spontaneously organized spaces such as gatherings at bars (which, not incidentally, presents an additional barrier for persons in recovery from substance abuse), restaurants, private rooms, or during rushed hallway or elevator exchanges.

A conference as a whole can be described as a kairotic space. It can also be described in terms of *genre*. In their 2002 collection *The Language of Conferencing*, editors Eija Ventola, Celia Shalom, and Susan Thompson argue for recognition of the academic conference as "a social event comprising interrelated genres" with distinctive customs, languages, and social norms (9). Various discourse communities, the editors explain, will make various assumptions about how a conference should unfold, but in the main, conferences are presumed to be "primarily spoken and often spontaneous or quasi-spontaneous . . . essentially dynamic in their unfolding, and in some respects therefore relatively unpredictable" (10). Ventola, Shalom, and Thompson emphasize the challenges this oral/aural and unpredictable environment poses to those in less powerful positions. The focus in *The Language of Conferencing* tends to be upon the difficulties faced by nonnative speakers of the conference's main language, as well as novice participants; however, we can extrapolate from the authors' research to draw inferences about the problems that this genre poses for persons with mental disabilities as well. Ventola, Shalom, and Thompson emphasize the importance of "interpersonal management and politeness features" at conferences, and they rightly argue that these features pose quite different challenges for participants than those posed by written/published research (10).

The larger genre "the conference" comprises various subgenres, described by Celia Shalom as "research process genres" including "the paper presentation, the poster session, the plenary lecture and the book of abstracts," as well as "social genres" that include "coffee breaks, outings, lunch and the conference dinner" (52). To Shalom's list of subgenres, I have argued, we should also add *policy/procedure genres* (Price, "Access Imagined"). Documents classified as policy/procedure genres include the call for submissions, instructions on registering and arranging for travel and accommodations, and guidance on access and disability accommodation. In my study of seventeen policy/procedure documents from a variety of professional societies and disciplines, I found that the accommodations most frequently mentioned were wheelchair access; mobility aids such as scooters; alternative-format copies of presentations; and sign language interpretation. An important assumption to avoid here is that particular accommodations are "for" particular kinds of disabilities. For example, while it might be assumed that printed copies of papers are only for people with hearing impairments, in fact they may aid a wide range of people, including those who have difficulty focusing on, remembering, or processing oral language, whether that difficulty stems from fatigue, an illness, AD/HD, or a brain injury. With that said, however, it is notable how few of the statements mention disabilities other than those that involve impairments of mobility, seeing, and hearing.

An exception is the American Public Health Organization's "Accessibility Guide,"[11] which not only addresses both chemical sensitivity and chronic pain, but offers a detailed comment on how to enact accommodation of these disabilities:

> Specific requests will be made to the hotels that chemicals not be used on the meeting room carpeting within 4 days of the commencement of our meeting and that only unscented products be used in guest rooms. In addition, APHA requests that its meeting attendees refrain from the use of perfumes, hair sprays and other chemicals, for the comfort and health of all our registrants. . . . APHA members with disabilities (including chronic pain) have indicated that in crowded locations and at other times at APHA they experience perhaps unintended pushing or well-intended taps that have caused pain or have caused them to lose their balance. Please be aware of this and be considerate of all our members. (5)

Although this guide does not discuss the barriers that may be faced by conference attendees with mental disabilities, the directions given here move in that direction. The attention to the stress of contact with crowds, including "unintended pushing or well-intended taps," for example, is useful not only because such actions could cause pain or loss of balance, but also because of the mental stress they can create. Unfortunately, aside from the APHA, few of the policies I studied for "Access Imagined" mention chronic pain or fatigue, chemical sensitivity, or mental disabilities, and very few discuss accommodation of these issues at any length.

Even within the relatively proscribed format of a panel presentation, participants are likely to encounter spontaneous, and potentially stressful, modes of exchange. Pauline Webber's study from *The Language of Conferencing* focuses on a subgenre that may be particularly problematic for persons with psychosocial disabilities: the question-and-answer session following a panel presentation. This space may pose special problems both because it is spontaneous and because it is one of the sites at a conference where agonistic exchanges are likely. As Webber specifies,

> According to the conventions of the genre, participants use informal language, politeness devices, address forms and other resources which lower interpersonal distance, but in spite of this there may be tension and conflict in the interaction. . . . [T]his is certainly not just a chat among friends, however friendly it may appear at certain moments. Co-presence involves risk. In spite of the first-name familiarity, the jokes and the apparent modesty in the choice of language found here, speakers are on their guard and prepared to face criticism. (247)

Not only is conflict generally assumed in Q&A sessions, as Webber points out, but it may—depending upon discipline and other features of rhetorical context—be a tacit expectation. Webber quotes one of her research participants saying that "controversy should be welcomed [at conferences], since it is only through controversy that science advances" (248).[12] However, when we consider the environmental difficulties that may already be present during a session, then add to this the presumption that exchanges should involve "controversy," we can observe just how inaccessible this portion of a panel presentation might become for a person with difficulty navigating kairotic space, whether she is a presenter or a potential questioner.

Compounding these difficulties is the fact that "liminal," that is, marginally positioned, conference members (Shalom 66) may find that such exchanges are their *only* opportunities for speaking roles at conferences. In other words, if a person does not have a programmatic speaking role and is not part of the "insider" group that can access informal postsession gatherings, the Q&A session is one of the few spaces left open in which to gain academic capital through synchronous participation. Yet this space, which arguably should be structured to be *especially* welcoming of novices and liminal members, may in fact be one of the least accessible. Fortunately, other subgenres do exist to offer such opportunities, including workshops and special-interest groups (SIGs); and several professional organizations have made impressive efforts—often led by SIGs—to accommodate conference-goers with disabilities of all kinds. Such efforts, at this point, are largely labors of love carried out by a few highly dedicated people and groups. Professional organizations as a whole do not prioritize the inclusion of persons with disabilities at conferences; and where inclusion is attempted, it tends to imagine the disabled conference-goer as a person in a fairly narrowly defined position, with little concern for the flexibility of design that could enable access-as-practice.

Aside from the studies in *The Language of Conferencing*, there is a dearth of research on participants' interaction in conference spaces. Given the importance of conferences as a measure of academics' productivity, this lack is troubling. Ventola, Shalom, and Thompson suggest two reasons why little research exists: the conference's "intrinsic complexity as a focus of research" and the fact that collecting data in these spaces is "notoriously difficult" (361). Despite these difficulties, some researchers, especially in the field of computers-human interaction, have begun to find ways to collect data in the kairotic spaces of conferences, including the much-neglected but crucial arenas of social exchange. Among recent studies is one by Joseph F. McCarthy and coauthors, which confirms both the complexity of the conference as a research setting and the importance of pursuing such research nevertheless:

> One of the appeals of a conference is that it creates a context to support mutual revelation: allowing attendees to learn more about others and their work, as well as being open to opportunities to tell others about themselves and their own work. Thus, many conferences offer a variety of sub-contexts for different kinds of interactions, including formal presentation such as keynotes, papers and panels; informal presentations such as may occur around demonstrations or posters; and the more casual exchanges that typically take place during breaks and receptions.
>
> However, such opportunities for "give and take" tend to be unevenly distributed among the conference attendees, depending on one's status in the community, level of participation in the formal conference program, and more subtle issues such as one's native language and level of extroversion. (39)

Power differentials of all kinds, including the ones that McCarthy and coauthors mention—native language and level of extroversion—will affect a conference-goer's ability to access and participate in the kairotic "give and take" spaces of academic conferences.

To address these inequities of exchange, McCarthy and coauthors propose an augmentation they call the "proactive display": "a large computer display outfitted with sensors that can detect people nearby and re-

Persons at a conference gathered near the Ticket2Talk display. Image courtesy of Joe McCarthy and interrelativity.com.

spond to them in contextually appropriate ways" (39). What this means, in brief, is that information is shared more democratically during kairotic exchanges. For example, one "proactive display" the authors describe is an application called *Ticket2Talk* (T2T), which can be set up in an informal space such as a coffee-break area, or an area with couches and tables. The T2T monitor displays information about participants who are standing within range of the monitor. This information is gathered from participants ahead of time, and includes name, affiliation, photo, and a larger image of "the one thing you would be happy to talk about with anyone at the conference." Information is sent to the monitor by means of electronic tags inserted into conference-goers' badges.

McCarthy and coauthors are careful to note that conference-goers control the information that is displayed about them, and that the device should be used in a spirit of "plausible ignorability," that is, with the assumption that no conference participant is obligated to respond in any particular way to the information provided (42). In short, as the authors explain, the streaming information on the monitor "provide[s] an opportunity to learn about others nearby" (42). The presence of this augmentation means that highly charged kairotic situations, such as introducing oneself or attempting to attach names to faces, become more workable for persons who are processing information via various modes and abilities.[13]

Augmentations such as Ticket2Talk (as well as CART, sign interpretation, and others) may be unfamiliar to conference-goers who have not encountered them before. However, I will also note, from my own perspective, that accessibility measures that are designed flexibly tend to benefit a broad range of participants, not only those with certain kinds of disabilities. For example, CART is helpful not only for hearing-impaired participants, but for those who process information at differing speeds, those with unimpaired aural abilities who have difficulty interpreting aural/oral information, and those who are less familiar with the discourses or names being used. Such accommodations also cost money, and professional organizations commonly cite budget limitations as the reason that they do not provide better access. But budgets are rhetorical devices, designed within normative discourses of power and ability. We might justifiably ask why it is deemed acceptable to design conferences as events that involve expensive airplane travel and accommodation in elegant hotels, but not as events at which all participants can access the information exchanged once there.

Another concern often raised about flexible design is that it changes the normative structure of a conference in ways that are unfamiliar and disquieting to members. This was the case when Joseph F. McCarthy and danah m. boyd studied the introduction of a different adaptive technology at the 2004 Conference on Computer Supported Cooperative Work (CSCW), which took place in Chicago. McCarthy and boyd introduced a "digital backchannel" into the conference's oral/aural spaces, including panels and plenaries. The backchannel was essentially a "chat" space, with separate subsections corresponding to separate events. Attendees could log on to a chosen backchannel, then type and read commentary while the "main" (oral/aural) event took place. Although most users of the backchannel were also physically present at the conference, the researchers found that at least two participants joined remotely "to see how the conference was going." This suggests possibilities for potential conference attendees who are not able, for reasons of impairment, finances, or other limitations, to make physical appearances at a conference but who would like to participate. McCarthy and boyd found that participants used the backchannel for purposes ranging from clarification about events taking place at a panel ("whats the name of the question asker again?") to metadiscussions on content ("can we use his conclusions in non-gaming environments?") to access difficulties ("font on the main screen isn't large enough for the back of the room"). In some cases, as when the font-size problem was raised, the issue was addressed immediately.

Of course, not all persons will be able to attend to oral/aural events while also attending to a stream of backchannel information. Indeed, as McCarthy and boyd note, many backchannel comments focused on participants' difficulty in dividing their attention: for example, "Crap, I was reading this and missed everything he just said." However, the point of flexible design is not to require each individual to attend to every mode simultaneously, but to offer a *variety* of modes that provide support in different ways. Thus, if a participant finds it difficult to focus on information that is presented in a long, unbroken, oral/aural stream, the backchannel may provide just the metastream that enables him to remain engaged.[14]

McCarthy and boyd report that the backchannel, or more exactly, audiences' use of it, was discomfiting for some presenters: "Several presenters were uncomfortable with so many people attending to their laptops, and no way to distinguish those who were engaged in the backchannel from those who were using their laptops for tasks unrelated to the presentation." (An instructor who has lectured to a roomful of students staring into laptop screens may recognize this feeling.) Yet a world that is constantly mediated by digital technologies is not really such an unfamiliar space; our beliefs about acceptable behaviors, and especially acceptable ways of paying attention, shift with time. Consider, for example, the fact that it is quite acceptable to use the technologies of pen and paper to take notes during conference sessions; indeed, it is almost expected. We are accustomed to thinking of this as an *appropriate* way to divide our attention. But the sight of a person punching keys on her cell phone during a panel—despite the fact that this is becoming an increasingly common method of note-taking—is often considered the height of rudeness.

We cannot mandate who pays attention, and how they choose to do so, in kairotic professional spaces. What we can do is imagine ways to redesign those spaces so that they include a greater variety of paths toward access. This will sometimes entail uncomfortable shifts. In recent years, I have taken to knitting at conferences, since it is an excellent stim activity and also allows me to divide my attention in ways that are productive for the workings of *my* mind in particular. If I try to do something verbally based during a presentation, I find that my attention does not divide well. *An ethically designed kairotic professional space assumes that partici-*

pants are operating within it to the best of their abilities: this is the core assumption that underlies true collegiality. Attempts to police others' attention are both uncollegial and unproductive. And, pragmatically, they are doomed to failure.

Conclusion: Recommendations for Professional Practice

In this closing section, I offer a number of concrete suggestions for ways to change the academic profession that concur with Philip Lewis's and others' arguments for the benefits of structural collegiality and shared governance, not only as an ethical project, but as one that will ultimately construct a more workable (I might even say *productive*) academic culture.

My suggestions here are meant to be taken in a way similar to the suggestions offered at the close of chapter 2: that is, not as mandates or precise recipes, but as a range of possible efforts that can offer us a "way to move" (Dolmage 24) toward more accessible design of our professional practices. Just as classrooms are shaped through factors including pedagogical style, class size, discipline, and institutional requirements, so too are professional spaces shaped through contextual factors. Restrictions upon budget and time are two reasons often cited for the failure of institutional discourses to change. (Dubrow reports wryly: "Asked what would most encourage collegiality, one professor answered succinctly, 'Money'" [51].) Another significant limitation may be posed by the requirements of organizations larger than individual schools, including accrediting institutions and legislative measures. However, like the classroom, an institution's professional climate is a rhetorical space, and while some features of this space may have to remain rigid (for the time being, at least), others can flex. I offer these proposals in a spirit of pragmatic hopefulness, with attention to the value of dialogue and small changes that may accrete into larger ones. To reiterate a point made in regard to classrooms, social change begins on Monday morning.

1. SHIFTING ATTITUDES: FEEDBACK AND LISTENING

In *The Difference that Disability Makes,* Rod Michalko points out that institutions often take a "minimalist" stance toward access, defining it in terms of specific adjustments made for particular individuals who are perceived as lacking in some way (128–31). Michalko argues for a shift from this particularized view to a broader, spatial and social view—a shift that is the essence of universal design. *Accommodation,* while helpful, is often used to indicate specific measures intended to "fix" specific situations for individual "problems." *Access* means designing spaces—including kairotic professional spaces—in ways that are flexible, multimodal, and responsive to feedback.

I want to highlight this issue of *feedback,* and argue for a reconceptualization of it that adheres to the principles of universal design. Feedback is usually understood as case-specific concerns voiced by individuals. Instead, we should consider feedback in a larger sense, as information coming back to us about our practices at diverse times and through diverse channels. How many times have you been asked for your "feedback" by means of a single sheet of paper, handed out in the last few minutes of a conference or workshop? (Full disclosure: as a compositionist, a sometime administrator, and a believer in process-oriented pedagogies, I have distributed more than a few such sheets myself.) But how accessible is such a request for feedback, given its brief time frame, its written form, and the possible concerns about confidentiality that may result? I don't wish to argue for elimination of this method, or other heavily proscribed methods such as online surveys, but rather to point out how limited is the scope of what we usually think of as feedback. We must proliferate our ways of asking—and listening—for feedback.

For example, statistics about the presence of "othered" faculty in academe can be considered feedback. In "Faculty Diversity: Too Little for Too Long," Cathy A. Trower and Richard P. Chait report that 87 percent of full-time faculty in the United States are white, and 64 percent are male; only 5 percent of full professors in the United States are "black, Hispanic, or Native American"; and the percentage gap between tenured men and tenured women has remained the same for thirty years (34). Among faculty with disabilities, information is difficult to locate (Anderson), but the numbers that can be found are breathtakingly low; one study of U.S. law schools reveals that just over *1 percent* of their faculty were reported as having disabilities (Mikochik, cited in Anderson).[15] Specific information on faculty with mental disabilities is even more scarce. Current research indicates that persons with these kinds of disabilities are among the most likely to be discriminated against in employment markets generally (Gouvier, Sytsma-Jordan, and Mayville). Anecdotally, Peter Beresford remarked in 2004, "As far as I know, I am the first person actively involved as a mental health service user to be promoted to professor" ("Including Everyone's Knowledge"). A few other full professors can be found, including Elyn R. Saks, who has schizophrenia and is a professor in the School of Law at the University of Southern California. However, it is undeniable that such positions held by mentally disabled persons are few and far between.

Those of us who do hold tenure-track or tenured positions may rely on a strategy of silence in order to protect ourselves. In "Invisible Disorder: Passing as an Academic," Hilary Clark claims that "There is no illness, except perhaps AIDS, that bears the shame still attached to mental illness and that is hidden so well in the academy" (128). Any acknowledgment of disability can be dangerous: in her introduction to the anthology *Disabled Faculty and Staff in a Disabling Society*, editor Mary Lee Vance notes that "Several writers nearly backed out of this project because they feared the retribution and retaliation they might face as a result of exposing their situations" and that only thirty-three of the forty writers who submitted manuscripts ended up staying with the project (5). Thus, can we expect to receive direct "feedback" from persons who are already isolated and stigmatized, and who are so vulnerable to losses of income and insurance? I'm delighted to give and receive directly voiced feedback when I can; however, being queer and mentally disabled myself, I can well understand that silence may be the most empowering strategy one has available at a given time. For this reason we—faculty, administrators, and public advocates—must understand that feedback comes in many forms. The shameful statistics on employment levels of persons with mental disabilities, the silence around mental disability in academe, and our scarcity in faculty positions generally, are also feedback, if we pay attention to them. Here, we might usefully return to Krista Ratcliffe's theory of rhetorical listening. Rhetorical listening moves beyond scenarios of guilt and blame, asking instead that participants in discourse think in terms of *accountability* and *collective action*. It offers a useful theoretical framework for the actions I propose in this section, for such actions must stem from the understanding that "productivity" in academic discourse is a shared responsibility, a complex network of differences and commonalities, and must accrue to the benefit of diversely situated persons rather than those few in the most powerful positions.

2. ENACTING ATTITUDES: PRACTICAL MOVES

Attitude shifts rarely occur in the presence of theory alone; they require practice, in both senses of the term. With this point in mind, I want to offer some concrete examples of ways to create change. Drawing upon Philip Lewis's notion of "bicollegiality," I discuss changes that can take place on an individual level ("practical collegiality") as well as on a larger, institutional level ("structural collegiality") (76–79). It is important that we not place the onus for a more inclusive academic climate only upon individuals' attitudes and ways of behaving. The exercise of power through institutional authority, allocation of money and time, and kairotic structures, plays a crucial role. However, we also must recognize access as a collective responsibility, and hence as something in which individual actions do play a role. In their study of "hidden" disabilities at a community college (including faculty with anxiety, depression, AD/HD, chronic pain, and Asperger's), Avinger, Croake, and Miller suggest a number of ways that colleagues can "be affirming" toward those with such disabilities. They may "stand by [a colleague] who is under scrutiny," may offer collective support (for example, in a collaboratively composed memo to administration), or may become an "agent for change" through supportive committee or policy work (213).

It is an often-cited truism of academic culture that the infighting is fierce because the stakes (at least in terms of money and prestige) are so small. However, the less-often cited converse is just as true: a small gesture or a few well-placed words can have enormous impact. Once, at the beginning of the fall semester, I was supposed to show up for an orientation event called "Meet Your Department," and I happened to be having a day of deep fatigue and confusion. Rather than pleading flu, or car trouble, or any of the other small lies I regularly use, I told my department chair the truth: I was tired and my brain wasn't working well. Without missing a beat, she replied, "You stay home and feel better. I need you to teach well next week, so you just rest." Her basic assumption was to trust me, and to believe my judgment about how I would work best. That single gesture of trust and respect has resonated through my work—not only with her, but in my department generally—ever since.

Conversations about research can also be sites for the practice of professional access. Clark reports that when she explains that her research agenda focuses on narratives of mental illness, "I have seen unabashed shudders and heard comments such as 'I wouldn't go there!'" (128). When discussing this project, I have sometimes received similar responses. However, I have also had positive interactions about my research. For example, in 2008, members of our departmental reading group invited me to bring an article pertaining to DS. Our conversation at that gathering inspired interest in Ato Quayson's *Aesthetic Nervousness,* which became the focus of a later gathering. On these occasions, my colleagues in the Department of English—most of whom are literary scholars—put time and effort into learning about my more rhetorically focused approach to DS, and also offered their own perspectives from literary studies. Not incidentally, one of these gatherings included a conversation about the supposed link between mental illness and violence. My argument that this link was largely mythical was received with some discomfort (in my subjective interpretation), but also with genuine interest. I vividly recall how I felt after those two gatherings: anxious and exposed, but also thrilled that my research interests had crept out of my office and into a slightly larger conversation. It would not have happened if my colleagues had not been skilled rhetorical listeners.

Intervention in conversations that denigrate or otherwise marginalize mental disability is another means of practicing accessibility at an individual level. I can think of myriad occasions on which I have practiced such interventions; one was the exchange, mentioned above, when my colleague mentioned her assumption that mentally ill persons are usually threatening or violent. But still more valuable to me have been those occasions on which my nondisabled allies have chosen to speak out, not specifically on *my* behalf, but as part of a more general agenda toward social justice. For example, during a seminar I once attended, the topic was disability studies, and one participant began discussing research that had been conducted on the question of—if I recall correctly—whether sharks have consciousness. After a few minutes of this dialogue, one of the seminar leaders spoke up and noted that, in his experience, scholarly conversations about disabled persons seemed often to gravitate to the subject of animals. Without lecturing, and speaking from his own experience, he reminded us of the long and destructive history of comparisons between disabled persons and animals. This is an aspect of rhetorical listening that Ratcliffe calls *interruption:* in this case, speaking as an ally to intervene in cultural structures and practices (75). I was grateful for his intervention, and for the calm way he guided us in a different direction. I was especially grateful that it had not fallen to me (as "the disability person") to make this point, which I certainly would not have accomplished so gracefully.

A key question in working toward accessible forms of feedback is "What do you need [as a learner]?" This question is very different from the apparently similar "Is there anything I can do?" The latter, a yes/no question, focuses on individual remediation; the former, an open-ended question, focuses on the *situation.* Keeping it at the forefront of our daily exchanges reminds us that what one person prefers may not be another's preference; in other words, there is no "one size fits all" for access. For example, I detest telephone interviews (in fact, I detest using the phone in general, unless I am text-messaging), because of the lack of contextual visual information. However, Brenda J. Lightfoot, who identifies as having a "vision impairment" (97), notes, "I have always felt more comfortable in phone interviews than in-person interviews. Perhaps this is because I am not distracted by sights or extraneous outside noises, or because I don't have to wonder what my interviewer(s) think of my appearance" (99). *What do you need?* is an important part of the micropractice of accessibility.

3. ENACTING ATTITUDES: STRUCTURAL MOVES

At least as important as these microlevel and individual efforts is the other side of Lewis's "bicollegiality": the structural. Attitudes are expressed not only in personal conversations, but in the infrastructure of kairotic spaces and especially the allocation of resources. It is difficult to make concrete suggestions for structural alterations to kairotic spaces, because the project is so enormous: DS truly is trying, as Harlan Hahn once remarked, "to change the world" (*Vital Signs*). Again, however, I am a pragmatist. I've worked as an administrator, I've written budgets and argued for funding, I've learned to celebrate limited successes and to let certain battles go. Thus, my desire here is to offer workable steps that may form the beginning of a new way to move, with the understanding that this is *only* the beginning.[16]

Let's start with the job search. Sara F. Rose suggests that, if professional organizations conduct interviews at a large central conference, perhaps those organizations could establish a few accessible hotel suites for interviewees or interviewers who wish to use them. I imagine that such suites would be not only wheelchair-accessible, but could also include nonfluorescent lighting, a fragrance-free environment, and a quiet location. Importantly, the location of such suites should also be stable: instead of shuttling between spaces that are separated by blocks or even miles, disabled candidates could learn the location of the accessible suite *once,* and return to it repeatedly. A corresponding measure could be the establishment of a "retreat room" for candidates, providing quiet, food and water, an attendant to help navigate, and a place to lie down if necessary. For on-campus interviews, committees should discuss scheduling with each candidate, asking about kairotic considerations such as time between events. Again, the question "What do you need?" can be a helpful touchstone. This question is not a magic solution; disclosure is, as discussed earlier, a complex and highly contextual enterprise. However, simply raising the question indicates a committee's awareness that interviewing is not a "one size fits all" project, but a rhetorical enterprise that must be as responsive as possible to feedback.

On the job, we must consider ways that our definitions of "productivity" might proliferate. Heather Dubrow's discussion of collegiality makes clear that a collegial climate is one that reconsiders "productivity" itself:

> To foster collegiality, both institutions and departments in them could profitably rethink their reward systems, an issue recently studied by the MLA Task Force on Evaluating Scholarship for Tenure and Promotion. Witness the privileging of the single-authored monograph at the expense of types of writing that involve collaboration in their production or application (coauthoring scholarly articles, editing collections, translating someone else's writing). (57)

The report to which Dubrow refers, published in *Profession* 2007, recommends "a more capacious conception of scholarship," including greater attention to new media, collaborative projects, book reviews, and possible reconception of the doctoral dissertation as "monograph in progress" (63–64). Such proliferation is welcome, and in fact is already occurring in many locations. For example, many humanities departments have added "or the equivalent" to the conventional tenure requirement of the book-length monograph, and in some cases specify what that "equivalent" would mean in terms of alternative scholarship; in addition, many institutions accept peer-reviewed online publications as equivalent to print publications. Some faculty have gone further, calling for recognition of the scholarly activities inherent in teaching and service work (Gouge, Brady, and Singh-Corcoran; Long).

Despite these changes, one conventional tenet of "work" as a faculty member, as defined by the MLA task force, remains stable: "Scholarship, teaching, *and* service should be the three criteria for tenure" (63; emphasis added). I want to question the dominance of this triad. Is it indeed necessary that every faculty member excel in all three areas? In practical terms, the answer is no: a large percentage of faculty working in higher education today occupy roles that are predominantly teaching- or service-oriented. And a smaller percentage occupy roles (of notably higher prestige and remuneration) that are predominantly research-oriented.[17] In fact, the idea that a teacher in higher education should also do "research," or "work that discovers new information," arose fairly recently in historical terms—in the United States, during the early twentieth century (Rhode 31–32). Yet we continue to think of the prototypical faculty member as a three-trick pony, equally skilled in research, teaching, and service.

Michael Murphy, envisioning an alternate professoriate within the field of rhetoric and composition, offers another view. While emphasizing that so-called part-time positions should not continue in their present lower-status and lower-income states, he suggests that nevertheless we should recognize that there is "something strangely healthy" (16) about the adjunct phenomenon:

> [Part-time] teaching doesn't have to be either simple or accommodationist, as it many have assumed—that academia's potential for doing critical intellectual work and even for exerting an ameliorative influence on the culture around it may not depend absolutely on the preservation (or, perhaps, *restoration*) of the traditional professoriate. In fact, given the pressures now being exerted on academia, it may well be only by recognizing, legitimating, and actively cultivating the contributions of "instructors" with viable career tracks and legitimate identities that the possibility of such critical intellectual influence can be *saved.* (17)

The "but" in Murphy's argument—that such positions cannot hope to serve the goal he envisions if they continue to exist in their current low-status and low-pay positions—is the rub. Murphy does not discuss health insurance, but for faculty with disabilities, this can be a deal-breaker: if an instructorship offers intermittent or no health insurance, while a tenure-track professorship offers stable health insurance, there is no choice. (That has certainly been true in my own career as an adjunct, then tenure-track, faculty member.) Yet, as Murphy points out, many institutions, including UCLA, Georgia State, CUNY, and American University, have already established faculty positions in "security of employment" tracks (37)—many of which provide insurance and long-term assurance of employment.

Unfortunately, in the larger scheme of things, separate is rarely equal. A key structural shift that would benefit not only faculty with mental disabilities, but all faculty (except perhaps those few in the positions of greatest power and prestige) would be a radical reconfiguration of the research-teaching-service triad, with a proliferation of differently structured positions according to need, ability, and desire.

Structural access must be practiced by professional organizations as well as schools, and an important site for such changes will be the professional conference. As suggested earlier in this chapter, we might reconceptualize "the conference" in ways that diffuse its expense, its stress, and its emphasis on fleshly presence in kairotic space (not to mention its carbon footprint) in various ways, including use of digital media. Assuming that the large national conference persists, however—as I expect it will, at least in the foreseeable future—various interim measures, some quite simple and inexpensive, can be taken. For example, policy documents can be refigured so that they are more accessible for all participants, and so that they place the onus of accessibility on all members of the organization rather than those who self-identify as disabled (Price, "Imagining Access"). Other measures might involve material practices at the conferences themselves. For instance, Autreat, the annual conference run by Autism Network International, uses a system of color-coding on conference badges to indicate each person's preference regarding level of face-to-face interaction (Robertson and Ne'eman). If this sounds esoteric or unworkable, consider an accommodation that many societies have already incorporated: the "newcomer" badge. While wearing a "newcomer" badge, a conference participant can access additional support spaces, as well as (hopefully) expect smiles, greetings, and offers of help from more seasoned participants. This example points out the intersection of individual and structural dimensions of access: if a conference is a generally exclusionary or hierarchically organized professional society, the newcomer badge will have little meaning, or could even have a negative effect. Friendly greetings cannot be mandated, but are a form of rhetorical listening at a small (and often highly persuasive) level.

4. SYNERGY BETWEEN THE INDIVIDUAL AND THE STRUCTURAL: MENTORING

Although this section has separated individual and structural shifts in an effort to make the recommendations more useful for diverse practitioners, such shifts must occur in synergy, and will have mutually reinforcing effects. A practice that merits particular attention because it manifests this synergy between micro- and macroshifts is *mentoring*. The conventional view of mentoring is that of a more experienced faculty member guiding a person at a lower level of experience and status (e.g., an untenured faculty member or graduate student). Peer mentoring, which takes place between persons at similar levels, has also been gaining in popularity for at least twenty years. However, both models have proved problematic, according to Holly Angelique, Ken Kyle, and Ed Taylor, in part because "opportunities for faculty from marginalized groups to find likeminded colleagues can be quite limited" and because the competitive culture of academe can inhibit faculty members' desire to work in others' best interests (196). Moreover, mentoring can become more a process of assimilation than development, so that its outcome becomes "recycling the dominant power within workplace relationships" (198). In response to these limitations, Angelique, Kyle, and Taylor propose an alternative system called "musing":

> Framed within a radical humanist philosophy, musing is a process of creating peer communities that facilitates connections between naturally developing relationships, shared power, and collective action. Through mentoring as musing new faculty have the potential to evolve as change agents in the institution, instead of assimilating into the existing system. (196)

To support their argument, Angelique, Kyle, and Taylor describe the evolution of Penn State Harrisburg's New Scholars Network (NSN), which operates as a collective that both provides internal support for its members and also functions as a base from which to "take risks and negotiate the power structure of the university" (206). This sort of collective action is in some ways similar to union organizing, which is commonly practiced by graduate students, tenure-track faculty, and occasionally adjunct faculty at various schools. Unlike union organizing, however, "musing" as described by Angelique, Kyle, and Taylor occurs on a small scale, and includes academic and social support as central to its mission.

Although "musing" is an important alternative to conventional dyadic mentoring, I argue that dyadic and triadic structures should be retained as well, because universal design is achieved not through a "new, best" way but by offering flexibility and a proliferation of possible ways. The danger to avoid is finding oneself either without mentors at all, or stuck in a dyadic relationship that is not mutually beneficial; in other words, as Linn Van Dyne points out, an element of "reciprocal selection" must be a part of the establishment of mentoring relationships (162). But how shall a faculty member with a highly stigmatized and perhaps non-apparent disability go about finding a "like-minded" colleague? In other words, when one's professional survival may depend upon "passing," how can this process of reciprocal selection proceed?

One possibility is to rethink what can be meant by "like-mindedness." Certainly it may be helpful to "cultivate comrades in madness, friends who know mania and depression firsthand" (Scott 202). However, colleagues in diverse positions may prove valuable mentors as well. I have very few mentors with mental disabilities, but among my most helpful mentors have been persons with interests in disability studies, minority politics, and social justice; who have family members with mental disabilities; or who simply have a genuine interest in learning about my position, sharing their perspective, and offering guidance and support based on *both* what they know and what they learn. In other words, "like-mindedness" may stem from a variety of stances, and is not especially predictable. For this reason, mentoring structures must follow principles of universal design. In addition to factors such as rank and discipline, mentor-mentee combinations should be responsive to ways of learning, social styles, and communication preferences. Mentoring systems should also include provisions for feedback and review: although formal mentoring relationships are usually established in a one-time, information-poor decision framework, this approach should be revised toward a more recursive process, so that neither mentor nor mentee is locked into a relationship that may not be mutually beneficial.

The rather idealistic arrangement that I am describing cannot reliably take place in an environment that is not already making shifts on both individual and structural levels toward greater accessibility. Overall, we need the ethos of academic discourse to change. The present ethos presumes that academic discourse is an individualistic, competitive, and agonistic enterprise. We must shift in ways that make more room for collaboration, mutual recognition, and rhetorical listening. For those who now feel that I am describing an encounter group rather than a professional practice, I will add that we don't have to eliminate disagreement, agonistic exchange, and competition from academic discourse. The attitude shift I am describing is similar to what Cornell Thomas and Douglas J. Simpson call "radical tolerance":

> Pseudo-tolerance, or tolerance that is based upon the fallacious idea we must abandon any strongly valued difference, is unlikely to lead to cultural, ethnic, religious, and sexual inclusivism. Such shortsightedness will result, not in equal respect of persons, social justice, community concern, political freedoms, and substantive distinctions, but in the resurrection of the out-dated and inadequate concept of the cultural and educational "melting pot" and the creation of an environment in which covert and overt ways of eliminating cultural, ethnic, religious and other differences are employed. What is called for instead is radical tolerance—tolerance that creates a "cultural gumbo," in which every ingredient retains its distinct flavor while becoming part of the collective. (4)

As I argued in the previous chapter, and as Thomas and Simpson affirm, this aim is not a simplistic bumper-sticker approach ("Celebrate Diversity!"). It is fraught with complication and demands ongoing dialogue and revision.

Mental disability as an abstract concept props up much of academic discourse. Faculty are "nutty professors," we are "eccentric" or "odd"; according to the often-repeated bromide about academic culture, "the inmates are running the asylum." And, apparently paradoxically, academic discourse also presumes the necessity of a "sound" and "agile" mind in order to maintain collegiality and productivity. The abhorrence of mental disability is usually practiced in ways that are hard to notice unless one is already attuned to this issue. We must stop assuming that the existing infrastructure is the sine qua non of academic discourse, and instead recognize ways that it can be redesigned for the benefit of all.

CHAPTER 4

Assaults on the Ivory Tower

Representations of Madness in the Discourse of U.S. School Shootings

> In the liberal view, violence occurs at the very limit of the social order, where it displays the fragility of meaning, identity, and value; and the "progress" of modern society can be measured in the successful substitution of persuasion and consent for violence and force. But this view draws attention away from the fact that violence also (and increasingly) arises from within the authority of existing social, political, and economic arrangements and serves quite effectively to reinforce their legitimacy.
>
> —*Lynn Worsham,*
> "Going Postal: Pedagogic Violence and the Schooling of Emotion"

In 2007 and 2008, two mass shootings occurred on two U.S. college campuses, Virginia Polytechnic Institute (Virginia Tech) and Northern Illinois University (NIU).[1] The shooter at Virginia Tech was a twenty-three-year-old undergraduate English major named Seung-Hui Cho; the shooter at Northern Illinois was a twenty-seven-year-old graduate student in sociology named Steven Kazmierczak. At Virginia Tech, Cho killed thirty-two people and wounded twenty-three; at NIU, Kazmierczak killed six and wounded eighteen. Both shooters killed themselves. The extreme nature of these events, the fact that both killers were university students who committed their crimes on campus, and the fact that both completed academic writings that appear to have bearing on the crimes, have brought forth a new onslaught of opinions about the relationship between mental disability, violence, and academe.[2]

My concern in this chapter is the way that these two events, and especially the shooters, have been portrayed in written and visual representations. However, before I proceed, I need to include a note about the painful nature of this material. I am not involved directly with either school or the persons who were affected by the events; I am not part of "the inaudible knowledge inherent to everyday life on campus" (Nickel 159). In my efforts to shape a discussion that is both useful and sensitive, I have been guided by Kathleen W. Jones's highly personal and intelligent account, "The Thirty-third Victim." Jones, a faculty member at Virginia Tech, writes that "the memories are still incredibly raw" (78), and makes a plea that we remember Seung-Hui Cho as an individual who committed suicide, amidst all the public constructions of the shootings on April 16, 2007. My own construction is not an analysis of either shooter as an individual, nor is it an indictment of the members of the Virginia Tech and NIU communities. Rather, this chapter focuses on the ways that *accounts* of Cho and Kazmierczak inflect public myths about mental disability, race, class, nationality, and gender, as well as myths about the proper functioning of higher education itself.

I am acutely aware that such analysis may seem beside the point for those with a more personal stake in either shooting—or could even seem like an apologia for two men who committed murder and injured or traumatized countless people. My own status as a survivor of trauma has made me, if anything, more aware of the possibility that what I am now writing may be, in the colloquial term, "triggery." My intention in this chapter is not to pass judgment on either Cho or Kazmierczak, nor to "heal" or further distress victims and survivors. Nor is it to pass judgment on any particular writer about the events. Rather, it is to critique the *rhetorical structure* through which news of each shooting unfolded, and to demonstrate the ways that prevailing myths about mental disability and violence shore up an ongoing structural violence in American society. As I wrote this chapter, I kept coming back to the statement made by one of Cho's professors: "All our hearts are broken" (Falco). I believe that analysis can incorporate heartbreak, can even help show ways to move through heartbreak; that is why I have written what you read here.

I begin, then, with the words—the explosion of words that emerged following each shooting, and what I think those words might teach us.

The coverage that followed the events ranged from sober *Wall Street Journal* accounts to lurid *Esquire* articles to online blogs and bulletin boards. Much of it focused on the killers themselves: what they looked like, talked like, what they wrote, what medications they took (or refused to take), whom they dated, what their parents' professions are, what sorts of weapons they used and how they acquired them—on and on and on. I argue that such representations function as case studies of the killers, and as records of mental pathology escalating "inevitably" toward extreme violence. Each killer is relentlessly individuated, and the tiniest details of his life taken apart and reconstructed in a narrative aimed to show that he was a "time bomb that sputtered for years before he went off" ("Framing"). Through these representations, Cho and Kazmierczak are diagnosed with a host of disorders, and the disorders taken as evidence of the progression of each man's life toward its violent conclusion.[3]

One of the most detailed (and gruesome) case studies is David Vann's thirteen-page article in the August 2008 issue of *Esquire,* titled "Portrait of the School Shooter as a Young Man." To introduce this article, editor David Granger writes that Vann's story "begins to answer the one question we have to ask before we get to why: Who?" (16). It would seem that most writers who have discussed the events agree with Vann and Granger. In fact, it appears that *who* doesn't just come before *why,* but is posited as the key to learning *why.*

In the days immediately following each event, details of the shooters' lives were dug up and reported pell-mell, as fast as the news wires could collect and distribute them. Headlines[4] shouted:

"Before Deadly Rage, a Life Consumed by Troubling Silence" (Kleinfield)
"From Disturbed High Schooler to College Killer" (Golden)
"Inside Cho's Mind" (T. Moran)
"Bright Daughter, Brooding Son: Enigma in the Cho Household" (Kang, Drogin, and Fiore)
"Steve Kazmierczak: The Secret Life" (Fast)
"Who Was the Illinois School Shooter?" (Friedman)
"Portrait of a Killer" (*Guardian*)

Headlines like these (I have selected just a few from dozens of choices) portray Cho and Kazmierczak as individuals whose "secret lives" must contain the details that explain their violent acts. Such representations do not merely reflect, but also help construct, prevalent beliefs about mental disability, violent behavior, and academe. They locate madness *within* the individual killers, marking the "crazy," "troubled" aspects of their personalities, and hence reify "our" (the putatively normal readers and creators of such representations) status as normates.

Underlying this approach are several intertwined assumptions: that madness is a defect of the individual, that it is "strangely twinned with crime" (Foucault, *Madness* 228), and that it must be cured or contained. Peter Beresford eloquently explains how these myths intertwine:

> [A] powerful medical psychiatric tradition has for more than a century now shaped attitudes, responses and understandings towards mental health service users. It has framed us as pathological, as defective, as problems, as unpredictable. It has focused attention on us as individuals; that something is wrong with us and sometimes suggested that what's wrong will always be there and all that can be done is contain it and us—whether in institutions or by drugs. . . .
>
> Psychiatry has helped us become confused about what bad and mad mean. Increasingly when some terrible crime is committed, there is some awful act of violence, abuse or assault, then we are encouraged to feel the person must be mad to do such a thing. . . . While psychiatry may say it cannot treat the people so identified, it will be happy to attach labels to them. So they are included as mentally ill and increasingly shape public and personal understandings of madness and distress and couple it more and more closely with crime, violence and threat. ("Violence and Psychiatry")

Both Cho and Kazmierczak were mental health service users. My concern is not to argue whether or not they *were* mentally ill; they certainly were labeled as such by various doctors and institutions, and based on the information available, both were in great distress. Rather, I want to look at how madness is constructed in the representations of Cho and Kazmierczak that appeared in various media, including mainstream news, academic discourse, online blogs and discussion groups, and government reports.

In these representations, madness is generally assumed to be the *cause* of the shooters' actions. My rereading makes an alternative argument: that in fact, madness operates in the representations as a *mechanism* through which the shooters are placed in a space of unrecoverable deviance. This move enables such accounts to separate Cho and Kazmierczak—and by extension, madness itself—from everyone else. By individuating the shooters and detailing every nuance of their "odd" or "disturbed" behavior, these representations reify the belief that madness and sanity are two extremely separate spaces—one dangerous, one safe. As Richard Miller puts it, they assure readers that the shooter "wasn't anything like anyone we've ever known or been" ("Fear Factor"). To extend the metaphor of academe as an ivory tower, these representations attempt to form a moat that both *defines* and tries to *protect* academe as a sanctuary of reason. The moat separates the "normal," noncrazy people, from the crazies, who are "time bombs." Shoring up the moat are not only the endless case studies of Cho and Kazmierczak, but also the many descriptions of U.S. campuses as being "under siege," or the objects of "campus terrorism," as well as the widespread policies that have emerged to ensure "preparedness" for such disasters. Perhaps most significantly for a DS reading of these events, the wave of shootings in schools across the United States is frequently called an "epidemic."[5]

While all this energy goes to digging the moat around the tower, what gets lost is the *social* in *psychosocial.* To what extent should it matter that any given student's chance of being shot on campus is infinitesimal? Amid all these calls for "public safety," are we thinking about the systemic violence done by schools and service agencies to students who exhibit differences of all kinds, including not only mental, but racial and class differences? Might we consider links between this so-called war on our campuses and the fact that persons fighting the United States's literal wars are developing depression, anxiety, and PTSD while being denied adequate care? As Miller asks in his discerning essay "The Fear Factor": "Are these the details that should most concern us at this time?"

"From the Beginning": Case Study and Individuation

About a week after Seung-Hui Cho killed thirty-two persons and himself at Virginia Tech, the *New York Times* ran an article that began:

> From the beginning, he did not talk. Not to other children, not to his own family. Everyone saw this. In Seoul, South Korea, where Seung-Hui Cho grew up, his mother agonized over his sullen,

> brooding behavior and empty face. Talk, she just wanted him to talk. . . . Interviews with investigators, relatives, classmates and teachers offer inklings of how he progressed from silence to murderous rage. (Kleinfield)

The article continues in this dramatic style through Cho's childhood in Seoul, move to the United States, experiences in grade school and high school, and matriculation at Virginia Tech. The story culminates on April 16, slowing to a minute level of detail: "[On Monday morning] Mr. Cho dabbed moisturizer on his eyes and slid in contact lenses. He brushed his teeth." It closes with a passage describing the letter and video Cho had sent to NBC: "In death, Seung-Hui Cho finally spoke." This article is one of many that attempt to reconstruct Cho's entire life, from birth onward, in an effort to attach some rational cause to the killings. These stories function like medical case studies in several ways: they focus on pathology and deviance; they locate pathology within the individual; and they assume that violent behavior can be explained by examining the individual's deviance from childhood. Their choices of language and style create an overdetermined narrative of madness leading inexorably to a violent explosion. In doing so, they reify the myth that madness leads to violence, as well as the myth that academe is a madness-free zone that should be protected from the dangerous incursions of insanity.

An important strategy used in these case studies is *juxtaposition,* the placing of pieces of information side by side to imply a connection. This strategy is especially prevalent in early writings about the shooters. Here is an example from a profile written about Kazmierczak, released the day after the shootings at NIU:

> Stephen [*sic*] Kazmierczak, the 27-year-old who opened fire on a crowded Northern Illinois University lecture hall, killing five, and then himself on Thursday, was discharged from the United States Army in February 2002 for unknown reasons, ABC News has learned.
>
> Kazmierczak enlisted in September 2001, and was separated before he completed basic training, a defense official told ABC News.
>
> Reasons for his separation include not revealing a condition during initial screening, or not adapting to military life.
>
> The Privacy Act forbids the Army from characterizing the reason for Kazmierczak's discharge.

> Kazmierczak had most recently been studying mental health issues at the University of Illinois, and had taken a job at a prison, according to his academic advisor. (Friedman)

Without including explicit connections between the paragraphs, this article moves across five points: first, the shooting; second, Kazmierczak's separation from the army; third, the possible reasons for separation, which include "not revealing a condition during initial screening, or not adapting"; fourth, Kazmierczak's interest in "mental health issues" as a topic of study; and fifth, his employment at a prison. The paragraph breaks separate these pieces of information, but also imply that they constitute a logical, even causal progression. Perhaps as a means of reinforcing the connections the reader is asked to make, some of the same juxtapositions appear in telegraphic form in the article's subheadline: "Kazmierczak, 27, Killer of 5 Students, Studied Mental Health Issues, Worked at Prison."

In "Media Depictions of Mental Illness: An Analysis of the Use of Dangerousness," Ruth Allen and Raymond G. Nairn argue that such omissions invite the reader to "supply the missing elements, explicitly becoming a co-creator of the text and its meaning" (379). Moreover, media accounts generally do not leave the reader much flexibility in how to fill in those missing elements; rather, "the reader is compelled to draw on existing stereotypic knowledge to explain the behaviour and, in so doing, to confirm the relevance and adequacy of that knowledge" (379). We can observe this strategy at work in Friedman's article as it juxtaposes Kazmierczak's choice to shoot people, his separation from the military, his association with prisons, and his interest in mental illness. As Allen and Nairn emphasize, the strategy of juxtaposition and omission does not merely invite the reader to draw certain conclusions; it also *implicates* the reader in those conclusions, so that the reader becomes a cocreator of the association between violence and mental illness.

An interesting feature of Friedman's article about Kazmierczak, and other early writings about him, is that they appear a bit confused by the glowing testimonials he received from friends and teachers. Not worthy of appearing in the headline, but included in Friedman's article, is a quotation from one of his professors, Jan Carter-Black, who said that Kazmierczak was "a very committed student, extremely respectful of me." Despite this comment, the overdetermined role of Kazmierczak's deviance in Friedman's article is clear. Immediately after Carter-Black's positive comments, and a note that he had received a dean's award, comes the information that he "was a co-author of an essay entitled 'Self-Injury in Correctional Settings: "Pathology" of Prisons or Prisoners.'" This is followed, improbably, by a quotation from an unnamed "music site message board," on which an unnamed commenter referred to Kazmierczak as "mental." Another article, published by CNN.com, even seems to gloat at Carter-Black's realization that her highly regarded student had committed murder: having published the same statement, that she knew Kazmierczak as "extremely respectful," CNN adds a video link that reads, "Watch Carter-Black deal with painful news" ("University Shooter"). By inviting us to view this supposedly pivotal moment, CNN frames it as a revelation, as though the scales had dropped from the teacher's eyes: Kazmierczak was crazy all along. A few days later, more damning evidence was found: Kazmierczak had been taking a "cocktail of 3 drugs" for anxiety and depression (Boudreau and Zamost). The use of the term *cocktail* implies a sense of the illicit, although the three drugs in question—Prozac, Ambien, and Xanax—are routinely prescribed together. Still, even before the "cocktail" revelation, the case studies had labeled him mentally ill by association.

In the case studies of Cho, evidence of his status as a "nutter" (Goldsworthy) was easier to obtain. Just two days after the shootings at Virginia Tech, CNN published an article headlined "Professor: Shooter's Writing Dripped with Anger." Like the articles about Kazmierczak, this article uses juxtaposition to encourage the reader to construct a narrative about a deviant individual who eventually exploded into violence due to his mental illness:

> A year and a half before Cho Seung-Hui went on a deadly shooting spree on the campus of Virginia Tech, a professor was so concerned about his anger that she took him out of another teacher's creative writing class and taught him one-on-one.
>
> The former chairwoman of Virginia Tech's English department, Lucinda Roy, said the anger Cho expressed was palpable if not explicit.
>
> Cho, an English major, never wrote about guns or killing people, she said. But his writing was disturbing enough that she went to police and other university officials to seek help. (Watch the professor tell how her student frightened her [video link].) ("Professor")

Little evidence appears in this article to explain what made Cho's anger "palpable," although later the writings are described by a student as "very graphic" and "extremely disturbing," and a link to the full text of Cho's plays is provided. As with the case studies of Kazmierczak, the aim of the juxtapositions is to explain Cho's actions in terms of his mental pathology. "He left students and professors alike unnerved in his presence," the article reports, and had been urged to "go to counseling" because of what a fellow student called the "twisted" nature of his writing ("Professor").

The interstices between these juxtaposed pieces of information encourage the reader to draw stereotypical conclusions about madness, violence, and academic discourses. The narrative goes something like this: Each young man had a history of association with mental illness. Eventually he committed horribly violent acts. His reported mental illness was a contributing factor in his violent behavior. His previous writings provide evidence: in Cho's case because these writings were "twisted," and in Kazmierczak's, because they addressed the topic of mental illness. Cho's "sullen" and "unnerving" presence is taken as evidence of his life's progression toward violence, while Kazmierczak's image as a "committed" and "respectful" student is framed as having been only a mirage, whose dissolution should be dramatized by a video of his teacher "deal[ing] with the painful news." Each man is presumed to have been a "time bomb that sputtered for years before he went off" ("Framing").

Marking Deviance

Although mental disability is the primary form of deviance marked in the case studies of Kazmierczak and Cho, it's important to note that these writings also stigmatize other aspects of the men's lives, including race, class, religion, and even body size. In his portrait of Kazmierczak, theatrically written in present tense, Vann sketches Kazmierczak's childhood:

> Steve grew up watching horror movies with his mother. Fleshy, enormous, laid out beside him on the couch. Middle of the day, and all shades are drawn. Dark. She's protective, doesn't want Steve to go outside. Won't let him play much with other children. She's not mentally right, according to Steve's godfather, but what can he do? A family feud.

> Horror movies and the Bible, those are what animate this living room, those are Steve's inheritance. A close fit, the plagues, the tortures of Job. God's sadistic games, teaching his flock to appreciate the value and meaning of their lives. The flesh of no consequence. Late night, his mother can't sleep. An insomniac with anxiety problems. A history of depression on his father's side, Steve's grandfather an alcoholic. So they continue on, still watching. (116)

Horror movies, fatness, darkness, mental disability, apocalyptic religious beliefs, alcoholism: all these crowd together in Vann's terse sentences to form a collage of stereotypical deviance. This marking continues throughout Vann's article: Steve built pipe bombs, Steve looked at "porno" (117), he got a tattoo, he dressed as Jigsaw from the *Saw* movies for Halloween. While the primary emphasis remains Kazmierczak's mental disabilities—every trip to a group home or psychiatric ward is documented, along with medication shifts and suicide attempts—these other marks of deviance are used to further stigmatize the madman at the story's center.[6]

In my review of writings about the Northern Illinois shootings, I did not come across a single reference to Kazmierczak's whiteness. This is unsurprising: although most school shooters are white males, the factor of whiteness in these incidents is "continuously masked and divorced from any sense of responsibility" (Brandzel and Desai 69), and no one ponders the stigmatizing effect of this fact on white males in general, although there is considerable hand-wringing about what is wrong with "our youth," with both "us" and "youth" implicitly marked as white.[7] In 1999, shortly after the Columbine shootings, Orlando Patterson asked why the actions of white youths Eric Harris and Dylan Klebold had touched off "an orgy of national soul-searching," while crimes committed by young African American or Latino men inspired no such reflection. Astutely, Patterson argues that what is really at stake in such orgies and omissions is the popular notion of what constitutes normality:

> What is at issue here is the principle of infrangibility: our conception of normalcy and of what groups constitute our social body—those from whom we cannot be separated without losing our identity, so that their achievements become our own and their pathologies our failures.

As Patterson's argument suggests, the deepest fear engendered by the news of sudden, apparently senseless murders committed by supposedly "normal" persons is not that we, the watching and listening public (again, implicitly marked as white), will be directly threatened. Rather, our deepest fear is that their actions challenge our constructed notions of normality itself. Accordingly, we search for markers of deviance that will separate the killers from "us."

Patterson's remarks were prescient, which becomes sadly apparent in the case studies of Cho, which extensively mark his race, ethnicity, immigration status, and class. He is called an "Asian immigrant" (Kang, Drogin, and Fiore), a "resident alien" ("Professor") who "had a green card" ("Source"). Often such racial or national markings mix with class markings, as in this article from the *Los Angeles Times:*

> The three-story beige town house on Truitt Farm Drive stands as the Cho family's symbol of middle-class success, precisely what they were searching for when they left a dank basement apartment and a life of struggle in South Korea. . . .
>
> Asian immigrants tend to emphasize education and success, and by all accounts, the Chos were no exception. (Kang, Drogin, and Fiore)

These presumptions about "Asian immigrants" run through many of the case studies of Cho. While the *Los Angeles Times* reporters cite a professor of ethnic studies to back up their claim, other accounts blithely discuss the significance of Cho's race and class without referencing anyone in particular. An example, from the *Washington Post,* reads:

> Investigators said Cho was a Korean national with a green card and used the Asian style of putting his last name first, which the news media generally followed. But Cho had spent nearly twice as much time in the United States as in Asia. He is part of what Korean Americans call the "1.5 generation"—children who immigrated to the United States and who live in both Korean and American cultures but sometimes feel completely at home in neither.
>
> As his name was broadcast to the world, Koreans abroad and in the United States struggled with their reactions, *cultural analysts say.* The South Korean government expressed fears of a backlash

> against all Koreans. Korean pastors and civic leaders who had no relationship to the family or Virginia Tech apologized on behalf of the shooter. *Academics said* the reactions revealed how personal the shooting has been for Koreans and Korean Americans. It was as if Cho was one of their own family members. Shame and blame boiled to the surface. (Cho and Gardner; emphasis added)

This passage lacks specific evidence for the applicability of the stereotypes in Cho's case: the opinions are not attributed to anyone in particular, but to vaguely situated "cultural analysts" and "academics." Only two persons are cited in this section of the article, one of whom actually refutes its pronouncements: Josephine Kim, a professor from Harvard, is paraphrased as saying that "the Korean American community should not feel responsible for an incident it had nothing to do with." The other person cited, from Princeton Theological Seminary, is quoted as saying that "there would be some reluctance and some hesitancy in admitting [a mental illness]" by "Korean immigrants." But in fact, this was not true for the Cho family: when Seung-Hui was diagnosed with a mental disability, his parents made extensive efforts to seek support for him, including educational accommodations and art therapy. Like Vann's case study of Kazmierczak, this description of Cho's life refers to darkness—its subhead reports "Family 'Humbled by This Darkness' "—and seizes upon every possible detail to form a portrait of deviance. It even describes the mildew coating the basement apartment the family had rented years before in Seoul.

In their study of media accounts of the Virginia Tech shootings, Amy L. Brandzel and Jigna Desai argue that Cho's race is both hypermarked and unmarked. Popular media rendered him as Korean, rather than Korean American, and also as "sexual deviant," "yellow peril," "gook," and "model minority" (Brandzel and Desai 73). Yet these same media are curiously quiet about the racialized nature of the harassment Cho experienced in school. Brandzel and Desai argue that this simultaneous hypermarking and demarking occurs because, otherwise, popular accounts of Cho might have to recognize the narrative presented in his own writings, photos, and videos: "the racially oppressed retaliating for [his] isolation from the privileges of normative citizenship and for economic and social inequities" (77). In other words, it is more comfortable to fit Cho into popular racist discourses such as the "inscrutable" or "robotic" Asian killer (74), rather than reconsider the structures of oppression against which Cho explicitly spoke—and, perhaps, acted. I concur with this argument from Brandzel and Desai, although I believe another factor should be added to their analysis of the raced, gendered, and classed narratives into which Cho was written: his diagnoses of mental illness. The case studies of Cho, like those of Kazmierczak, enthusiastically diagnose both men with a range of mental illnesses, drawing upon and reifying the presumed connections between deviance, mental illness, and violence.

Diagnosis and Blame

Much is made of Cho's and Kazmierczak's experiences with the mental-health service industry, and especially their "failure" to take drugs or attend therapy consistently. For example, one headline from the *Guardian* reads, "Portrait of a Killer: Virginia Tech Gunman Was a Loner with Mental Health Problems Who Shunned Treatment." This invites the reader to participate in a narrative of blaming the shooters for failing to overcome their mental disabilities. If they had only gone to therapy and taken their medications, the narratives suggest (and in some cases, directly say), they would never have done such terrible things. Blame is also extended to other parties in the stories, including the men's parents and friends, their therapists, and their schools. The supposition underlying this narrative is that madness can be overcome, and that the key to this process of overcoming is *control* or *containment* of the mad person by means of medical treatment or incarceration.

News reports about Cho dig into his childhood, marking early "warning signs" to establish not only that he was crazy, but that he had always been crazy. The *Washington Post* states that "Warning signs about Seung[-]Hui Cho came early in his life" and dwells on Cho's "antisocial behavior," which largely consisted of not speaking and of writing about violent events (Cho and Gardner). (Cho and Gardner's *Post* article also notes, as few other accounts did, that Cho had been ridiculed by his classmates for being so quiet: "Some remember classmates derisively offering dollar bills to Cho if he would just talk.") Although some persons who knew Cho are quoted saying that they found his quietness "docile" and "well-behaved" (Kang, Drogin, and Fiore), writers of the case studies generally choose more portentous adjectives: "haunted" (Kleinfield), "sickly" ("Portrait"), and "brooding" (Kang, Drogin, and Fiore).

Diagnostic accounts of Cho reach a climax in the *Report of the Vir-*

ginia Tech Review Panel. Researched and authored by a panel formed by Virginia governor Timothy Kaine, the *Report* aims to study the shootings and make recommendations "that will reduce the risk of future violence on our campuses" (viii). An entire chapter of the *Report* is dedicated to the "Mental Health History of Seung Hui Cho." This chapter draws on interviews with Cho's family, teachers (both high school and college), staff at counseling centers where he was treated, transcripts and school records, and Cho's own writings from various classes. Like earlier newspaper accounts, it attempts to explain Cho's violent actions by piecing together evidence from his life experiences, and, as its title indicates, the primary topic of interest in his life is his mental health.

One of the most intriguing themes in this chapter is its repeated references to Cho's difficulty with speech. He was diagnosed in high school with "selective mutism," which the *Report* summarizes as follows:

> Selective mutism is a type of an anxiety disorder that is characterized by a consistent *failure* to speak in specific social situations where there is an expectation of speaking. The *unwillingness* to speak is not secondary to speech/communication problems, but, rather, is based on painful shyness. Children with selective mutism are usually inhibited, withdrawn, and anxious with an obsessive fear of hearing their own voice. Sometimes they show *passive-aggressive, stubborn and controlling* traits. The *association between this disorder and autism* is unclear. (35; emphasis added)

Although the language of this description is restrained in comparison to the more lurid newspaper and magazine accounts, note the value judgments it attaches to silence. According to the *Report,* someone with selective mutism is "unwilling" to speak (rather than "unable" or "afraid"). The absence of speech is also characterized as a "failure." It is associated with "passive-aggressive, stubborn and controlling traits," and also has some murky association with autism that is not discussed further. The rhetorical term for this last strategy is *paralipsis:* paraliptic statements suggest truths while simultaneously denying doing so. Saying to a friend, "I'm not even going to comment on how ugly that sweater is" is an example of paralepsis. Through this strategy, the *Report* manages to establish a connection between Cho's condition and autism while also maintaining deniability for doing so.

The *Report*'s extensive attention to Cho's quietness as a "failing" (36) stands in stark contrast to its lack of attention to social factors that may have contributed to it. For example, the *Report* offers a description of an early medical trauma that seems to have been the beginning or trigger of Cho's quietness; however, it does not remark on the significance of this trauma, nor does it mention the experience in its many recommendations for ways to address problems in the health-care system. The anecdote reads:

> When he was 9 months old, Cho developed whooping cough, then pneumonia, and was hospitalized. Doctors told the Chos that their son had a hole in his heart (some records say a "heart murmur"). Two years later, doctors conducted cardiac tests to better examine the inside of his heart that included a procedure (probably an echocardiograph or a cardiac catherization). This caused the 3-year-old emotional trauma. From that point on, Cho did not like to be touched. He generally was perceived as medically frail. According to his mother, he cried a lot and was constantly sick. (31–32)

Let me be clear: I am not pointing to this incident as some sort of diagnostic keystone that "explains" Cho's violent behavior, nor am I interested in mining the details of Cho's past, as all these case studies do, in order to draw yet another map of mental disturbance creeping inexorably toward violent behavior. Rather, I am pointing out how little attention is paid, even in an exhaustive account like the *Report,* to the many traumas Cho seems to have undergone, including not only this incident but also hate speech and harassment (discussed further below). The information in this anecdote could provide an opportunity to consider what trauma and mental disability are like as experiences; however, that opportunity is not taken up. Although the *Report* spends a great deal of time enumerating the failures of various health-care agencies, these are perceived as failures to *contain* and *control* Cho, rather than failures to listen to, or attempt to alleviate, his obvious distress.

The *Report*'s documentation of Cho's contacts with mental-health professionals and brief experience of involuntary commitment is an example of this tendency. According to school records, Cho made several attempts to obtain counseling from Virginia Tech's Cook Counseling

Center and was not successful. However, the report does not mention the effects this might have had upon him, focusing instead on the failure of the counseling centers to take adequate notes or follow up on the case. Again, the incident is framed as a failure of *control* rather than a failure of *care*.

> On Wednesday, November 30, at 9:45 am, Cho called Cook Counseling Center and spoke with Maisha Smith, a licensed professional counselor. This is the first record of Cho's acting upon professors' advice to seek counseling, and it followed [an] interaction he had had with campus police three days before. She conducted a telephone triage to collect the necessary data to evaluate the level of intervention required. Ms. Smith has no independent recollection of Cho and her notes from the triage are missing from Cho's file. A note attached to the electronic appointment indicates that Cho specifically requested an appointment with Cathye Betzel, a licensed clinical psychologist, and indicated that his professor had spoken with Dr. Betzel. The appointment was scheduled for December 12 at 2:00 pm, but Cho failed to keep the appointment. However, he did call Cook Counseling after 4:00 pm that same afternoon and was again scheduled for telephone triage. (45–46)

I have experienced telephone triage through a large university's counseling center before. Simply put, it's no fun. When I made my own first call to seek help from my university, I was met, as Cho was, with an impersonal telephone "triage" process, followed by the information that I would not actually be permitted to meet with a counselor until weeks later. Note that the appointment time Cho was given, December 12, came nearly two weeks later than the date of his initial call. When one is experiencing mental distress, two weeks is a very long time. I can't assume that Cho's feelings were the same as mine, but I would argue that the experience of having to wait so long for a first appointment, missing it, calling immediately, and being sent right back to triage must have been stressful, at the least. Yet, instead of acknowledging the stress of this process upon Cho, the *Report* again focuses on recording the center's bureaucratic failings: "No referral was made for follow-up services either at Cook or elsewhere . . . [A]ny written documentation that would typically have been associated with the [phone] consultation is missing from Cho's file" (46). The *Report* mentions, but does not dwell upon, the fact that Cho never got to see a counselor at Cook Counseling. When it states that Cho was *again* triaged by another agency about a month later (following an involuntary commitment hearing due to a message he sent to a suite mate saying, "I might as well kill myself" [47]), the *Report* notes merely that "the triage report is missing . . . and the counselor who performed the triage has no independent recollection of Cho" (49). It then concludes, "Cho never returned to Cook Counseling Center" (49).[8]

This lack of attention to Cho's experience or point of view continues through the *Report*'s approach to his isolated social life. Evidence from the *Report* indicates that Cho was bullied and intimidated in school from a young age. However, this information is passed over rather quickly and does not detail the cruelty of these experiences, which have been described elsewhere to include students laughing at him, ridiculing him in class, and offering him dollar bills if he would speak (Brandzel and Desai; Cho and Gardner; "Ex-Classmates"). Despite the possible significance of this harassment, the *Report* chooses to provide a paraphrase of a statement from Cho's sister Sun Kyung that downplays it:

> His sister said that both of them were subjected to a certain level of harassment when they first came to the United States and throughout their school years, but she indicated that it was neither particularly threatening nor ongoing. (37)

By all accounts, Sun Kyung operated much more easily in social space than her brother: The *Los Angeles Times,* for instance, says that she "soar[ed]" in high school, traveled abroad for a "transforming" internship, and had a "rich" social life in college (Kang, Drogin, and Fiore). Given this different profile, it would seem that her experience of harassment might have been very different than Cho's. One of Cho's high-school classmates reported that when Cho read aloud in class, for example, other students "started laughing and pointing and saying 'Go back to China'" ("Ex-Classmates"). Yet the *Report* assumes that Sun Kyung's experience must reflect her brother's as well. Moreover, the language of the *Report* places the onus for being harassed upon Cho himself. For example, it states, "Cho continued to isolate himself in middle school" (34) and that "[in high school] his manner of speaking and accent sometimes drew derision from his peers" (37). Note the way these statements arrange agency so that the responsibility lies with Cho: he isolated *himself,* and it was his manner that *drew* the derision.

A similar tendency to blame Cho for his difficulty operating in kairotic space seems to have been practiced by some of his professors, whose judgments are recorded in the *Report.* For example, instructor Carl Bean constructs Cho as having been even more willfully disruptive, even conniving:

> [Bean] told the panel that Cho was always very quiet, always wore his cap pulled down, and spoke extremely softly. Bean opined that "this was his power." By speaking so softly, he manipulated people into feeling sorry for him and his fellow students would allow him to get credit for group projects without having worked on them. Bean noted that Cho derived satisfaction from learning "how to play the game—do as little as he needed to do to get by." (50)

This interpretation of Cho's behavior depicts him as a kind of evil genius: not a person in distress or afraid, but someone deliberately "manipulat[ing]" people and a system in order to get what he wanted. Although the *Report* details Cho's diagnoses of selective mutism and an unspecified mood disorder, it quickly brushes off the notion of mental distress in favor of Bean's evil-genius interpretation. Immediately after Bean's statement, the *Report* muses, "This [Bean's] profile of Cho stands in contrast to the profile of a pitiable, emotionally disabled young man, but it may in fact represent a true picture of the other side of Cho—the one that murdered 32 people" (50). According to this comment, the best one can hope for, if mentally disabled, is to be considered "pitiable"; and in Cho's case the "true" interpretation is not even pitiability, but "the other side"—that one is a murderer.

My rereading of these case studies is not meant to exonerate Cho, nor to demonize the people around him, many of whom, by all evidence, went to great effort to listen to, understand, and help him. Rather, I want to move away from narratives of blame, and pay attention instead to the ways that Cho's portrait is drawn through these representations as *willful* deviance *resulting in* murderous violence. We do not actually know very much about the relationship between mental disability and violence, despite long-standing scholarly and popular fascination with this topic.[9]

But if we are ever to learn more, we will have to move beyond narratives that simply reify the myths we already think we know.

Digging the Moat, Part 1: Privacy as the "Price" of Public Safety

The goal of the *Report of the Virginia Tech Review Panel,* as explained by Kaine in its foreword, is to "make changes that will reduce the risk of future violence on our campuses" (viii). One of the changes it calls for is greater sharing of information between institutions about persons diagnosed with mental illnesses, and even a change to laws specifically designed to protect personal rights and privacy, including FERPA (Family Educational Rights and Privacy Act), HIPAA (Health Insurance Portability and Accountability Act), and the ADA (Americans with Disabilities Act). When Cho matriculated at Virginia Tech, the *Report* states, his record of having received therapy and been in "special education" classes did not follow him. The *Report* states that although it "does not make a recommendation here" regarding information sharing, it immediately goes on to suggest various ways that such information *could* be shared, even without the adult student's consent:

> It is common practice to require students entering a new school, college, or university to present records of immunization. Why not records of serious emotional or mental problem[s] too? For that matter, why not records of all communicable diseases?
>
> The answer is obvious: personal privacy. And while the panel respects this answer, it is important to examine the extent to which such information is altogether banned or could be released at the institution's discretion. No one wants to stigmatize a person or deny her or him opportunities because of mental or physical disability. Still, there are issues of public safety. . . .
>
> Perhaps students should be required to submit records of emotional or mental disturbance and any communicable diseases *after they have been admitted but before they enroll at a college or university,* with assurance that the records will not be accessed unless the institution's threat assessment team (by whatever name it is known) judges a student to pose a potential threat to self or others.
>
> Or perhaps an institution whose threat assessment team determines that a student is a danger to self or others should promptly

> contact the student's family or high school, inform them of the assessment, and inquire as to a previous history of emotional or mental disturbance.
>
> This much is clear: information critical to public safety should not stay behind as a person moves from school to school. Students may start fresh in college, but their history may well remain relevant. Maybe there really should be some form of "permanent record." (38–39)

While denying that it is making any official recommendation, the *Report* nevertheless proposes several ways that a student's record of "emotional or mental disturbance" *could* follow him or her from school to school. Startlingly, it also mentions that "any communicable diseases" could appear on this record, thus raising the possibility that a student's HIV (or hepatitis, or herpes, or any other communicable disease) status could be shared as well. The *Report*'s preference seems clear: where mental illness or "communicable diseases" are concerned, privacy should be less important than perceived threats to public safety. Even before the *Report* appeared, its vision had already begun to come to pass: in March 2008, the Federal Education Department proposed a new set of rules to loosen FERPA guidelines on what information about students can be shared, and with whom. Ada Meloy, general counsel of the American Council on Education, stated that "there is more understanding that to err on the side of withholding information can have dire consequences" (Lewin).

The *Report* is only one of many calls for elimination of civil rights for persons with mental disabilities in the interest of "public safety." While the *Report* is careful to qualify its recommendations, other proponents of eliminating civil rights are more strident. For example, Kristin Ruth Tichenor, vice president of enrollment management at Worcester Polytechnic Institute, published an article in the *Chronicle of Higher Education* calling for "federal legislation that will mandate full disclosure of disciplinary and criminal action on the part of students as they move from school to college, or from one college to another" (21). This might sound fairly harmless until we recall the kinds of behaviors for which students are routinely "disciplined": lack of attendance, not participating in approved ways in class, or having difficulty operating in kairotic space in ways that are deemed "appropriate." What if a student barks as a way of expressing anxiety? This is a behavior mentioned by James C. Wilson in his memoir of his son, Sam, who is autistic. Wilson describes a range of Sam's behaviors, each of which is a form of communication:

> When Sam barks, I know he's nervous. When he starts tapping loudly on walls, I know he wants my attention. When he races around the house, I know he's flying high and ready to go off. When he stares at me sullenly, I know he's angry or depressed. And so on. There's no failure of communication, no misunderstanding. Sam talks perfectly well, but he communicates just as effectively with his body. Sometimes more effectively. (114)

It's unlikely that any of the behaviors Wilson describes—barking, tapping, racing around, or even sullen staring (recall the many pejorative descriptions of Cho's "sullen" face)—would be tolerated in most school environments. Such behaviors would be "disciplined." And the records of all this discipline, if Tichenor's call for federal legislation were brought to fruition, would follow the barking, tapping, staring student from school to school, marking her not as someone who communicated in unconventional ways, but as a threat.

Sociologist Katherine S. Newman, coauthor of *Rampage: The Social Roots of School Shootings,* presents perhaps the most direct proposal for control and containment of persons with mental disabilities: just lock them up. Shortly after the shootings at Virginia Tech, Newman published an article in the *Chronicle of Higher Education* that anticipates, and in fact amplifies, the review panel's call for tracking and containment:

> The Americans with Disabilities Act teaches us that people with mental problems can lead productive lives and should be shielded from discrimination. But we pay a high price for clearing the slate, and an even higher price for the civil liberties that prevent us from locking up someone who is simply writing scary stories or sending bizarre e-mail messages. We strip information from the system that might yield clues to an unraveling mind when we destroy disciplinary records. . . . Part of the story lies in the unwillingness of our society to lock up people who have committed no illegal acts. (20)

Newman's argument takes the information-sharing suggestion to its extreme: literal containment. Not only should information about persons with "unraveling mind[s]" be shared, she suggests, but such people should be "locked up" even when they have "committed no illegal acts." Like the *Report,* Newman shapes her argument as one that serves the cause of public safety, repeating the phrase that both describes and heightens the very common fear of these very rare events: "as educators," we "wonder which of our campuses might be next" (20).[10]

The foregoing arguments rely on two major assumptions that bear further consideration: first, that persons with mental disabilities are dangerous; and second, that "public safety" is best protected not through changes to social structures, but through control and containment of these supposedly dangerous people.

Let's start with the first assumption, that mental disability is a significant predictor of violent behavior. The *perceived* link between such disabilities and violence is well documented.[11] However, empirical evidence of such a relationship is more difficult to determine. In a 1991 review of research (situated within psychology), John Monahan found that such a relationship does appear to exist. However, he explains at length that the predictive power of this relationship is heavily limited, and should not bolster calls for laws to restrict freedom, nor should it heighten social stigma. He cites two reasons for this conclusion. The first is that "being a former patient in a mental hospital—that is, having experienced psychotic symptoms in the past—bears no direct relationship to violence" (519). And the second, "more important," reason is that most persons with "mental disorder" are not violent:

> By all indications, the great majority of people who are currently disordered—approximately 90% from the ECA study—are not violent. None of the data give any support to the sensationalized caricature of the mentally disordered served up by the media, the shunning of former patients by employers and neighbors in the community, or regressive "lock 'em all up" laws proposed by politicians pandering to public fears. (519)[12]

In other words, the public perception of the madness-violence link is not baseless. However, it is so limited that to call for widespread tracking and incarceration of persons with mental disabilities approaches the arbitrary.

A 1999 study by Bruce G. Link and colleagues, taking a sociological perspective, follows up on Monahan's earlier work and expands on the fragility of the supposed connection. The authors argue:

> [T]he magnitude of the association [between mental illness and risk of violent behavior] is modest in comparison to the fear engendered by stereotypes of dangerousness. The odds-ratios relating psychotic/bipolar disorders to violent behaviors are within the range of odds-ratios for other predictors of violence such as age, gender, and education. If a community were to use the risk of violence as the sole basis for the exclusion of people with mental illnesses, such a community might just as well exclude men in favor of women, teenagers in favor of people who are 50 years old, and grade school graduates in favor of college graduates. (330)

A decade after the research from Link and coauthors, another review of the literature—this one situated within psychiatry—appeared (Choe, Teplin, and Abram). This 2008 review, which examines only studies of "severe mental illness" (defined as psychotic and major affective disorders), presents findings similar to those of Link and coauthors: there is a "small attributable risk" of violence by persons diagnosed with severe mental illness (161). However, the authors emphasize, as the studies preceding theirs have, that this risk is much smaller than that attributable to other factors, including gender and age. Furthermore, their study emphasizes, violent victimization *of* people with severe mental illnesses is extremely high. Overall, Choe, Teplin, and Abram contend, "the stereotype that persons with severe mental illness are typically violent" is not supported by their research (161). Unfortunately, although decades of research from multiple disciplines disavow the stereotype of the violent mad person, these findings have not percolated into popular or even governmental accounts of school shootings. For example, nearly every school shooter on record in the United States has been a young man, and with heavily marked exceptions, most are white. Yet "risk" factors such as maleness, youth, and (in Kazmierczak's case) whiteness are apparently of little interest in the case studies drawn of them.

Now to the second assumption—that "public safety" relies upon tracking and incarceration of persons with mental disabilities. In terms of probabilities, this would be a highly inefficient course of action. Even a cursory examination of college life in the United States shows that a college student's chances of being shot during a "rampage" are infinitesimal compared to her chances of being harmed due to alcohol use, intimate partner violence, or driving to class. As James Alan Fox puts it, "for the 18 million college students in America, the odds of being murdered on campus are so low one might need a course in college math to calibrate them" (64). This has not stopped colleges from instituting new policies to address "active shooter scenarios," however. Unsurprisingly, this rush for preparedness has a distinctly capitalistic flavor. For example, a commercially produced twenty-minute DVD titled *Shots Fired on Campus,* which aims to teach students, faculty, and administrators to develop a "survival mindset," was released in 2008. According to Eric Hoover, writing for the *Chronicle of Higher Education,* colleges can purchase a campus-specific version for $495, with extra media files available for an additional $1,000. Hoover reports that, as of June 2008, about fifty orders had been filled, and "its creators expect to sell several hundred more this fall" (1). Another high-tech solution, a "web-based incident reporting platform" (312), is proposed by Hughes, White, and Hertz in their article "A New Technique for Mitigating Risk on U.S. College Campuses." And on July 30, 2008, the U.S. Department of Education awarded thirteen grants, totaling $5.2 million, to colleges and universities "to prevent violence and prepare institutions to respond quickly and efficiently."

Despite all this "preparedness," ironically, the greatest risk associated with students who have mental disabilities is that they will harm themselves. In a 2006 review of campus mental health services, Carol T. Mowbray and colleagues found that "college counseling centers may be dealing with students with suicidal ideation and potential suicide attempts in nearly one out of every two cases they see" (234). Persons with mental disabilities also face an increased risk of being the targets of violent acts as compared to the general population (Choe, Teplin, and Abram). Furthermore, the risks to students with mental disabilities go beyond immediate bodily harm: for instance, a 2005 survey of campus disability services by Mary Elizabeth Collins and Mowbray points out that "An estimated 86% of individuals who have a psychiatric disorder withdraw from college prior to completion of their degree" (304). *Eighty-six percent.*

If we are seriously concerned with public safety as it pertains to persons with mental disabilities, it would make more sense to provide adequate support services, and to work to reduce bullying, hate speech, and

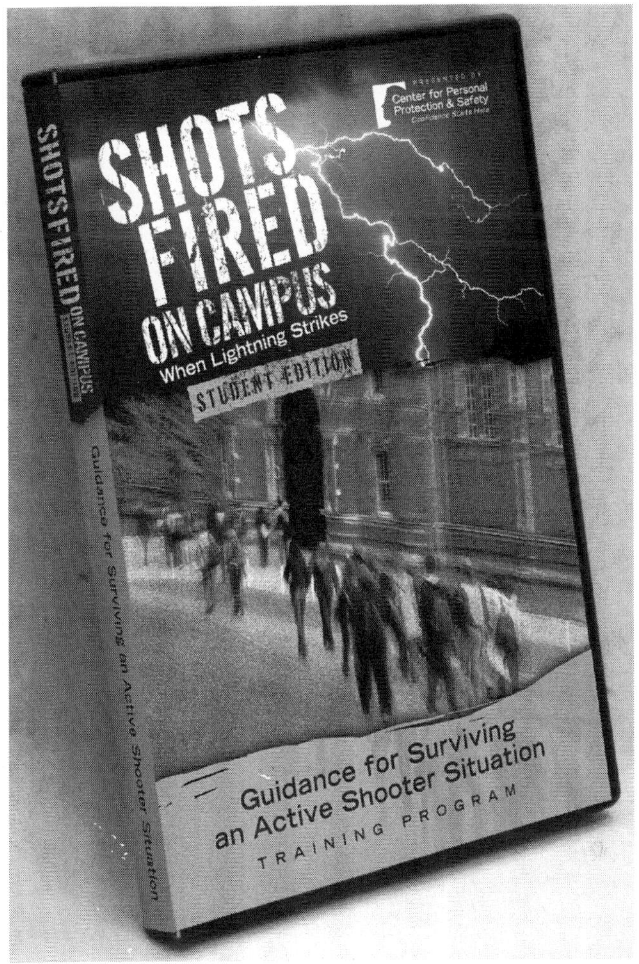

Graphic from videos4training.com showing the cover of the DVD *Shots Fired on Campus: When Lightning Strikes,* which includes an image of a lightning bolt as well as a blurred photograph of students outside a university building.

other forms of stigmatization—for differences of all kinds, including disability, sexuality, race, gender, and class. At present, services on U.S. campuses that do exist for persons with mental disabilities tend to be targeted at documentation, individual accommodations, and referral, rather than at remediating hostile or inaccessible environments. This fact was confirmed by Collins and Mowbray's study, which surveyed disability services offices from 275 schools and focused specifically on the offices' services for psychiatric disabilities:

> In addition to fear of disclosure and stigma as barriers, multiple respondents also noted a lack of awareness (among students and faculty) about [psychiatric] services offered through disability services offices and lack of optimal programs, services, and staff resources. In contrast, it is interesting to note that, among the list of services provided in disability services offices, activities to address these barriers, such as faculty and student presentations or distribution of brochures about available services, are carried out to a much lesser extent. That is, the most commonly reported services are those related to documentation of the disability and individual support for students (including referral to off-campus services). (Collins and Mowbray 312)

This finding suggests that we have far to go in our efforts to remediate environments in the interest of true public safety and well-being. And the issue of educating faculty raises another question, one that was already a hot topic before 2007 and that has now risen to the level of conflagration. The question is often phrased this way: "Am I a teacher or a therapist?"

Digging the Moat, Part 2: "I'm a Teacher, Not a Therapist"

In chapter 1, I discussed the frequent disclaimers made by teachers (and the frequent reminders we receive from authorities) that we are not therapists, and suggested that this tendency relies in part upon a desire to position medical discourse as the ultimate authority on disability in the classroom. I now return to this point in the context of discourses surrounding school shootings, arguing that another ideology shoring up the teacher/therapist divide is the desire to expel madness—and its presumed manifestation in violent acts—from the classroom.

The forces that seek to separate the affective, emotional, and generally "psychological" aspects of mind from the presumably safer rationalist aspects in the classroom are old and deep. The fact that college teachers are likely to engage on a regular basis with students who are crying, shouting in anger, or disclosing traumatic experiences is generally met with one directive: Send them to the campus counseling center. Make a referral, make a call, perhaps walk the student over there yourself—in whatever form, remove the excessive affect from the sphere of your teaching. Most interesting to me is not the fact that this divide exists, but its rhetorical forcefulness. If I had ever had any impression that my students' emotional lives might be within my purview as a writing teacher, I would have been disabused about ten minutes into my first TA training session.

Even before the shootings at Virginia Tech and NIU, university instructors, especially writing teachers, took up the question of emotion in their teaching practice within an "atmosphere of apprehension" (Richmond 73). For example, in 1993, when Wendy Bishop called for greater attention to the politics of emotion in writing instruction, saying, "The analogies between writing instruction and therapy have something to offer me and something I need to offer to the teachers I train," she also included the standard disclaimer: "I don't feel like rushing out and practicing without a license." Around the same time, in *College English* Carole Deletiner published an article titled "Crossing Lines" that detailed emotional topics her students wrote about, and her own emotional responses in return. Michelle Payne describes the "backlash" (3) that Deletiner met in subsequent comments published in the journal:

> [Respondent Kathleen Pfeiffer] figures "emotional" writing as threatening to the purpose of the university, as a "radical deconstruction of community and communication" (671); it seems, in fact, to be so unrelated to the real work of the university as to be laughable, worthy of caricature. Such writing is only valid (and yet still not valid at all) within the context of popular culture, in twelve-step programs, popular psychological understandings of the inner child, victimization, and dysfunction. . . . Teachers are obliged to keep threatening emotions at bay, to reinforce cultural dictates about how emotion can be expressed and understood. If they don't, the very foundation of university education will come undone. (2–3)

Although Payne does not refer to the long rhetorical history equating knowledge with rationality, she accurately describes the climate of academic discourses before 2007. For the most part, emotion was considered inimical to learning. Emotional writing by students or professors was assumed to belong, as Payne puts it, to the "weepy world of confessions" (1)—not to the clear, rationalist world in which knowledge was acquired and critical minds labored.[13]

But the writings of Cho and Kazmierczak changed this. Cho's violent plays, and Kazmierczak's work on mental illness, were not confined to Facebook pages or emails; they had been written for classes, turned in, read, discussed, graded—even, in Kazmierczak's case, published. The moat had been breached. This has brought forth a torrent of speculation about the relationship between teaching, therapy, writing, free speech, and violence. Although much of this speculation, predictably, seeks to repair the imagined damage to the moat protecting academe from violent mental illness, some writers take a more nuanced and complex approach.

Most of what has appeared so far relates to Cho's writing. This may be because it contained more overtly violent themes, because (as of this writing) the NIU incident is more recent, or because Kazmierczak destroyed much of what he had written by discarding his computer's hard drive and his cell phone's memory card. However, some news outlets have gone to great trouble to dig up Kazmierczak's written work. For example, the *Chicago Tribune* obtained his graduate-school application essays by means of the Freedom of Information Act, published excerpts from them, and claimed that they offered "unprecedented and chilling insight into [his] mental-health troubles" (Cohen and St. Clair). It is also notable that some representations of Kazmierczak tend to assign a therapeutic role to his academic work. In a *Huffington Post* article, Jonathan Fast wrote: "He would discover why he cut himself by writing a paper about self-injurious behaviors. He would cure his psychiatric problems by attending social work school." Although unsupported, these statements imply that Kazmierczak deliberately sought to "discover" and "cure" himself through writing (though, the narrative implies, in vain).

Benjamin Reiss argues that, following the Virginia Tech shooting, the classroom may become "a barely acknowledged zone of quasi-psychiatric surveillance" (27). This is evident from the May 2007 issue of the *Chronicle of Higher Education,* which featured a compendium of opinions by "writers and creative-writing professors" regarding Cho's writing. These opinions separate academic discourse from madness through various means, the most direct of which is simply maligning persons with mental disabilities. For example, Kerryn Goldsworthy says that creative writing classes "bring nutters out of the woodwork." She then amplifies this derogatory remark:

> There has been at least one person in every writing class I have ever taught who was either in need of, or already getting, professional help. Those are inevitably the students who are most resistant, recalcitrant, and disruptive. (60)

A host of questions arises upon reading this: first, how does Goldsworthy determine which of her students are "in need of" professional help? Also, what basis does she have for arguing that students who are receiving care for mental disabilities are the "most resistant, recalcitrant, and disruptive"? No explanation is given. Another professor, William O'Rourke of the University of Notre Dame, says that Cho was a "monster" (60). This point is debatable, depending upon one's definition of *monster,* but O'Rourke's own definition of the term appears straightforward: "[I]t wasn't so much Cho's writing that has been exposed that showed that, but his lack of contact, his absence of speech, his signing his name as a question mark, his aloneness" (60). According to this definition, then, what makes Cho a "monster" is not his violent actions or writings, but his failure to comply with approved social norms.

A second means of establishing a divide between academic discourse and madness used in the *Chronicle* compendium is to assert that persons with mental disabilities are bad writers. Goldsworthy claims, for example, that "disturbed work is inevitably bad writing." Novelist Stephen King expands on this view:

> For most creative people, the imagination serves as an excretory channel for violence: we visualize what we will never actually do. . . . Cho doesn't strike me as in the least creative, however. Dude was crazy. Dude was, in the memorable phrasing of Nikki Giovanni, just "mean." . . . On the whole, I don't think you can pick these guys out based on their work, unless you look for violence unenlivened by any real talent. (60)

Like Goldsworthy, King evidently feels entitled to use derogatory terms to describe mental disability. His main point is that being "crazy" is incommensurate with having writing talent. What would lead a reasonably knowledgeable person to make such a remark? I can't guess, but I take the comment, whatever its motivation, as another bit of evidence indicating how deeply held is the widespread desire to dig a moat between madness and academic discourse.[14]

The desire to shore up the moat can be observed in another collection of writings, this one from *Academe,* the bulletin of the American Association of University Professors (AAUP), which in November 2007 published a collection of articles related to campus shootings. In "Creative Writing Class as Crucible," Monica Barron rehearses the familiar narrative that creative writing professors frequently receive violent writings from students. One semester, she says, she received so much violent writing "that I started a file and told a friend, if I end up dead, go to my office and get the file marked 'suspects.'" Her article details her interchanges with one student in particular, then shifts to a description of Cho:

> One April morning in Blacksburg, Virginia, a young man packed up his guns and went to school for the last time. He was done struggling to be part of any community of readers or writers. He was entering the community of killers.

This theme of *community* continues throughout the article, which says in closing:

> What I want is for my writing students to see my responses as those of a reader and lover of literature and as those of teacher, editor, and facilitator. Most of all, [I] want my students to think constructively, as Seung Hui Cho could not, of themselves as members of communities and as producers of work that evokes emotion in others, for better or for worse.

"Community" is a commonly used metaphor for writing classes, and often for academe in general. With finality, Barron excludes Cho from those communities: when he became part of the "community of killers," he was "done struggling to be part of any community of readers or writers." (Recall that the "community" metaphor was also invoked by Pfeiffer in her pronouncement that "emotional writing" in the classroom is "a radical deconstruction of community" [qtd. in Payne 2].) Although I appreciate Barron's careful consideration of the ways that emotion can and should be part of the rhetorical situation of the classroom, I am discouraged by the way it establishes a divided space, within which are readers and writers, and outside of which are killers. The lines just aren't that simple, and we do ourselves and our students a disservice when we pretend that they are.

Another of the *Academe* articles is straightforwardly diagnostic: written by a psychiatric nurse, Ellen Gecker, it is titled "How Do I Know If My Student Is Dangerous? A Psychiatric Nurse Explains When to Refer a Student for Help." To be fair, this piece is actually less sensationalistic than its title would suggest. Gecker emphasizes several times that "only in extremely rare cases does mental illness lead to violence—and, of course, violence is not always a product of mental illness." However, by its very presence it reinforces the presumption that teaching and mental disability are separate domains: a psychiatric nurse has been called in to the pages of *Academe* to explain madness to its readership of university professors. The article's overall tone is diagnostic, offering a bulleted list of "cues" that will help readers pick out mental illness in their students. These include "a flat affect," "unusual emotional reactions," "difficulty conversing," and "social isolation." And the final recommendation is, once again, referral (out, away). While Gecker is careful to say that "most of the time you are not in any danger, even if there are mentally ill students in your classroom," it is unlikely that this article, however well meant, will provide its readers with anything more than a checklist of reasons to further stigmatize mentally disabled students, or for that matter, any student who fails to meet social norms.

Alternative perspectives do arise, however, both in the *Chronicle* compendium and in the special issue of *Academe*. In "What's Writing Got to Do with Campus Terrorism?," for example, Chris M. Anson constructs a debate between two rhetors, named "Nothing" and "Everything," who lay out two vastly differing points of view on the question in the article's title. "Everything" seems to stand for the popular view that mental disability is threatening and can be diagnosed through writing:

> EVERYTHING: Writing gives us a powerful tool to identify . . . well, malfeasants and lunatics. You know, members of the fringe. You see, writing is like a camera in the room of the miscreant's mind.

NOTHING: I'm not sure I follow, exactly.

EVERYTHING: Members of these groups have a need to disclose, to share their twisted thoughts as if to persuade us of their rationality. But in doing so, they give us clues. The anonymous evildoer lays down a crumb trail to his whereabouts. . . .

NOTHING: Come on, Ev. You know better than that. Writers can dissemble. Who's to say that the product of a writer's mind offers anything but the most cracked mirror of real thoughts and beliefs?

By echoing the hyperbolic language of popular media ("lunatics," "twisted")—not to mention the U.S. government ("evildoer")—and questioning it, Anson both acknowledges and critiques the desire to merge madness with evil, and to draw a sharp line between mad or evil people and "normal" people. Although my own sympathies lie more with the "Nothing" character, by presenting two such polarized views, Anson offers the reader the opportunity to arrive at a conclusion (or non-conclusion) that differs from both. His article also raises one of the most vexing questions raised by Cho's writing, and one that, in the rush to diagnose, has received less attention than it should: free speech. "Everything" supports the notion of tracking and surveillance, while "Nothing" argues just as stridently for complete freedom of expression:

EVERYTHING: But if we look, we see. If we seek, we find. We're talking about terrorism. Dead students. Anguished communities. Families torn asunder. Tragedy of the worst kind. And preventable. . . .

NOTHING: Freedom means freedom to write. Anything.

Anson defers an answer to this debate. I'm not sure I have one either. I've been teaching zwriting for fifteen years now, and the problem comes up again and again: what do you do when a student submits writing that appears simply to be hate speech? Or contains threats of violence? Or imagines violence against herself? I can't pretend that I handle such issues deftly, nor do I wish to imply that I eschew the support of campus counseling services. I've walked students over there myself, and expect to do so again; and sometimes, although not often, it was something in a student's writing that began the conversation. (I've never based a referral solely on something a student wrote, although I imagine there's always a first time.) What Anson provides, through the structure of his Nothing/Everything debate, is the invitation to keep these questions open, keep the conversation alive. The final remark in his article, from "Everything," is "I don't think that's the last word." The only thing I feel sure of is this: attempting to diagnose, imprison, and vilify my students in order to expel them from the "community" of my classroom is not the answer.

Richard E. Miller, another *Academe* contributor, has been considering the problem of violent student writing for over a decade.[15] His deep perspective on this topic contributes to the complex reading he offers in his *Academe* essay, "The Fear Factor." Miller refuses to individualize Cho's madness, and in fact, calls attention to the problematics of doing so: his article begins with the familiar case-study-style narrative, but quickly stops short, asking, "Are these the details that should concern us most at this time?" Miller then turns to an examination of the politics of fear as they have circulated in the United States since the events of September 11, 2001,[16] and even acknowledges, "Seung-Hui Cho was afraid, too." He also suggests a concrete teaching practice, "reading in slow motion," which he argues offers students the time and space they need to engage in deep and empathetic reflection:

> Our job [as teachers] is to establish an environment that promotes reflection and to provide our students with multiple opportunities to experience mental acts that take them to the edge of the unknown. . . . If we are to offer an alternative to the violent options that are now always just a click away, then we've got to foster an equally powerful counter-experience—one that cultivates optimism and resourcefulness and resilience. Confronting the limits of one's understanding is a scary business, but this is the task that lies forever before all who are committed to the life of the mind.

Not incidentally, Miller's suggested strategy, "reading in slow motion," is also an access strategy for some persons with mental disabilities. It offers a way to read in crip time, accessing a text repeatedly, making connections in more dimensions than are offered by the conventional academic pace of absorb-respond-move-on. In the article overall, Miller neither condones violence nor dehumanizes Cho. Instead, he manages to *con-*

sider—rather than scramble to protect—the blurry spaces between academic discourse, mental disability, and violence.

Perhaps the most moving statement about Cho's experiences in and with academic discourse is the one from Edward Falco, a Virginia Tech professor, who taught Cho in a playwriting class. Shortly after the shootings, Falco sent the following message to the other students in the class:

> There was violence in Cho's writing—but there is a huge difference between writing about violence and behaving violently. We could not have known what he would do. We treated him like a fellow student, which is what he was. I believe the English department behaved responsibly in response to him. And please hear me when I say this: It was our responsibility, not yours. All you could have done was come to me, or some other administration or faculty member, with your concerns—and you would have been told that we were aware of Seung-Hui Cho, we were concerned about him, and we were doing what we believed was appropriate. Look, all our hearts are broken. There's no need to add to the pain with guilt. (60)

I find this message extraordinarily hopeful, for several reasons. First, it refers to all persons respectfully and without resorting to derogatory remarks. Second, it does not attempt to pretend that the mystery of Cho's violent actions has an easy answer. Third, it names Falco's own emotion and indicates to his students that emotion is an appropriate response—"all our hearts are broken."

We will not find answers to the terrible events of April 16, 2007, and February 14, 2008, by searching inside the heads, or through the pages, of Cho and Kazmierczak. We might as well dissect a human body in an effort to find its soul. In the fear and sorrow following the shootings, representations of these two men have both played upon and reinforced a series of commonsense assumptions. By constructing intricate case studies of the shooters and examining their deviance, we convince ourselves that each shooter was, indeed, not a "normal" person subject to unbearable social circumstances, but in fact a "time bomb waiting to go off" ("Framing"). We imagine that their disabilities caused the violence, and extrapolate from this step to imagine that all persons with mental disabilities are potential threats. This results in a culture of hatred and fear in which persons with mental disabilities are stripped of their rights and further stigmatized, and the very real violence—both personal and institutional—that they face is ignored. Larger social forces contributing to a culture of violence are brushed off. It is easier to focus on individuals, because when we presume that the problem lies within individuals, we can continue to believe that the problem will go away if the individuals are cured. Or incarcerated, or expelled, or eradicated.

If there is any hope to be found in the terrible mystery of sudden violent attacks, it will not come from attempts to vilify or diagnose students or faculty with mental disabilities, or to take away their civil rights. Nor will it come from videos, software, or federal grants that encourage students, faculty, and staff to develop their "survival mindset." Creating an academic environment marked by fear and hatred of madness will do nothing to end violence. The hope I find is in voices like Falco's, which offers simply the truths he knows: The shooter was a fellow student. We were concerned about him. All our hearts are broken.

CHAPTER 5

"Her Pronouns Wax and Wane"

Mental Disability, Autobiography, and Counter-Diagnosis

> If it is a crazy story surely it will do no harm, and if it is not, why had it not ought to come out.
>
> —*Elizabeth T. Stone,* "A Sketch of My Life"

In September 2008 I visited a Barnes & Noble bookstore in Atlanta and was confronted by a large table display bearing a sign that read "Memoirs of Affliction." I was partly amused and partly disgusted—and not at all surprised. Disability memoirs have proliferated in recent decades. By no means does this indicate a surge of public interest in disability studies, that is, a decreased appetite for stories of "tragedy" and "overcoming"; as G. Thomas Couser has documented in numerous books and articles, the politics of life writing by people with disabilities is filled with complications. But the increased interest in disability life writing, Couser argues, does attest to a shared sense of fascination with the experience of non-"normal" embodiment and how that embodiment is represented (*Signifying Bodies*). And although there are many problems to consider when "disability" intersects with "autobiography," Couser demonstrates that there are also many opportunities to recognize the transgressive power of such life writing, for we can find many "narratives from hidden corners" ("Conflicting" 89) that rebel against familiar scripts of disability as an individualized, medicalized phenomenon and instead engage in acts of resistance against oppressive discourses. This chapter examines three such transgressive texts: *A Mind Apart: Travels in a Neurodiverse World,* by Susanne Antonetta; *Lying: A Metaphorical Memoir,* by Lauren Slater;

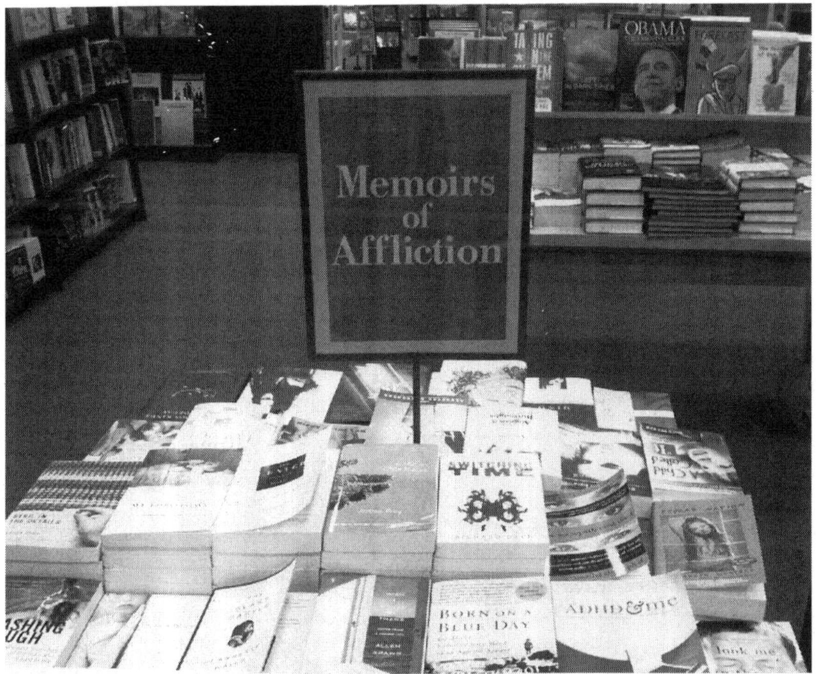

A table display of books in Barnes & Noble (Atlanta) with a large sign reading "Memoirs of Affliction." Photograph by author.

and "Her Reckoning: A Young Interdisciplinary Academic Dissects the Exact Nature of Her Disease," by Wendy Marie Thompson. Their authors occupy various relationships to academe: Antonetta (as Suzanne Paola) works periodically as a writer-in-residence or teacher at literary conferences; Slater is a clinical psychologist and writer; and Thompson is a postdoctoral fellow in history and Asian American Studies. More significantly for this study, their narratives exemplify what I have called micro-rebellions in academic discourse. They challenge both existing theories of autobiography and the genre itself through a strategy I call *counter-diagnosis*.

In this segment of my critical discourse analysis, I confine myself to a single rich linguistic feature: pronouns. I'm particularly interested in the operation of pronouns in disability discourses because they offer a significant window onto the ways that power dynamics around disability are maintained. The "us-them" binary, often invoked in DS literature, is a ready example. Beyond this, pronouns can take on extraordinary meanings when used by persons with mental disabilities. What we mean by *I* is not necessarily normative; neither is what we mean by *you, she,* or *we.* As Antonetta writes of her friend N'Lili, who has multiple personalities and identifies variously as *I, they,* and *we,* "Like the moon her pronouns wax and wane" (108).

Scholars of disability autobiography have pointed out various reasons that we might regard this genre with caution, not to say pessimism. One concern, as David Mitchell and Sharon Snyder note, is that such narratives often reify the dominant script of disability as an individual tragedy (and potential source of triumph when "overcome"), while also solidifying the normate reader's sense of his own "comparative good fortunes" (10). Another concern, explored in depth by Couser, is the history of exploitation of persons with disabilities by those who write about them, including medical professionals and so-called cowriters of works that may then be labeled autobiographies (*Recovering Bodies; Vulnerable Subjects*).

Building on the insights of Couser and others, disability autobiography is a growing field within DS. This work often draws upon feminist, queer, or post-colonialist theories of autobiography, which have been asking for quite some time whether various representations of the subaltern can speak. Such accounts take seriously the hegemonic history and effects of the genre, so much so that some propose the use of alternative or additional terms, including *auto/biography* (Stanley), *auto/body/ography* (Mintz), *autobiographical manifesto* (Smith), *autobiographics* (Gilmore), *autography* (Perreault), *autogynography* (Stanton), *autopathography* (Moran), *autrebiography* (Loftus), and *testimonio* (Beverley). However, while these resistant theories of autobiography have permeated DS research,[1] they rarely examine mental disabilities. One exception is Stephen T. Moran's "Autopathography and Depression," which studies autobiographies of depression. Unfortunately, Moran selects for attention only "unusually articulate" and quite canonical "sufferers"—Ernest Hemingway, F. Scott Fitzgerald, and William Styron (79). His analysis therefore does not offer much insight into the transgressive power of autopathography as it might operate when inhabited by "sufferers" who are *not* as (conventionally) "articulate." A response to this problem is offered in Prendergast's "The Unexceptional Schizophrenic," which argues for attention to writings by schizophrenic people who are *not* "exceptional," and whose stories are thus not easy to pin down theoretically. Following Prendergast, I believe that further study of autobiographical writings by people with mental disabilities will refigure key assumptions of autobiographical discourse, including rationality, coherence, truth, and independence. In the present study, I am arguing that Antonetta, Slater, and Thompson[2] claim authority not in spite of, but through and because of, their mental disabilities. This is the counter-diagnostic move.

In counter-diagnosis, the autobiographical narrator uses language (here, pronouns) to subvert the diagnostic urge to "explain" an irrational mind. Richard Ingram has suggested that because authorities such as psychiatrists may appropriate the stories of persons with mental disabilities, "perhaps it is better to arrest the progress of existing narratives by interrupting them with multiple complications, to render them confused, to deflect them from their righteous paths, to fragment them" (212–13). The counter-diagnostic story does not merely parallel or replace the conventional diagnostic story: it ruins it altogether, attacks its foundations, queers it.

As my use of *queer* suggests, the diagnostic story in many ways resembles the queer genre of the coming-out story. For example, conventional disability narratives and conventional LGBTQ coming-out stories often hinge on a moment of revelation through labeling: "At last I have the name that makes sense of my foregoing experience!" But the story is of course not so simple. As I have written elsewhere, "The phrase *coming out* implies that the event is sudden and recognizable—a flinging open of a door, a step over the threshold. But, in fact, coming out is more like moving through a hall of mirrors" ("Then You'll Be Straight" 98). Tobin Siebers adds to this point that "coming out" may be confounded by sociopolitical pressures: "Closeting involves things not merely concealed but difficult to disclose—the inability to disclose is, in fact, one of the constitutive markers of oppression" ("Masquerade" 2). The inability (or disability?) to disclose can take many forms. One example in the area of mental disability is the common response to the announcement "I have depression": "Oh yes, I sometimes get depressed too."

Anne Wilson and Peter Beresford describe psychiatry as a "diagnostic empire" (141) and call for a social theory of madness and distress that "*vigorously contest[s]* the role of the psychiatric system and, in particular, of medical/psychiatric records and discourses" (155). Such contestation can be found in the narratives I examine here. However, I should emphasize that Antonetta's, Slater's, and Thompson's narratives neither embrace diagnosis as truth nor reject it as useless: instead, they draw power from the shape-shifting nature of counter-diagnosis, accepting, rejecting, mimicking, and contesting the diagnostic urge in various ways. Counter-diagnosis is an oxymoronic form.

Incoherence and Coalition: The First Person

It would be difficult to overstate the degree to which scholars of autobiography have considered, wrestled with, and at times despaired of the *I*. This mysterious entity has sparked tremendous debate, including what Paul John Eakin calls a "face-off between experiential accounts of the 'I,' on the one hand, and deconstructive analyses of the 'I' as illusion on the other" (4). (Monique Wittig, in fact, discarded the pronoun *je* altogether, replacing it with *j/e*.) I am less interested in taking a side in these debates than in attempting to read various *I*'s on their own terms. As Eakin puts it, we will most usefully approach autobiographical narratives not by bringing a predetermined frame to the *I* but rather by "*asking what such texts can teach us about the ways in which individuals in a particular culture experience their sense of being 'I'*—and, in some instructive cases that prove the rule, their sense of not being an 'I' " (4). In each of the narratives studied here, *I* is positioned in ways that take advantage of its fragmentation, proliferation, and otherwise unruly existence.

The first counter-diagnostic strategy I call *creative incoherence*. While the conventional *I* of autobiography is unified, and tends to progress through a linear narrative, the *I*'s of these narratives are strategically disorganized and incoherent. *Incoherent* may be used colloquially to mean completely lacking in understandable meaning; however, I am using the term in a sense that draws upon its etymological roots, which translate loosely as "not sticking together." This understanding of incoherence is informed by Charlotte Linde, who describes coherence in life narratives as the outcome of a negotiation between reader and writer:

> [Coherence] is not an absolute property of a disembodied, unsituated text. The speaker works to construct a text whose coherence can be appreciated, and at the same time the addressee works to reach some understanding of it as a coherent text and to communicate that understanding. The coherent text that the addressee constructs may not, of course, be the same as the text that the speaker believes was constructed. As long as the gap is not too great, the discrepancy will probably not be noticed. But if it be-

> comes very large, further negotiation about the meaning of the text may be necessary. (12)

It is this "further negotiation" that is most relevant to analysis of the texts at hand. I argue that *A Mind Apart, Lying,* and "Her Reckoning" purposefully open a large gap between what Linde calls "speaker" and "addressee"; they invite (even demand) negotiation, often remarking directly on the space between the narrator's consciousness and the reader's. *Incoherence* as I am using it should therefore be thought of as a-coherence, or sometimes anti-coherence; it is turned to strategic advantage rather than accommodated as impairment.

In "Her Reckoning," Thompson announces at the outset, "Please keep in mind that I have always found it difficult to write in a consistent linear fashion. Rather, I tend to weave together not only concepts, but genres as well" (373). Her account includes both prose and poetry, and skips between voices, as in this passage:[3]

> There are studies documenting the survivors of genocide and de/colonization, relocation and internment . . .
>
> I have read other stories too, reports about survivors of war and the horror of killing fields. How after witnessing such madness and atrocity, they went completely blind and, once arriving on asylum or reunification to North America, had baffled doctors who had no way to medically justify what caused this loss of sight because the irises and retinas were all healthy. There was simply a refusal to see anymore.
>
> Conceivably a gesture towards maintaining sanity.
>
> *My skeleton reads DNA inferiority complexes*
>
> ❦ ❧
>
> I survive by what I see, by what I am, by who died before me and paved my road with their backs. Take living back when a racist white supremacist society prided itself for lynching my father's kind. Colored. (378)

This passage, like Thompson's full essay, is a palimpsest of genres, voices, and perspectives. Deliberately, it breaks various conventions of standardized English, including grammatical "complete sentences" as well as "correct" punctuation. The linguistic strategies of "Her Reckoning" serve to position a narrator who is "an outsider, a mixed-roots Afro-Chinese American sister" who refuses the coherence of stereotype that might be suggested by this positioning and instead offers a hearty "Fuck trivial measurements of authenticity held up to the phenotype of existence" (375). Not quite sensible, this poetic line is nevertheless unmistakable in meaning.

Antonetta similarly embraces incoherence as a creative meaning-making strategy. She announces near the beginning of her narrative that it will be "a bipolar book," and explicates this term in neuroatypical fashion:

> My husband, Bruce, reads this [introduction] and says, Tell them it's a bipolar book.
>
> Hey, out there. It's a bipolar book.
>
> Though I, too, have to ask him what that means. He says, alinear, associational: I always have many things happening in my mind at once. To be honest, I am some of the many voices in this book. (12–13)

Here, as with Thompson's narrative, we see the refusal to apologize for a disorganized *I*. We also see a hint of a strategy Antonetta uses often in her counter-diagnostic story—the proliferation of *I* into *we* (discussed in more detail below).

Slater's use of the incoherent *I* is perhaps the most radical: beginning with the title of her book, *Lying: A Metaphorical Memoir,* she constructs a narrative in which virtually every presumption of autobiography, including a truth-telling narrator, is up for grabs. *Lying* narrates the emergence of a factually inaccurate diagnosis (epilepsy) in order to convey the "narrative truth" of the unnamed disorder at the heart of the book (219). Having presented a memoir that describes her numerous epileptic seizures, as well as radical surgery (a corpus callosotomy, or severing of the two hemispheres of the brain) to correct those seizures, Slater suddenly announces in the book's afterword that epilepsy has been used as a metaphor:

> In *Lying* I have written a book in which in some cases I cannot and in other cases I will not say the facts. . . . *Lying* is a book of narrative truth, a book in which I am more interested in using invention to get to the heart of things than I am in documenting actual life

> occurrences. This means that the text I've created uses, in some instances, metaphors, most significantly the metaphor of epilepsy, to express subtleties and horrors and gaps in my past for which I have never been able to find the words. (219)

This is counter-diagnosis with a vengeance: a case study in which truth—or, to use the medicalized term, accuracy—is blithely left by the wayside. With a mentally disabled *I* telling the story, empirical truth is no longer a given feature of diagnosis.

Undeniably, in the choice to appropriate another disability to stand in metaphorically for her own, Slater is on risky ground. Her choice has been sharply critiqued by Couser, who argues that "in exercising prose license she commits herself to an essentializing and mystifying characterization of a still stigmatic disability . . . [and] promotes discredited assumptions about the condition [of epilepsy]" ("Disability as Metaphor," 142, 152). I agree with these points and would add that Slater risks playing into the accusations of "malingering" so often leveled at disabled persons—especially those of us who have no objective evidence to offer, but only reports of what is happening inside our minds.[4] However, I also want to suggest that perhaps in its very shamelessness lies its value. With this flamboyant gesture of untruth, the narrator of *Lying* refuses to become the exposed, confessing narrator of conventional disability autobiography—the narrator who, as Mitchell and Snyder caution, may serve merely to "[place] physical and cognitive limitation and difference on display to be consumed" (10). Instead, the narrator of *Lying* invents her own diagnosis to unnerve the normative gaze.

A second strategy of the *I* in counter-diagnosis is *proliferation*—the construction of many selves to tell a single "person's" story. Antonetta's assertion that she is "some of the many voices" (13) in *A Mind Apart* is one example. This counter-diagnostic strategy contributes new insight (or perhaps I mean new obfuscation) to a concept of great interest in DS autobiography: the difficult question of dependence/independence/interdependence. In *Vulnerable Subjects: Ethics and Life Writing,* Couser examines a number of autobiographical genres, including "auto/biography," which he defines as "memoirs of proximate others, such as close relatives or partners, which are collaborative in some sense or degree" (40). My analysis takes up Couser's point but enlarges the genre to suggest that the "proximate others" may be aspects of a split self. In clinical terms, "splitting" is an undesirable event; it is what happens when a troubled consciousness divides itself, retreating into a fugue state or other alternative (protective) state of consciousness. Therapy for persons who experience splitting is generally aimed at eliminating the phenomenon by helping the therapized person "integrate" her consciousness. However, in counter-diagnostic narratives, a proliferation of selves may be a desirable state.

In *A Mind Apart,* the state of having many selves, or being a "many-head" (2), is described as having its own unique advantages, and in fact generally preferable to being a "one-head" (109): "I like my mind the way it is" (89). Antonetta connects her own multiple selfhood to a more literal notion of community—in her case, a geographically scattered alliance of neuroatypicals connected largely via letters and the Internet. The book's subtitle, *Travels in a Neurodiverse World,* indicates its emphasis not on Antonetta's individual experience, but rather on the varied and collected experience of all the persons described and addressed therein, many-heads and one-heads alike. While musing on the state of being many, Antonetta calls upon her community of neuroatypicals to ask their perspectives. As it turns out, many of them feel similarly:

> I like my mind the way it is, like a striving city, or a small town at least, noisy and architectural. I want to believe there is value in this, and in my beautiful friends. . . . I check in with my online tribe to see how many of them would want to be bipolar again [if given a choice]. One man writes:
>
> > I choose not to look at bipolar as an illness at all. In fact, I couldn't imagine myself as not being bipolar, nor would I want to be . . . I do not wish to be anyone else but me. . . .
>
> "Look at how normals live and treat each other," says a man named Harry, wanting no part of that. (89–90)

Throughout, *A Mind Apart* forges a series of constantly shifting alliances—narrator and reader (discussed further in the section on second-person pronouns); human and (other) animal; present-day human and prehuman; and, of course, neuroatypical and those "who don't have a syndrome you could find in the DSM-IV" (2). This counter-diagnostic strategy, with its celebratory tone, could be read as somewhat naive (Morrice); however, it effectively opposes the conventional diagnostic impulse to isolate the mentally disabled subject. It also opposes the habit of conventional disability autobiographies to "offer the narrator as a disputatious figure critiquing the less than humane responses of a flat, often hostile, and uniformly able-ist culture" (Mitchell and Snyder 9). *A Mind Apart* (despite its title) consistently locates its narrator within richly varied contexts and communities.

Like Antonetta, Thompson uses *we* to form coalitions across time and space; however, unlike Antonetta, Thompson acknowledges the painful conflicts that occur within communities, and focuses specifically on the intersection of postcoloniality with mental disability. She notes that, despite early recognition of her many minoritized identities, she did not recognize her "mental affliction" (373) as a site for collective understanding until later in life. This lack of recognition, she points out, is not a personal failing, but was governed by cultural imperatives as to who may and may not claim mental illness. Thompson's proliferate selves are portrayed as having *been* split by a racist and classist culture:

> As I began configuring my racial self, my sexual self, my gendered self, I never realized mental illness was connected to experiences of trauma (cultural, racial, class, diasporic, environmental, social) because so often mental illness is constructed into a "white people" disease or a "rich people who have time for therapy" disease. (374)

Situating herself as a "young, queer, black-Chinese, working-class female" (373), Thompson explores the ways this experience has affected her ability to narrate her experiences of mental disability. Her present situation, she reports, is marked by a sense of "passing for normal, performing the gestures of a composed, competent, young, female academic of color" (379). This vision of *we* emphasizes the struggle of coalition, its pain and betrayals, as well as its opportunities, and recalls Couser's warning that representation of self/other "is always at once a mimetic and a political act" (33). Thus, *we* space should not be taken as an easy Three Bears ("just right!") kind of solution: it is a space of possibility, but of discomfort and uncertainty as well. From her position—markedly less privileged than Antonetta's or Slater's—Thompson calls attention to the pain and betrayals, as well as the promise, inherent in the finding coalition among the multiple *I*.

Mind Games: The Third Person

As Slater's, Thompson's, and Antonetta's subversive approaches to the coherent and singular *I* indicate, counter-diagnostic narratives wreak havoc upon what Philippe Lejeune has called "the autobiographical pact." In brief, the autobiographical pact is a tacit agreement between author and reader, sealed by authorial signature, promising that the author has made "a sincere effort to come to terms with and to understand his or her own life" (*Autobiography* ix, 11–12). Even in the case of pseudonymous autobiographies, the author's identity is "claimed at the level of enunciation"; that is, authorial presence is conferred by the existence of the text (13). While his most famous essay, "The Autobiographical Pact," says little about third-person pronouns, a few years later Lejeune returned to the question of what might happen to this pact if a self-referential author were represented not as *I,* but as *he* or *she.*[5] Examining works that practice this strategy, including *Roland Barthes* by Roland Barthes and *The Autobiography of Alice B. Toklas* by Gertrude Stein, Lejeune suggests that they "illustrate that the coherence attributed to genres is exaggerated" ("Third Person" 46). (He also, with unintentional irony, refers to such narratives as "borderline cases" [27, 46] within autobiography.) However, despite his acknowledgment that the autobiographical *I* may be destabilized when it shifts to the third person, Lejeune seems determined to hang onto its rational ability to direct the narrative from a consistent, *I*-like position. For example, he says that, when using the self-referential third person, "an author *pretends* to speak about himself as someone else might" or "invent[s] a fictive narrator" (27). He repeatedly underscores the point that such figuration is a "game" (42) and argues that "If the game were no longer a game, the 'I' would cease to be consistent, the necessary conditions for communication and writing would vanish" (40). In short, for Lejeune, a crucial feature of the autobiographical pact is a rationalist sense of agency shared by author, narrator, and reader; without such a shared rationalism, "communication . . . would vanish."

While Lejeune reads first- and third-person alternation as a Lacanian expression of "the impossibility of expressing identity" ("Third Person" 39), I argue that, in autobiographies of mental disability, such alternations may in fact be direct expressions *of* identity. In other words, when the so-called rational world does not truthfully reflect one's experience, autobiography may be used not just to "play" with the autobiographical pact, but to rewrite its terms altogether. The use of third-person pronouns in these narratives refuses coherence, truth, and resolution, but instead of causing communication to "vanish," these counter-diagnostic refusals construct a different kind of meaning.

Thompson first identifies her disability as it was defined to her: a mysterious entity represented by the third-person pronoun *it.* This underscores the omission of a-rational minds in Lejeune's accounting; even in the most "exceptional" ("Third Person" 39) autobiographies, he does not seem to have found an instance that uses *it* to describe a self. In a paragraph that sketches her childhood and adolescence, Thompson uses the rhetorical strategy of anaphora (repetition) in a way that grammatically fixes *it* in place (at the beginning of each sentence) while simultaneously demonstrating the pervasive power *it* has had over her life:

> [M]y parents figured that I would eventually "grow out of *it.*"
>
> *It* was my anti-social, very emotionally secluded childhood. *It* was my silent way of internalizing trauma and abuse. *It* was the way I tried to take my life at fourteen, then at fifteen after reading about self-injury in a teen fiction library book, the way I repeated it on my body for years after. *It* almost got me arrested and put into juvenile hall at sixteen after fighting my father because I wanted to run away. *It* was supposed to go away with the prescribed Zoloft that I never took, but instead sold to my then physically and sexually abusive homeless boyfriend's childhood gang friend. (373–74)

In this passage, Thompson uses the pronoun *it* to set up two themes the essay continues to explore: first, a rejection of the rationalist and chemically driven diagnoses of the medical profession; and second, a genre-jumping style that moves abruptly between prose and poetry. A later passage, presented as a journal entry from her undergraduate experience, notes, "I already know everything that's wrong with me; I just lack the sophisticated psychiatric language to define myself and my condition to everybody else" (374). "Her Reckoning" seizes the pronoun *it* as a move toward an alternative rationality, one that both describes and obfuscates, and refuses to be pinned down in "sophisticated psychiatric language." *It* is part of Thompson—even, in extreme terms, *is* her—but is also not of her.

Thompson also uses the strategy explicitly named by Lejeune, that is, self-reference as *she.* After moving more or less chronologically from adolescence to undergraduate to graduate school, "Her Reckoning" is suddenly interrupted by a two-page poem titled "Cuts," which shifts between time frames and is connected to the prose narrative only by juxtaposition and theme. "Cuts" offers another examination of a health-care professional, and again this third-person figure represents the distanced force of "psychiatric language" that is incommensurate with the narrator's own reality. This figure, called both "a nurse who moonlights / as a school counselor because of / budget constraints" and also "the lady," asks a series of diagnostic questions: "Are you having problems adjusting? / Family problems? When did this all / start? Are you at risk of suicidal / behavior?" Note the similarity between Thompson's approaches to *it* and the demonstrative pronoun *this,* both of which mark an insidiously vague territory. Thompson places emphasis upon *this* by enjambing the subject *this all* and its verb *start,* thus holding it up for scrutiny. She then rewrites *this all* as a more complex and less coherent space, a counter-diagnostic narrative whose subject, *she,* may or may not be narrator of the essay's prose sections:

> The girl shakes her
> head, unable to explain the book,
> the razor, the experiment to link
> the book with the razor. What did
>
> those girls do? She knew it was
> fiction. It was in the library's Young
> Adult Fiction series. (376)

Faced with the annihilating impulse of *it* and *this,* through poetry the narrator of "Her Reckoning" is conducting a diagnosis of her own. This counter-diagnosis makes no promises: we are not told that *she* is the *I* of the prose narrative, but offered only juxtaposition as well as thematic connections (including cutting) between the two. In a move that recalls Slater's pleasure in lying, the poem "Cuts" also implies that perhaps the girl's actions are unreal: "She knew it was/fiction." The authority of such gestures rewrites the autobiographical pact, and in doing so, upends the diagnostic urge for empirical observations that can be labeled as symptoms.

Antonetta, like Thompson, shapes her counter-diagnostic story in part by self-reference in the third person. Antonetta refers to the various parts of her mind playfully, as in this passage that describes her reaction to an infestation of mice in her home:

> I become more and more terrified of the sound [of the mice], and in what's no doubt some weird displacement, I develop a phobia

> that we're all going to get hantavirus—a fatal disease carried by mice, but deer mice, not house mice like our cartoonish creatures. Phobias live their own lives, however, and mine becomes overwhelming . . . [My husband] Bruce keeps trying to reason with me, which makes things worse; personally, I don't mind, but my phobia gets furious about it. (40–41)

In this counter-diagnostic story, Antonetta does not detach from the phobic *I* to demean her, or to discount her fears; indeed, the phobic self is clearly established as having her own life. Antonetta treats this other self with gentle humor: while *I* can understand Bruce's reasonable objections, the phobic self "gets furious." In addition to this phobic form of herself, *A Mind Apart* introduces "Manic Girl," whom the nonmanic *I* "find quite extraordinary, as she does me" (126). And—not mentioned within the narrative of *A Mind Apart,* but subtly present—is a second name, the name under which the book was copyrighted, similar to but different from Susanne Antonetta, the announced author and narrator.[6]

Slater's approach to counter-diagnosis in the third person is the most literal: she invents her own case history. Chapter 4 ends with a third-person epistolary description of the surgery that split the narrator's brain, concluding, "Love, Lauren." The page turns, and chapter 5 opens this way:

> THE BIOPSYCHOSOCIAL CONSEQUENCES OF A CORPUS CALLOSTOMY [SIC] IN THE PEDIATRIC PATIENT
> Dr. Carlos Neu, M.D., and
> Patricia Robinson, P.T.
> ABSTRACT
> Sixty percent of patients with temporal lobe epilepsy display dysfunctional psychological profiles that include emotional lability. (98)

The reader has already met Dr. Neu in *Lying:* he is described in an earlier chapter as "a little frumpy and old-fashioned, with thick eyebrows and a curly beard" (74). But here he is again, this time assuming the role of author, his "signature" on this imagined case study written by Slater. This is a transgression of the autobiographical pact apparently not imagined by Lejeune: various sections of a book "authored" by real-yet-imagined persons. In the case study, Slater is "Case study LJS, a pediatric TLE patient" who can "contribute to the ongoing body of knowledge and evolving question sets in the study of epilepsy" (100). The article describes the surgical procedure and details the process of "patient LJS's" recovery.

I am tempted to read this case study as a kind of kernel of truth in *Lying,* based in part on Slater's other works that reference her mental disabilities;[7] for instance, the "article" goes into some detail about the patient's "disturbing depressive tendencies" and speculates that she may have a "mood and/or anxiety disorder" (105). However, this impulse in itself is the diagnostic urge, the desire to figure out what is *really* wrong with Lauren. And that is precisely the counter-diagnostic strategy of *Lying:* it dangles an illusory promise of truth before its reader, and calls our attention once again to the appetite for diagnosis.

Unveiling the Jury: The Second Person

Addressing the reader directly as "you" or as "reader" became popular in Victorian novels, particularly realist novels by women; an example is *Jane Eyre*'s famous pronouncement, "Reader, I married him." In *Gendered Interventions,* Robyn Warhol argues that this strategy was an attempt on the parts of female novelists to claim authority in a literary field dominated by men. Warhol's argument can be applied to disability autobiography to illuminate the power shift achieved through direct address. While conventional disability autobiography, as Mitchell and Snyder suggest, tends to assume a normate reader who is free to gape at the freakish narrator, the autobiographies studied here employ *you* in a way that disrupts that dynamic and relocates the dominant gaze. The strategy goes beyond simple reversal, producing a variety of counter-diagnostic effects.

Antonetta's *A Mind Apart* confronts the reader early in the narrative: "And you, reader, the mirror, as Baudelaire wrote, the veiled jury. I must account for you" (13). It then leads this *you* through a series of meditations that deconstruct the usual assumptions about readers and narrators in disability autobiography. For example, Antonetta does away with the presumption that the reader is a priori sane:

> You have sat in a chair, reading, alive in the present of your body and the earth and the gasses you breathe: and also in the book of your head. . . . In fact, you are more likely than anything to be like me: anxious—which 25 percent of people have been, clinically,

> needing treatment—and depressed, which 10 percent of the U.S. is in any given year, or plagued by other irritations born of those neuronal connections that helped scalp the planet millennia ago. (122)

This passage uses *you* to develop the theme of neurodiversity explored throughout *A Mind Apart:* rather than sane/insane, or any other reductive binary, Antonetta prefers to view humanity as a "garden" of neuroatypicals, all of us odd in our own ways (217); at one point, she muses, "I wonder about your mind" (117). Throughout, *A Mind Apart* consciously resists the stare-at-the-freak convention of disability autobiography, and even offers specific commentary on why it does not include graphic descriptions of the narrator's "crazy" behavior: "I don't want, in writing, to put myself into that zoo. I want to say: This is another way to be human" (95). Antonetta also develops a metaphor of predator and prey, calling herself, as narrator, the "top predator" (152) in the relationship, and openly announcing, "I tease you, reader, by telling you what I'm doing" (152).

Antonetta's boldest use of *you* echoes the strategy used by Slater in *Lying:* breaking the autobiographical pact by not telling the reader the truth (or rather, *telling* the reader she is not telling the truth). Antonetta's lie takes this form: In the final chapter of *A Mind Apart,* she details her meeting with an orangutan named Chantek. Chantek lives "in a habitat on the grounds of Grant Park Zoo in Atlanta" (218) and has been raised signing. In an extended description of her encounter with Chantek, Antonetta says she was dismayed by his general uncommunicativeness with her. "Flummoxed," she reports, "I sit on a rock and sing" (225), then transcribes the lyrics to the spiritual "I'll Fly Away." But a few pages later, the narrative performs an abrupt turnabout:

> I did not sing to Chantek, except in my mind, looking at his bars, which my imaginings of our encounter had never contained. It shocked me, the ape in a cage (Lear said, *Unaccommodated man is no more but such a poor, bare, forked animal*). Unlike my son, I don't have the chutzpah to sit in front of strangers belting out my melody-induced belief that I'll fly away. Why do I lie to you? When the truth's persuasive enough, I think, and occupies this space almost wholly. . . . Perhaps to even out our relationship: I behind these lines, carrying out my fantastic gestures, you free. (229)

As this passage indicates, lying to one's reader can be a way to balance power, or as Antonetta puts it, "to even out our relationship." While conventional autobiography assumes an autonomous *I* who guides the narrative and a docile *you* who must follow, Antonetta understands that this dynamic in disability autobiography is not so simple: *you* may be the one outside the bars, and the *I* inside may need to take measures to transform the narrative cage.

Thompson's moves to seize and define *you* are more subtle than Antonetta's, but work toward a similar end. With the injunction to "keep in mind that I have always found it difficult to write in a consistent linear fashion," she maps the reader (implicitly) as *you,* the object of direct address (373). Like Antonetta's, Thompson's use of direct address seems aimed at balancing an uneven power relationship with the reader—in this case, by setting explicit rules. Unlike Antonetta, however, Thompson employs a *you* that migrates from person to person; and, as with the abrupt shift to the poem "Cuts," uses juxtaposition to deny consistent connections between pronouns and antecedents. After creating the reader as *you,* Thompson then moves to a more ambiguous use of the pronoun:

> I met a boyfriend who physically and sexually abused me worse than any father-like figure would have. Our interactions consisted of various assaults in public, forced intercourse, his threats of shooting me and killing himself if I ever left.
>
> I tried to run him over with my car.
>
> *Goddamn it you punch too many holes in walls, too many holes and I have not enough skin to patch them up with.* (375)

An initial reading of this passage seems to indicate, through juxtaposition, that *you* is the abusive boyfriend. It would seem evident that the person who "physically and sexually abused me . . . in public" would be the one who is punching holes in walls. However, this reading is undermined by the larger context of Thompson's essay, in which pronouns do not necessarily denote individuals, but also refer to larger cultural and political forces. "Her Reckoning" repeatedly connects individual experiences of mental disability to cultural experiences of trauma: "genocide and de/colonization, relocation and internment, natural disasters that show that even if the experience is erased from the history books and glossed over by the rest of the world, someone's child somewhere is born with that grief and will live it like an open wound, feel it deep in her bones, deep in his mind" (378). Given this, it is plausible that the *you* who punches holes in walls may not be the boyfriend but instead, or also, (a) violent dominant culture(s).

"Her Reckoning" includes yet another use of *you:* it serves as a means of communicating with other characters in the narrative. Near the essay's close, the narrator speaks directly to her father and grandfather, both dead, and both addressed as *you:* "To the father I want to say, you pushed the suggested depression roughly aside when I confronted you . . . And to the grandfather I want to say, I was never afraid of you" (378–79). Both Thompson and Antonetta demonstrate that using *you* is way to adjust the conventional power dynamics of autobiography, not through simple reversal, but rather, by playing with various possibilities for whom *you* might be.

Slater's use of *you* is both more mannered—two of the chapters in *Lying* are framed as letters—and more incoherent than in *A Mind Apart* or "Her Reckoning." At times *you* is the indefinite pronoun ("Sometimes you can crack open a cliché and find a lot of truth" [53]); other times, as in Thompson's narrative, *you* is used to address other persons in the book ("I applaud you, Mom, or at least the left side of me does" [93]). Here, I focus on the two chapters framed as letters. Chapter 4, titled "Sincerely, Yours," begins "Dear Reader" and details Slater's early adolescence. The narrative of this chapter proceeds with few uses of *you* until, as Slater announces, "we get to a little hoary truth in this tricky tale" (88). At that point, she informs the reader that along with epilepsy, she also developed Munchausen's, a psychiatric syndrome that the DSM-IV describes as "the intentional production of physical or psychological signs or symptoms" (American Psychiatric Association 513). Slater then abruptly directs *you* to "some quotes" from psychiatric journals "so you will understand Munchausen's Syndrome better" (88). The quotations are extensive, and immediately afterward, the narrator remarks, "Well, that should prove my point. You can fake epilepsy" (91). The letter continues, detailing the events leading up to the surgery in which the narrator's corpus callosum is severed, and concludes, "Love, Lauren" (97).

Importantly, before chapter 4, *Lying* does not indicate that the narrator's epilepsy is metaphorical or untrue. Although the entire book is filled with warning signs that this is no conventional autobiography—including, of course, its title—these details accrue slowly in the early parts of the book, and "Sincerely, Yours" is the first point at which *Lying* signals its extreme disruption of the autobiographical contract. *You* is, we might say, the instrument Slater uses to cut up the contract: speaking with apparent straightforwardness ("Dear Reader"; "so that you will understand"), this chapter of direct address is in fact the most transgressive of the narrative thus far.

The second letter, chapter 7, titled "How to Market This Book," carries the transgression still further. "How to Market This Book" shifts the role of *you:* instead of being "Reader," *you* is now "The Random House Marketing Department and my editor, Kate Medina" (159). And while the *you* of chapter 4 was positioned as a relatively passive witness to a story, this *you* is asked to adjudicate a persuasive case: whether *Lying* will be labeled fiction or nonfiction. Beginning fairly straightforwardly ("For marketing purposes, we have to decide. We have to call it fiction or we have to call it fact, because there's no bookstore term for something in between" [159]), it then evolves into a kind of list poem, in which the Random House / Kate *you* mingles with the general readerly *you:*

> 9. Nevertheless, confusions and all, Kate, I think I am a nonfiction writer, and I would like to be known as such. . . . Come with me, Kate. Come with me, reader. I am toying with you, yes, but for a real reason. I am asking you to enter the confusion with me, to give up the ground with me, because sometimes that frightening floaty place is really the truest of all. . . .
> 10. Together we will journey. We are disoriented, and all we ever really want is a hand to hold.
> 11. I am so happy you are holding me in your hands. I am sitting far away from you, but when you turn the pages, I feel a flutter in me, and wings rise up. (163)

This passage is the climax of Slater's uses of *you* to shatter the complacency of the reader's gaze into the autobiographical text. To return to the figure of coming-out story as hall of mirrors, Slater confounds the normate reader's power to gaze at her by building a hall of mirrors around *you,* drawing *you* into the "frightening floaty place" with her.

Scholars of disability autobiography have shown that we have good reason to be cautious about this genre. In this ableist world, autobiographical narrative is often just one more tool used to grind us down. Yet narratives written as counter-diagnostic stories can also be used to disrupt conventional dynamics of power, to claim the advantages of disability, and to call for the "one-heads' (and other abled persons) to join us in coalitions. Autobiographies of mental disability have something important to add to the study of disability autobiography: they show unique talent for refiguring the rational, thus exposing the possibilities that may emerge when we dance on generic truths. Without question, we may be punished for such dances—medicated against our will, written against our will, ostracized, disbelieved, institutionalized, abused. However, if we use counter-diagnoses to "vigorously contest" (Wilson and Beresford 155) such measures, we will continue to move toward more robustly truthful ways of living and telling our stories.

CHAPTER 6

In/ter/dependent Scholarship

WITH LEAH (PHINNIA) MEREDITH, CAL MONTGOMERY, AND TYNAN POWER

I didn't pay much attention to independent scholarship until I arrived on its doorstep, so to speak, by way of mental disability. I can date my attentiveness to an email exchange with Cal Montgomery in 2007. In April of that year, I wrote to Cal—having read her work in *Ragged Edge Online*—to ask if we might meet at the upcoming SDS conference. Cal responded warmly to exchanging ideas by email, but said she would not be at the conference, since she had attended some years before and found it an "access nightmare." Although I probably should have realized earlier that SDS, even with its efforts to provide access for all members, remains an inaccessible space for many, Cal's note was nevertheless a revelation. Her chance remark led me to further research into the accessibility of conference spaces (Price, "Access Imagined"), and has helped me develop my theory of kairotic space—particularly the disturbing question of whether the kairotic spaces of academe are *by their very nature* poorly accessible to those with mental disabilities. It also led me to conduct further research into independent scholarship.

Institutions of higher education in the United States now employ *more* independent scholars than their counterparts—should we say "dependent scholars"? However, the foregoing claim depends upon how one defines *independent scholar,* and definitions vary widely. Some suggest that all persons employed as instructors in higher education who do not occupy tenure-track or tenured jobs should qualify. For example, Barbara Currier Bell, writing in a 2004 edition of the newsletter from the Center for Independent Study, argues that only one-quarter of new faculty hires hold "regular," that is, tenure-track jobs, and notes that the majority of "term" hires are women. Bell suggests that "the 'full-service' white male professor is already the faculty equivalent of the spotted owl" ("Independents" 1). Scholarship in composition and rhetoric often uses the term *contingent faculty,* noting that such faculty are "often neither part-time nor adjunct in the true sense of those words" (Schell and Stock 15). Further investigation reveals a huge array of definitions and related terms, including *contract scholar, scholar-for-hire, hobby scholar, gypsy scholar, scholar-at-large, liberated scholar, private scholar, freelance scholar,* and most piquant, *intellectual* (Bell, "An Independent Scholar" and "Independent Scholarship"; Schell; Wentz).

An important distinction to note is between those whose primary means of support is teaching and those whose primary means of support comes from elsewhere. Discussions that use *contingent faculty* tend to focus on those whose livelihood comes from teaching—for instance, term hires or, in some cases, graduate students working as TAs. However, discussions that use *independent scholar* tend to define these workers differently. In a 2004 survey of the National Coalition of Independent Scholars, David Sonenschein found that only 7 percent of respondents who were working identified their primary work as teaching (17). I make this distinction not to pull the two groups apart, since they do overlap considerably and have many common concerns, but to clarify my own purposes for this chapter. While many academics with disabilities do work as contingent laborers because of institutional barriers that prevent them from accessing conventional tenure-track jobs, my interest for the present study is disabled academics for whom even the path to part-time teaching work is barred. For example, some scholars with mental disabilities may not be permitted to enroll in postsecondary institutions in the first place; and at least one postsecondary degree, if not two, is the usual prerequisite for university teaching work. My point here is that, although the situation of contingent faculty is important, such faculty members have already found ways past a primary access barrier—the "moat" that guards postsecondary education in general.

Fueling my interest in independent scholarship is a rhetoric of "choice" that seems to enter discussions of academics who do not teach, or teach only rarely. In their often-cited 1993 study *The Invisible Faculty,* Judith Gappa and David Leslie propose and elaborate four categories: "career enders"; "specialists, experts, and professionals"; "aspiring academics"; and "freelancers" (49–63). While Gappa and Leslie pay careful attention to limiting factors, including "lack of geographical mobility"

(56) and "gender bias" (57), it is notable that their profiles of contingent faculty include frequent mention of choice. For example, one person who "exemplifies the freelancers" "*prefers* not to have any greater involvement in the institution because she values the free time she can devote to her other roles and activities" (61; emphasis added). I am worried less by the data included in the study by Gappa and Leslie, a valuable work, than by who is left out: how many contingent faculty or "aspiring academics" do *not* have so much choice in their access to academic discourse? What are the stories of their decisions—and are we comfortable calling their decisions "choices," given how circumscribed access to academe can be? How well have these persons been represented in studies so far? How often is disability a factor in the hard "choices" that must be made?

Research on contingent faculty, while still receiving less attention than it should, nevertheless has proliferated and gained increasing authority over the last several decades. "Working Contingent Faculty in(to) Higher Education," by Eileen Schell and Patricia Lambert Stock, provides an excellent overview. Schell and Stock document the movement of research about and by contingent faculty from its origins in the social sciences, which tended to provide aggregated data and composite profiles, through further waves of research that include personal testimonials, "ideational" calls for large-scale reform (29), and reports of specific changes occurring in local contexts.

But it's important to notice that much of the research on contingent faculty is located *within* academe. For example, the article by Schell and Stock is the editors' introduction to a collection published by NCTE, an academic press, and I would be able to find most of the sources it cites by visiting databases such as JSTOR and MLA, consulting academic periodicals such as the *Chronicle of Higher Education,* and drawing upon the book collection of a university library. By contrast, much of the research about independent scholars exists in a kind of gray space at the margins of academic presses and databases. A great deal of the research I gathered for this chapter, including reports and newsletters published by the National Coalition of Independent Scholars (NCIS) and the Center for Independent Study (CIS), was sent to me personally by independent scholars working for various organizations.[1] As I continued to investigate the situations of scholars who do not teach for a living—whether by choice or because of institutional barriers—I realized that a kind of information firewall exists between independent scholars and the conventional locations of academe, serving to reinforce inequities of status, recognition, and material benefits. A poignant example of the power of this firewall comes from one of my personal communications with an independent scholar that preceded the writing of this chapter. Having learned my name through a listserv, this scholar emailed to ask if I would be willing to receive a copy of his life's work in the event of his death—an oeuvre that included, at the time of the email, six self-published books. This scholar knows that his work will not be immortalized in academically or commercially maintained archives, and therefore is exploring other means to ensure that his writing will survive beyond him.

How, then, shall I define "independent scholar" for the present study, given my attentiveness to the concerns of contingent faculty, but also my belief that there is a pool of academics "out there"—thinkers, writers, knowers—who are barred from access to conventional academic arenas such as classrooms and conferences? I begin with the definition offered by Ronald Gross and Beatrice Gross in their 1983 study *Independent Scholarship: Promise, Problems and Prospects.* Gross and Gross suggest that, while the range of people who might be called "independent scholars" is diverse, "they share two defining characteristics: they are pursuing serious, intellectual inquiries outside academe [characteristic 1], resulting in findings that have been accepted by fellow scholars as significant contributions [characteristic 2]" (2). I want to unpack each of these defining characteristics more carefully.

First, let's consider the status of "serious, intellectual inquiries." Who decides what is serious, and what is intellectual? We could say that independent scholars should publish peer-reviewed articles in scholarly journals, which are then indexed in heavily subscribed databases such as JSTOR, MLA, or PsychArticles. Yet many independent scholars operate outside, or at least at the margins, of these privileged domains. For example, Cal Montgomery, one of the independent scholars interviewed for this chapter, has published extensively in the online magazine *Ragged Edge Online*. Montgomery's contributions have been cited repeatedly in scholarly articles—that is, articles that appear in peer-reviewed journals indexed in databases such as JSTOR. Yet her articles *themselves* do not usually appear in these scholarly databases. Second, let us consider the status of "fellow scholars." While Tynan (Ty) Power, another independent scholar I interviewed, has attended, presented at, and in some cases organized conferences for groups including Al-Fatiha (an organization for LGBTQ Muslims), and has published in "alternative" locations such as the anthology *Pinned Down by Pronouns* (Conviction Books, 2003), it is questionable whether this sort of activity would meet the standard set by Gross and Gross of "serious, intellectual inquiry," nor whether Power's readers and listeners would be considered "fellow scholars." Much of Power's writing appears on the blog site LiveJournal, and is often password-protected. Some of the LiveJournal posts are quite clearly scholarly—for instance, an extensive post about Ramadan, combining Power's research on Islam and data from his personal experience, which is updated and reposted each year. Many members of Power's audiences are graduate students, professors, instructors, or researchers. And yet, since we exist on LiveJournal only as unaffiliated entities such as "mirrormargaret," it is debatable whether the interlocking threads of our comments would be deemed "scholarly" conversation, and by whom. To be fair, the report by Gross and Gross was published decades ago, well before the question of Internet authorship arose. Yet the questions remain: Who decides what is *serious* and *intellectual,* and which persons qualify as *fellow scholars*?

For the purposes of the present study, I want to extend the boundaries of the definition, and to change the terms a bit. I begin with this claim: Academic inquiry investigates questions salient to our material and discursive lives; conducts this investigation with a level of rigor appropriate to the context; and is attendant to responses from others concerned with similar questions. Anyone engaged in such inquiry, I believe, can lay claim to the name *independent scholar,* if wished. This is the working definition that led me to the selection of participants in this small qualitative study. These are people whom I know in contexts outside the study, and whom I know largely online—as friends on LiveJournal and Facebook, as email correspondents, as passionate writers and thinkers whom I never run into at conferences. That, to me, is part of the point: I *don't* meet them at conferences. An important aspect of this study's methodology is its aim to record experiences from persons whose views are not readily accessible through conventional academic channels.[2]

The Role of Disability in Independent Scholarship

Just as research by and about independent scholars is hard to find in conventional academic spaces, recognition of the significant role that disability might play in an independent scholar's life appears to be similarly unnoticed in research by and about independent scholars. In Sonenschein's 2004 study *Independent Together,* for example, a survey of 286

NCIS members collected extensive demographic information on topics including gender, age, race, ethnicity, region, marital status, degrees obtained, financial situation, and languages spoken or read. Yet in this sixty-three-page report the word *disability* does not appear once. To be sure, related data were collected—including information on members' health insurance, employment, and (in a few cases) roles as "caregivers" (50). While reading, I wondered: Isn't it possible that a significant proportion of independent scholars have disabilities? Why aren't their experiences better recognized?

I based this supposition on research by DS scholars who have documented the inaccessibility of academe's conventional system of tenure, promotion, and reward for persons with disabilities. A chilling example comes from Paul K. Longmore's "Why I Burned My Book." In this essay, Longmore describes his path toward academic employment, including encounters with undergraduate and graduate professors who told him things such as "no college would ever hire me as a teacher" (232), and eventual achievement of a Ph.D. in American history in 1984. Using his own experience as a case study, Longmore demonstrates the means by which public society at large, including academe, has made itself inaccessible to scholars with disabilities. For example, Longmore was blocked from gaining teaching experience as a graduate student, since even part-time work as a TA or instructor would have forced him to risk giving up government benefits that paid for his in-home assistants and his ventilator—"the aid that enabled me to live independently and, in fact, to work" (237). In other words, experience crucial to his professional development was disallowed on the grounds that engaging in such work would undermine his status as one who "needed" accommodations such as in-home assistants. According to government definitions, if one is disabled enough to receive benefits, one cannot work; and if one can work, then one must not be disabled enough to qualify for benefits. Longmore's essay vividly portrays this catch-22:

> Necessity has forced many of us [among the severely disabled] to maintain eligibility for federal Supplemental Security Income (SSI) or Social Security Disability Insurance (SSDI) or both . . . [which also] make us eligible for other, more essential assistance. For instance, throughout my adult life I have paid my personal assistants through California's In-Home Support Services program. Medi-Cal (the California version of Medicaid) has paid for my ventila-

> tors. Without this financial aid, I would have had to spend my adult life in some sort of nursing home. . . . Independent living has allowed me to work productively.
>
> The catch is that for most of my adult life, in order to maintain eligibility for this government aid, I have had to refrain from work. Using a combination of medical and economic criteria, *federal disability policy defined—and still defines—"disability" as the total inability to engage in "substantial gainful activity."* (236–37; emphasis added)

This is a rhetorical and material paradox similar to that noted in the ADA case-law discussion from chapter 3. In order to qualify as "disabled," faculty members must display a certain (implicitly measurable) "level" of impairment; yet if they display that level of impairment ("severe" or "total" or whatever), they are presumed unfit to work at their chosen profession.[3] Longmore's story is a saga of political action, letter-writing, and wrangling with bureaucratic definitions in his efforts to engage in work as an employed scholar while still obtaining the accommodations that would enable him to exist outside of a nursing home. Despite all his efforts, he learned that he would not be allowed to earn royalties from his first scholarly book (*The Invention of George Washington*), which had taken him ten years to write, without losing his SSI/SSDI benefits. In response, he burned a copy of the book in a public protest on October 18, 1988.[4]

Although wheelchair users, like Longmore, are the group most likely to be classified as "unemployed" because of a disability, those with mental disabilities constitute a large group as well. In its 2007 annual report, the Social Security Administration (SSA) reported that 2.2 million Americans receive Social Security benefits because of "mental disorders" (excluding "retardation"). This number represents more than 27 percent of all disabled beneficiaries. The large percentage of SSA beneficiaries with mental disabilities has attracted attention from scholars, mostly within public health, psychology, and psychiatry. For example, in 2008 Ronald C. Kessler and coauthors published a paper claiming that serious mental illness (SMI) caused an estimated $193.2 billion loss of personal earnings in the United States during the year 2002.[5] Tellingly, the press release from the National Institute of Mental Health (NIMH) announcing Kessler's findings is headlined "Mental Disorders Cost Society Billions in Unearned

Income." The original study does not say that mental disorders "cost society" anything, although it does use terms such as "societal burden" (708), which is a discipline-specific term in public health. Note, then, the way that the significance of the findings is twisted when it travels from original study to press release. The publicly available online NIMH press release, which is likely to have many more readers than the original study from the *American Journal of Psychiatry,* could have interpreted the findings from Kessler and coauthors in another way: namely, that *society* (in the form of access barriers) costs *people with mental illnesses* billions in annual income. Yet it twice uses the phrase "costs society," thus implying that the societal burden is the fault of persons with SMI.

At any rate, the problem remains clear: millions of people with mental disabilities receive benefits that depend upon the judgment that they are unable to work, or can work only in very limited capacities. If we put this number together with Longmore's point that receiving necessary benefits often bans the recipient from engaging in "gainful" employment, we can conclude that persons with disabilities who wish both to receive treatment or accommodations *and* to earn money for their work are caught in an insidious bureaucratic and rhetorical paradox. I noted in chapter 3 that academics with disabilities may "need" full-time employment in ways that nondisabled academics do not, in order to obtain health insurance. But it is also true that in some cases, academics with disabilities may "need" *not* to have full-time employment, lest they lose government-sponsored benefits. I call this *the un/able paradox:* If one is deemed "unable" to work, then one qualifies for the accommodations that would make work possible; yet if one makes use of those accommodations and does work, then one is deemed too "able" to qualify for accommodations, whose loss makes work (and in some cases, life) impossible.

Questions of health care, employability, and the intersection of one's everyday life with the terms of one's employment are shared by most academics (and most workers, for that matter). However, these questions take on highly complex and specific shapes when we consider the situation of academics with mental disabilities. Researching the experiences of academics with mental disabilities who operate outside the conventional structures of academe does more than bring forward the experiences of an underrecognized group; it also calls into question the very notion of "independence" in scholarship, including the process of scholarly research itself.

Disability Studies Methodology: Putting It to the Test

Sonenschein suggests in the introduction to *Independent Together* that in-depth, open-ended interviews would be "the next logical step" of investigation into the lived experiences of independent scholars (5). In the rest of this chapter, I report on interviews conducted in an effort to bring forward the perspectives and academic lives of three independent scholars, Cal, Phinnia, and Ty. I turned to qualitative research for this part of the study because I wanted to know more about the experiences of independent scholars with disabilities (mental disabilities in particular), and I was unable to find published work that spoke directly to my questions. I came to my questions by way of the research that is described in the first chapters of this book. An academic's job, I had concluded, involves the following actions: first, produce "work" (usually in written form); and second, gather in rooms (both classrooms and meeting rooms) with other people and talk about that work. But what if those seemingly simple requirements conflict with a person's modes of communication, learning, and knowing? I couldn't stop thinking about the statement from Clarice, a faculty member with Asperger's, quoted in chapter 3: "A meeting can be a disaster for someone on the spectrum" (Avinger, Croake, and Miller 211). With this in mind, I formulated three research questions:

1. How do independent scholars with mental disabilities[6] pursue academic work including writing, attending conferences, and networking with colleagues?
2. How do such persons construct their own positions in relation to academic institutions, including their own processes of self-naming and self-identifying?
3. What access barriers and benefits apply to persons with mental disabilities who pursue academic work?

I selected these three participants because I know their work well—both published and unpublished—and all three met my definition as independent scholars with mental disabilities. Importantly, as the study unfolded, it became clear that Phinnia, Ty, and Cal do not necessarily define *themselves* this way. Their own self-identifications are discussed below. This is an exploratory study, using a convenience sample, and is therefore limited. Future research projects will, I hope, address larger numbers of independent scholars with disabilities, using a variety of methods. My purpose at present is simply to open the arena, to offer suggestive questions for further investigation, and to relate these stories.

One of my primary concerns was how to conduct ethical and effective research with participants who occupy positions vis-à-vis academe quite different from my own; who have mental disabilities; and who are my friends. The issues I raise here are indebted to the work of feminist and DS researchers including Colin Barnes, Tim Booth, Michelle Fine, Gesa Kirsch, Patti Lather, and Mike Oliver. During the study, I attempted to adhere to an *interdependent qualitative research paradigm*—one in which the progress of research relies upon participants and continually seeks their feedback and guidance. To some degree, this is simply a way to name what has always been true in qualitative research: the researcher needs participants, and is dependent upon them, even as her power as interpreter and writer of findings is an ongoing problematic. Further than this, however, I believe that acting as an interdependent researcher, especially within a DS framework, should involve taking risks and operating in unfamiliar modalities. The usual model of qualitative research assumes that the "design" will be set ahead of time and that any responses that do not conform to the requirements of that design are unusable—in some disciplines, are "tainted" data. By contrast, an interdependent qualitative research paradigm suggests that the site of such "taint" is in fact where the action is: this is where questions arise, where researcher and participant must communicate, where compromises take place and participants' decisions will guide and even redirect the course of a study.

I knew from prior experience that all three participants had written at some length about their lives, including their disabilities, and in some cases treated the subject with casualness and humor. For example, one of the tags on Phinnia's blog is *my head is pasted on crooked yay,* used to mark entries in which she records her experiences with anxiety, medications, brain fog, and other issues having to do with her emotional state. But the reason I know this is not because I conducted any sort of "objective" scan of LiveJournal blogs; rather, I know it because she is my friend. This study applies what Lisa Tillmann-Healy has called "friendship as method," which involves "conversation, everyday involvement, compassion, giving, and vulnerability" (734). Friendship as method, Tillmann-Healy explains, involves increased risk for both participants and researcher(s) because, in their dual roles, all experience heightened levels of vulnerability (741, 743). An example of the complication this added to the present study was my concern about inadvertently revealing information that had been given to me "as a friend" but not "as a researcher." Over the years of our friendships, I have become privy to quite a bit of information about the participants through channels such as personal emails and password-protected blog entries. It would not be ethical, of course, to use such protected information without explicit consent. And yet that sort of information does not necessarily come in separable units. My knowledge of Phinnia's battles with public transportation, of Cal's frustrating history with the DS community, of Ty's familial losses—this knowledge infuses what I write about them and how I interpret their words, whether I refer to it directly or not. Complicating the situation still further is that sometimes, during the course of the study, participants would reveal information and then add a note such as "I'm not sure if I want you to put that in or not." In other words, *because* we were conversing as friends, we were divulging information that might or might not be appropriate for inclusion in a publicly presented study. As Carolyn Ellis has written, when conducting research with friends and other intimate acquaintances, "there is no leaving the field" ("Telling" 13). Because of these concerns, Tillmann-Healy argues that friendship as method "all but demands that writings be taken back to the community for examination, critique, and further dialogue" (744). I agree with this point, and would add that DS methodology places a similar imperative upon its researchers: if we are truly dedicated to "changing the social relations of research production" (Oliver), we must place co-interpretation at the center of our work.

I take the term *co-interpretation* from Thomas Newkirk's "Seduction and Betrayal in Qualitative Research." Newkirk's vision of how to "share" work with participants is especially useful for DS methodology, because it emphasizes *ongoing* discussion of data rather than simply mailing out a manuscript after data have been collected, analyzed, and written up. Newkirk argues that participants should have access to a researcher's emerging interpretations so that they can offer their own interpretations or "mitigating information" (13). In the present study, because participants' stated preferences were for online rather than face-to-face interviews, we had the luxury of time during which we could reconsider questions, pose counterquestions, clarify our ideas, and offer further information. It also provided the space for me to share other pieces of the book with them, including the project proposal, individual chapters, and emerging versions of this chapter. But the approach had a limitation as well, one that participants pointed out to me, and that I plan to change the next time I conduct a similar study: Ty, Phinnia, and Cal were isolated from each other during the data-collection stages. Because of concerns about confidentiality, I was careful not to reveal participants' identities to one another as interviews began; and even after each gave his or her permission to be named, I still didn't share their interview comments. In short, they didn't really "meet" one another until they received the common email that included my first tentative draft of the chapter. A fully co-interpretive approach, I believe, would rectify this problem by introducing group as well as individual interview opportunities. This would be easy to set up online, through a commonly accessible blog, "chat" space, or shared emails.

My caution about confidentiality, I think, was a symptom of my ongoing anxiety about the risks that friendship-as-method entails. Despite the study's layers of "mitigating information" (Newkirk 13), I still felt nervous about my choice of design; I was also strongly aware that mental disability is a highly charged topic, and talking about one's mental disabilities in almost any context involves considerable risk. Therefore, I made an early decision about one aspect of my approach to co-interpretation: anything a participant wanted to have removed from the chapter would be removed, without question. This promise was stated on each informed-consent form and routinely referred to throughout the study. Although in some cases qualitative researchers may choose to retain contested information in a final write-up since "we owe readers an account that is as comprehensive and complex as possible" (Tillmann-Healy 741), and in other cases may look for middle-ground choices such as noting a participant's concerns but still including the contested information, I decided that in this case I wanted to draw a firmer line.

As the interviews began, I held email conversations with each participant to explain my hopes for a co-interpretive exchange. For instance, I wrote to Ty:

> [I'd like to] set it up as a highly collaborative research project, with due credit to you written into the chapter's explanation of the approach. As in, I share my thinking with you (which includes you reading the ms. in progress, if you can stand it), and then we together decide how best to present your "case" as an independent scholar. We could structure it as a series of conversations (email

> and perhaps some in person, but it's critical of course that whatever methods we use follow best-access for you), maybe posing questions back and forth, etc. I'd really like it to be more dialogic, in other words, than "HERE IS THE CASE OF TYLER (NOT HIS REAL NAME)."

This aim, in my estimation, was largely successful, and participants affirmed my sense of its success. However, it also introduced yet another complication: the problem of *structure.* Early in our exchanges, Cal wrote to me, "I guess what makes me uncomfortable about this whole thing is that it doesn't seem very structured. I tend to need guidance in ways that most other people don't, and I end up completely confused about what I am supposed to do." In other words, through my efforts to create a co-interpretive environment, I had unwittingly set up a situation that was not accessible for her. In that case, I revised my approach by creating a list of questions, which I sent along—at Cal's request—a few at a time.

Cal's point about lack of structure guided my later exchanges with Ty and Phinnia. For example, when Ty and I began our conversations on email, I mentioned that we might also use LiveJournal as our medium, which would offer the advantage of "threading" each topic so that it would occupy a visually discrete space. Ty initially refused this suggestion. However, as our conversations progressed, email became less and less accessible for him. He wrote:

> Re: your chapter, I keep thinking about it and I do want to get back to it and I'm not sure that picking up email is going to be the best way just because email sometimes feels way overwhelming. (My inbox today, from the last few days, had 700+ messages . . . even though most were "junk" and many were not important, when I approach email with the idea of "check email, get back to Margaret, etc" I often don't get *through* the check email phase.) So maybe we *should* try private LJ posts or doing something like a Google doc. The idea of making you juggle different strands of conversation in different formats makes my head hurt, though, so let me know what will not make *your* head hurt :)

Accordingly, Ty and I moved our conversation to LiveJournal, where I set up a space that was accessible only to the two of us, and where we conducted a threaded conversation—again, over time—using the site's "Comment" feature.

The question of structure is intertwined with another methodological issue that I became increasingly aware of as the study progressed: *time.* Tillmann-Healy notes that studies using friendship as method must progress "at the natural pace of friendship" (734); this turned out to be true of the present study, and its pace was further affected because it unfolded in "crip time." In conventional interview studies, the researcher controls the amount of time to be invested by making decisions about the mode of interviewing (face-to-face, telephone, or online), how many questions will be asked, and how much time each participant will invest. In fact, some institutional review boards (IRBs) recommend that such decisions be announced ahead of time so that participants can be informed of how long their investment in the study will last. However, since I was attempting to use a more flexible methodology, I had no such guidelines to offer participants. Instead, I asked them to tell me how they wanted the interviews to unfold. I began by offering a choice of modes: face-to-face in person; by telephone; or online. All three participants chose the online option, but in quite different ways. Cal determined that she would prefer to receive the questions by email in short batches, three or four at a time; Phinnia asked for the questions by email, but all at once; and Ty determined, after some efforts on email, that a blog format would work better. Sometimes a month or more would go by before I received a response to an email I had sent. Periodically I would check in with participants, but I was hesitant to do so too often: they were working within constraints that included pain, brain fog, family obligations, anxiety, and work schedules. This is a situation in which my own mental disabilities offered an advantage. I know from experience that anxiety, pain, and fatigue can create a highly idiosyncratic work schedule, and that periodic "reminders" may be helpful, but that respect for the needs of one's own bodymind must be paramount. I also know from experience that people with mental disabilities rarely, if ever, receive sufficient recognition for the tremendous effort involved in carrying out what most people consider "everyday" tasks, and I included frequent acknowledgments of this in my responses to participants.

All these efforts were a part of a complicated exchange of encouragement, insight, and affirmation that formed this study's approach to reciprocity. Reciprocity is always intertwined with the issue of time to some extent, for the currency of exchange in qualitative studies is often measured in chronological terms: participants will invest x amount of time and will receive y in exchange. Sometimes the compensation is a small amount of money; sometimes it is a service offered by the researcher, such as free tutoring; sometimes it is as simple as an expression of thanks. In the present study, I attempted to compensate participants in ways that seemed in keeping with the approach of "friendship as method." I sent Cal and Ty each a book, and Phinnia requested a pair of hand-knitted socks.

In one sense, I am studying my peer group: we all have mental disabilities; all of us are white; and all of us are queer.[7] But in another sense, I am "studying down" (Fine; see also Kirsch), because I have a tenure-track job, and I am privileged in ways that make it easier for me to access academic spaces than for the study's other participants. I am the only one who can log on to a university website and request any book or article I wish through interlibrary loan, and the only one whose travel to conferences is subsidized by my employer. While Phinnia, Ty, and Cal can and do access materials and conferences through various means, it's important to mark the *ease*—that is, the privilege—of my own access. In part for this reason, I chose to practice a form of reciprocity that Tillmann-Healy calls "radical reciprocity," in which "we never ask more of participants than we are willing to give" (735). My practice of "radical reciprocity" included offering information about my own experiences of mental disability, both to participants during our interviews, and in the write-up of the study itself. I also offered to provide any books or PDFs they might need that related to their work on this chapter. Because I have the privilege of a tenure-track job, I am not classifying myself with them as an independent scholar. Rather, I am attempting to align myself with them in terms of other issues—particularly mental disability—in a move of solidarity. To return to Nagel's term, I am trying to gaze from *somewhere* rather than *nowhere*. At the same time, I want to center the participants' experiences rather than my own—for one danger of self-reflexivity is that it "risks turning representation into a solipsistic, rhetorical position in which the researcher (the self)—ah, once again—usurps the position of the subject (the other)" (Brueggemann, "Still-Life" 19).

To their words, then. After a brief introductory sketch describing each participant, the following sections are divided thematically. I relied on participants to help me determine the plausibility and integrity of each theme. When sending them a draft of the chapter in which I had assigned tentative categories to the data, I asked them to question the categories themselves, opening the possibility that my analysis might need to be reshaped according to their interpretations of the data. Although none chose to refigure the themes themselves, their comments in our subsequent exchanges considerably changed the content of each theme's discussion. The themes are

- Disability, impairment, and diagnosis
- Identifying as a scholar
- Isolation and community[8]

Sketch of Each Participant

Phinnia is thirty-two ("as old as my tongue and a little bit older than my teeth"). She lives in the Pacific Northwest with her husband and son; she also has two girlfriends, with whom she communicates daily online. She is a prolific blogger, posting anywhere from 250 to 3,000 words a day on topics including her fiction and poetry writing, her participation in other online communities, and her everyday activities. Everyday activities include working with her seven-year-old son, who is blind, autistic, and nonverbal, and advocating for and with him in his school and after-school environments. They also include wrangling rides for herself and her family on systems of transportation she has dubbed "failtransit." Phinnia uses a wheelchair and experiences severe joint and muscular pain; daily events around these topics are tagged on her blog with descriptors such as *medical-go-round* and *mind vs. body smackdown*. She regularly takes part in community writing events, both online and face-to-face, and has published her writing in journals including *Breath & Shadow* and *Electric Mandolin*. She identifies herself as a "self-historian" in reference to her nonfictional writing, and as a poet and short-fiction writer.

Ty, thirty-eight, lives in semirural New England with his partner and two sons. A transsexual FTM (female to male), he has published work in a wide range of venues, including the anthology *Pinned Down by Pronouns*. While working as a writer for a large educational publishing company, he created many research-based presentations on topics ranging from HIV prevention to pedestrian safety. He is a founding member of Al-Fatiha, an organization for LGBTQ Muslims, and has also been cochair and keynote speaker for True Spirit, the annual conference of American Boyz.[9] Ty is hearing-impaired, adding, "The term 'hearing impaired' is problematic because the Deaf community is often unwillingly included under its umbrella; however, I feel that for those with partial hearing it is preferable to 'hard-of-hearing,' which carries an implication that hearing is 'hard' (i.e., requires effort) rather than impossible for people with hearing limitations." He does extensive organizing and teaching work for his local Unitarian Universalist congregation, and is hoping to continue his graduate studies in communication.

Cal, forty-two, lives in the Midwest with a roommate and two dogs, Nate and Murdo. She has written for journals including *Ragged Edge Online,* and has presented at conferences including Autreat, the American Association of Philosophy Teachers, the Radical Philosophy Association, and Society for Disability Studies and, using a reader, has had her work presented at a Queer Disability conference. Her original academic training is in philosophy but she was "derailed," first by long-term institutionalization and later by access problems. Following a period in which she was unable to work, she is currently undertaking an independent course of study based on "all the things that I would have learned if I were going to school in disability studies (and if I had designed the program) before—I hope—returning to the fray."

Disability, Impairment, and Diagnosis

I specified from the beginning of the project—in the study's introductory letter and consent form, as well as during interviews—that two of the study's grounding terms (*independent scholar* and *mental disability*) are ones I bring to it, and I asked participants to talk to me about their own processes of self-naming and self-identifying. In reference to *mental disability,* all three participants expressed understanding of the reasons why I use this term, but chose to identify themselves in other ways. Phinnia, for instance, wrote:

> *Mentally disabled* to me implies a cognitive component, which doesn't really apply in my case. . . . I'd prefer to call myself "emotionally disabled" because it's closer to my self-concept: my emotions (fear, anxiety, depression, panic, etcetera) are really my disabling condition.

When I first began the process of interviewing, I was using the term *psychosocial disability* more often than *mental disability,* and Cal mentioned at one point that she thought the former term was a better descriptor. She wrote,

> I had the impression that you were using "psychosocially disabled" to include the people I consider to have "cognitive impairments" as well as those I've considered to have "sensory impairments," which is one of the things I liked about it.

Cal's use of *impairment* is a deliberate choice. She is cautious with the term *disability,* explaining: "I do not say that 'I have a disability' because to me that would be like a black person in a white-dominated society saying 'I have a racism.'" In her view, the U.S. social model of disability (or rather, the many views that claim to be "social model") tends to place the responsibility for lack of access upon individuals—even when claiming not to. Her language use, she explained, draws more from the British social model, in which "'impaired' has to do with inherent limitations, while 'disabled' has to do with socially imposed disadvantages that are neither caused nor justified by impairment. . . . In American thinking I don't tend to think the language really exists to make that distinction, which I think is vital." This is a point on which we differ; to my mind, "having a mental disability" does indicate disadvantages that are socially imposed rather than inherent. However, Cal's interpretation of my thinking—that it seemed more "American social model" than "British social model"—made me newly aware of how slippery distinctions of language can be, even in conversation between two people with apparently similar frames of reference. Particularly when conversing with Americans, Cal noted, "I use other phrasing to make it clear which of the many definitions of 'disability' that are out there I'm using." These include *disability-ASM* (American social model), *disability-BSM* (British social model), *disability-ADA/504* (Americans with Disabilities Act and section 504 of the Rehabilitation Act), and *disability-Amundson* (in reference to the work of Ron Amundson).

Cal later elaborated, "I do think we need a way of talking inclusively about people for whom *access to human interaction* is problematic" (emphasis added).[10] This point also emerged, although differently charged, in Ty's description of his disabilities. In Ty's case, his hearing (a "physical" or "sensory" disability) can operate causally to produce emotional effects:

> I definitely see my hearing as something that interacts with my anxiety. [For example], when I was in high school, I found out that

> on a day I was absent from math class, one of the students said, "Well it doesn't matter anyway, because she's not here even when she *is* here." Which I think had a lot to do with how much I missed because I didn't hear. But it definitely triggered anxiety . . . I sure didn't want to go back to class after that, definitely didn't want to ask questions or volunteer answers in class if they might be redundant, etc.

What I draw from these comments is that, although the participants identify in various ways, all three prefer to name themselves *in context* rather than abstractly. One of my interview questions asked, "Does [the term *mental disability*] feel like it applies to you? Why or why not?" and—in that acontextual format—the question didn't draw much response. On the other hand, as they were answering other questions about their work and their lives, Ty, Cal, and Phinnia made frequent references to their impairments or disabilities as a means to clarifying specific situations. An example of identification in context is Cal's choice to claim the label *crazy,* saying that, after years of institutionalization, forced medication, and ECT (electroshock) therapy, she feels she has "earned the right" to this label, although she has been urged by family members not to use it.

My question about the applicability of the term *mental disability* was not intended to be diagnostic, but it has some features in common with medical diagnosis—notably, its suggestion that it might provide a generalizable "truth" absent of context—which, I believe, is one reason participants rejected it. All three participants are familiar with the discursive and often oppressive nature of diagnosis. As a group, they have been diagnosed, at various times, with "disorders" including anxiety, depression, autism, multiple personality disorder (MPD), post-traumatic stress disorder (PTSD), bipolar disorder, catatonic schizophrenia, obsessive-compulsive disorder (OCD), and attention-deficit hyperactivity disorder (AD/HD). I am presenting their diagnoses in a group in an attempt to disrupt the medical and individualistic model of disability that would suggest that we ought to try to match different people's ways of learning and knowing to their diagnoses in a deterministic way. Although each participant refers to his or her diagnoses at various times, and in some cases chooses to claim one or another, this is not the most important information about them, and is more usefully considered as part of the rhetorical web within which they operate rather than as a set of labels that might determine some "truth" about them. For instance, Cal stated, "I really try to de-emphasize my diagnoses when I write," and explained her decision this way:

> I think that people [general readers] really want to read things by someone like me that explore my personal experience, and they don't consider that I can have anything to say other than personal experience, and that even if I did it would not be appropriate for me to do anything other than "interpret" autism for parents and professionals. But many people are open with their labels, or they are easily identified by others as having impairments that those others connect to decreased intellectual potential, and they are systematically not taken seriously by the people who read their work.

Here, Cal identifies one of the problems with being labeled, even by oneself. If the label is stereotypically considered to attach to "decreased intellectual potential"—as is true of most mental-disability diagnoses—then readers will tend to assume that the author's work is merely anecdotal, of little scholarly or analytic value. This observation testifies to the influence of the personal/critical divide that persists in academic discourse, with an added twist by way of mental disability: if one is seen as having "decreased intellectual potential," then one's writing must be *only* personal, or *merely* personal, rather than a critical commentary. Thus, Cal's published writing often sets aside the question of self-labeling. For example, the bio attached to her acclaimed article "Critic of the Dawn" reads simply, "Cal Montgomery is an activist, writer, and speaker focusing on disability issues."

Despite their awareness of the problems posed by diagnosis, all of the participants expressed an attendant awareness of its importance in their material lives—in particular, its relevance to the medications and quality of care they can access. For example, Phinnia celebrated the arrival of a pain-related diagnosis with the blog-entry title "can has diagnosis nao YAY."[11] Although chronic pain is often identified as a "physical" rather than a "mental" disability, it has many important ties to my broad definition of mental disability, especially since health-care practitioners tend to treat people reporting pain with suspicion. The common stereotype is that pain conditions are "all in the head" and that a person seeking pain medication "just wants the drugs" (i.e., is an addict). As a result, adequate pain diagnoses can be extremely hard to obtain, and the search for such a diagnosis may be taken by medical practitioners as an indication of mental disorder. Cal remarked on a similar diagnostic battle, one that resulted, like Phinnia's, in a potentially useful diagnosis and treatment: "This summer I finally got my pain specialist to take me seriously, and I am now on a drug that is seriously debilitating—a lot of the time I am awake for maybe three hours a day and I am having nausea and so forth—but that is worth it to me because I can once again read." Only rarely did participants self-identify by means of diagnostic labels; however, all are well aware of the material importance of diagnosis in their lives.

Identifying as a Scholar

The question of how they might identify in relation to the term *independent scholar* seemed to engage participants more than the question of identifying their disabilities or impairments. The Gross and Gross definition, discussed above, which suggests that an independent scholar should pursue "serious, intellectual inquiries outside academe, resulting in findings that have been accepted by fellow scholars as significant contributions" (2) was addressed at length. Ty's response to it focused on the problem of *audience:*

> In reading that definition, it seems to be validating independent scholarship by virtue of its acceptance as valuable to other scholars. A number of flaws in that definition jump out at me. For one, the expectation that an independent scholar's work will result in "findings" to be evaluated by others seems to be assuming that independent scholars have the same access to research funding, publication and presentation options (e.g. at conferences) as those who have ties to academe. How else would other scholars have access to their ideas to validate and accept them? I am sure there are "independent scholars" (such as those who work or volunteer for non-profits or lobby groups) whose work does allow them to conduct studies and publish findings, but to require that as a criterion seems to exclude the vast majority of non-academic scholars who might have valuable contributions to make.
>
> Another issue is that other scholars who accept and value an independent scholar's contribution may be, themselves, unattached to or alienated from academe. Would their acceptance "count"? This also brings us back to the first issue: if an independent scholar

> accepts another's work as valuable, that acceptance may not be presented in traditional scholastic ways, due to lack of access to publication.

Here, Ty points out the paradox raised by the Gross and Gross definition. If an independent scholar is to produce work that is "accepted" as "significant" by fellow scholars, that scholar must be able to *get* his or her work to an audience of fellow scholars. Yet the access barriers that accompany life as an independent scholar—for instance, as Ty mentions, having little or no access to research funding or conferences—makes it much more difficult to locate and reach that audience.

Moreover, as Ty points out, alternative audiences, such as those who attend community-organizing conferences or who operate mostly through public online communities, may be devalued. He offered an extended example of his work with several community-organizing groups and questioned how that work might "merit the label 'independent scholarship'" according to the Gross and Gross definition.

> I was a founding member of Al-Fatiha and, in 1998, was one of four people who were part of the first face-to-face meeting the group ever had (it was started and grew online, a fact which allowed it to become an international network for a very geographically-scattered population). From the beginning, I posted frequently about topics relating to gender identity and feminism, as well as about religious and spiritual practice. As the online group grew into a grassroots organization, the founder, Faisal Alam, appointed a shura (advisory board), of which I was a member until it was replaced by a Board of Directors. . . . At the second Al-Fatiha conference, in 1999 in New York City, I co-presented on gender identity and its relevance to the larger LGBT Muslim population. My co-presenter, Faris Malik . . . held a Master's degree in German literature, so it could be argued that he had some academic background; however, that did not provide a basis for validating his perspective on a topic so far removed from his academic field. Likewise, my own Master's degree in Mass Communication did not give me academic credentials to justify my presentation about Islam and gender identity. Still, it could be argued that in the area of LGBT Muslim issues, Malik and I were both knowledgeable, contributed new perspectives, presented our ideas and were ac-

cepted by each other, at the least, and by the conference attendees. Some of the attendees could also be considered knowledgeable and have written and presented on LGBT Muslim topics themselves; however, to my knowledge, only one has ties to academe.

> Does this merit the label "independent scholarship"? Using the Gross and Gross definition, probably not. There is no record of any "acceptance" the attendees may have conferred upon Malik or me, or any that we conveyed upon each other. Even if there were a record of the "acceptance" of our work, an argument has to be made for the scholarship of the attendees in order for that "acceptance" to carry any weight. Had I presented at an established academic conference about Islam, religion, gender, or queer studies, there would be validation of my work with Al-Fatiha as scholarship of some sort. Yet it was highly unlikely that an established academic conference would invite a non-academically credentialed individual to present in the first place.

Through this example, Ty illustrates what it means to exist at the margins of an academic system whose system of reward tends to operate through a process sometimes called "logrolling." Even systems such as anonymous peer review, which is supposed to be one of the main tools used by academe to maintain the integrity of scholarship, can be influenced by "personal friendships or animosities and desires to curry favor" (Rhode 58). To put it simply, in the current academic system, the rich get richer. This is not a new observation; however, it is rarely noted in reference to independent scholars with disabilities, whose intersectional positions are met by multiple and sometimes unique barriers.

Cal's take on *independent scholar* was similar to Ty's in her emphasis on the problematics of "acceptance" and audience. She wrote:

> I have a real problem with the idea that findings have to be accepted by fellow scholars as significant. I think peer review is to a great extent the way that we know whether someone is a scholar, especially in fields like disability studies where people have such diverse backgrounds and so few people are really qualified to judge a given individual's work. . . . I would consider a scholar someone who engages with a reasonably current (depending on the field) group of scholars, whether they are taking the significant contributions of others and working on them in a way that their peers would be

> willing to consider a significant contribution if the work were presented to the peers in a neutral way so that it could be considered without prejudice, or whether they are making contributions to which other scholars are responding. But I wouldn't consider that someone who is frozen out by academics who are operating from prejudice would be a non-scholar, even though people from other disciplines might not be able to tell that they are a scholar.

Here, Cal's argument is much like Ty's: that is, while there must be some set of common ways to measure the value of scholarly contributions, a definition that turns on "acceptance" ignores—in fact, conceals—the problem of access. She added that the access problem might extend to ways that people with certain kinds of disabilities are viewed before their work is even considered: for example, "I am regularly informed that people with IQ scores below 85 . . . cannot possibly benefit from postsecondary education and ought to be excluded from even open-enrollment schools." The absurdity of this suggestion is belied by Cal's own history: although her IQ was once measured (while she was institutionalized) and recorded as 80, she had a highly successful undergraduate career, was accepted to competitive graduate schools, and studied and taught successfully in graduate school for three years. Access barriers did influence her decision to leave grad school after three years, but it's obvious that the problem was not her "intelligence."

Unlike Cal and Ty, Phinnia does not identify any of her work as scholarly. Calling herself a "self-historian," she explained:

> "Scholar" to me implies a research focus. (For example in the term "scholarly article," which implies something in an academic journal setting, frequently peer reviewed.) My work is better classed as either fiction or autobiography (depending on the setting), and although [the latter] often blossoms from research, it's more subtly applied there, and [in the former case] doesn't apply at all, because it's coming from a personal space. Scholarly to me implies nonfiction.

Phinnia's definition of scholarship is therefore most in line with conventional academic definitions: "scholarship" is work that appears in academic journals and does not come from "a personal space." Although "personal"—even "fictional"—and "scholarly" work can intermingle in some contexts,[12] this is not the case in Phinnia's work. In fact, as our conversations continued to unfold, it became clear that defining her writing—both fictional and nonfictional—against "scholarly research" is a point of strength for her, as it affords her greater freedom of choice in genres and publication venues.

Phinnia's point that personal narrative operates differently from conventional scholarly research is certainly true from a practical standpoint: works such as Carolyn Ellis's "evocative autoethnography" or Kathleen Stewart's "cultural poesis" are the exception rather than the rule in academic discourse. Moreover, as Ellis herself has pointed out, the pressures of the academic reward system may discourage scholars in less-established positions from working in experimental or genre-bending forms. In "Evocative Autoethnography," Ellis looks back at the realist-ethnographic approach she took in her first book, *Fisher Folk,* and explains, "In 1979, I didn't wonder why sociology, my chosen discipline, couldn't be written more like a Tolstoy story; I couldn't afford to. I had a dissertation on fishing communities to finish, then a book to publish, then a tenure review to pass" (116–17). The pressure of being an "aspiring academic" (Gappa and Leslie) may therefore be seen as limiting: as Phinnia noted, "I have a certain amount of personal and academic freedom that I enjoy given that I report to no one." A similar advantage was noted by Ty: "I have the opportunity to screw up without a lot of people noticing, and without worrying about my professional reputation." However, he also made it clear that, from his perspective, this is "the only major plus" of working outside the privileged reaches of academic discourse.

Phinnia's take on academic and writerly freedom is heavily influenced by her awareness of the limitations that editors, journals, and even genres themselves can place upon one's writing. In a follow-up comment to my question "What feels most important about your written or scholarly work?" she emphasized the importance of "pleas[ing] myself" above other priorities.

> I write everything for myself first (even the things I write for other people are written in a format to please myself). I think that's an important distinction to make, because it contributes to something else I've mentioned, the fact that I'm not "responsible" to anyone else. It's something I'm struggling with about publishing, because publishing often requires you to write to a certain spec and I'm trying to figure out how far I want to take that. To a word length is

> one thing, but writing content is an entirely different animal. I have a lot of anxieties when it comes to editors and agents potentially changing things radically to make things "saleable." I'm not meaning that in a "my work is all perfect" sort of way, but I do know that the demands of the "market" are often way different than my own "tastes." The best example I can find is when they make a movie out of something and it's been cut to ribbons? I don't want that to happen to me. I wouldn't be able to respect myself. So that's a big hurdle I have to clear, undoing the association between "professional publishing" and "tearing things apart."

In this statement, Phinnia foregrounds a concern shared by many academic and creative writers: the problem of making one's own perspective "saleable" for the marketplace. Perhaps for this reason, Phinnia's marketplace is decidedly alternative: she publishes in new genres including fan fiction and flash fiction;[13] her poetry appears in small journals; and she generally does not aim for more conventional commercial or scholarly audiences. This decision complicates the suggestion from Gross and Gross that an independent scholar's work ought to be "accepted" by fellow scholars. Phinnia's work is indeed accepted, and enthusiastically; every piece of writing she publishes receives a torrent of admiring commentary on her blog. But she has chosen to build her own community of readers rather than attempt to conform to the more established (and more ableist) community of conventional academic and creative work.

Isolation and Community

The double-edged nature of scholarly freedom/isolation has received considerable commentary in writing about independent scholarship (Bell, "Independent Scholarship"; Sonenschein). Of the three participants, Phinnia seems to access most comfortably the writerly community of which she wants to be a part. For example, she is a member of numerous Internet communities devoted to her chosen genres; she also regularly takes part in community writing events near her home. This may be due, in part, to the fact that she identifies herself more as a creative writer than as a scholarly writer, and that communities for writers of her chosen genres have recently proliferated. By contrast, both Ty and Cal discussed at some length the barriers they have experienced in attempting to access conversations with like-minded academics.

For Cal, two spaces that present significant access barriers are classrooms and conferences. Reflecting on her experience in graduate school, she wrote, "I used to really enjoy the intellectual give-and-take you could get in an active academic department, but since becoming unable to speak I've found it much harder to participate in that sort of thing: other people can silence me simply by turning their heads, and most people seem to want to do that." (She had earlier explained that her ability to speak had been intermittent for years and "finally shorted out" in 2001.) Moreover, she understands little of what is said to her in an oral/aural context. For these reasons, both classrooms and conferences are highly inaccessible to Cal, and she has had a number of frustrating experiences at conferences, even ones that make significant efforts to be widely accessible, including SDS and Autreat.

Cal made the further point that, if one's "access to human interaction" is already problematic, this can set off a cascading reaction in which other forms of access become less and less possible:

> Access to the contents of texts and the contents of lectures is a big one for me, and I believe for some other people. Yes, ADA/504 should protect us, but if we aren't well-networked, we run into situations where we have to find a way to enforce our own rights, and we don't always know how to do that. . . . Once we don't have access to texts and lectures, we lose academic library access fairly quickly. (I would have library access if I went and pushed for it, but it's unclear to me whether or how I would access interlibrary loan. Previously I had library access but no access to ILL.) . . . And because many of us are working in low-wage jobs or living on disability payments (note that when I say "many of us" I am including myself as a part of the larger "us," but I am luckier than many people and can buy used books pretty regularly), creating our own libraries can be difficult. I'm very lucky there, just as I am lucky to have been able to read well enough to get by in my undergraduate years without really understanding lectures, so long as I was willing to turn to books to find out what was probably happening.

The cascading reaction Cal describes here begins with a single inaccessible environment—a classroom. If a person has a disability that makes speaking, listening, or being taken seriously problematic, virtually every classroom in the United States will present access barriers. And the next step usually required (in practice if not by law) is that this person will have to advocate for his or her own accommodations—*despite* the fact that communication itself is the arena of difficulty. Whether the next event is flunking out, dropping out, or a more euphemistic turn of events (such as "being academically withdrawn" from an institution), academic library access then disappears. And, as Cal points out, since many people with disabilities are already living on little money, the ability to build community by obtaining books and articles, and attending conferences, is often unfeasible.

While it would seem that publicly available Internet groups and journals could help bridge some of these gaps—as has been true for Phinnia—there are multiple problems with trying to attend, as Cal put it, "the University of Google." Most obviously, access to the Internet in the first place presents economic barriers. Even if one has reliable Internet access, much of the scholarship on the Internet is available only in password-protected spaces that require subscription. Subscriptions are available to individuals, but are extremely expensive; I think it's safe to say that most people who access subscription-only academic journals do so via some form of institutional affiliation. Investigating further, we find that are subtler problems to online access as well. For example, Ty told this story about an Internet-based group he founded in 1999 called Iman (for lesbian, bisexual, and trans Muslims):

> [Iman] was active in 1999–2001 and then kind of petered out because of the fact that Queernet—a site which hosted many of the GLBT email lists at that time—had a major crash and all list owners had to reset the lists from scratch. That meant that *many* groups ended very suddenly, including several of those crucial to my coming out. The Al-Fatiha "gaymuslims" list ended up moving to Yahoo groups, and others were added like "transmuslims," which has totally changed the nature of the lists because they are not as well moderated now and end up being spammed often.

The situation Ty describes is one example of the way that "infrastructure," in the sense used by Jeffrey Grabill, combines rhetorical and material effects to deny access. Once again, the rich get richer (or rather, the affiliated get even better affiliated)—in part because they (we) can rely on a level of consistency and safety in the materials and communities we access. If I am reading about Al-Fatiha in a scholarly database that includes the journal *Culture, Health & Sexuality* (see Minwalla et al.), I can count pretty reliably on two things: first, the article will still be there tomorrow if I want to go back and read it again; and second, I will not be randomly spammed by hate speech.

Ty's discussion of academic isolation and community seems to reflect more emphasis on internal processes than Cal's. Because of his hearing, he can, like Cal, be silenced "simply by [other people] turning their heads." In Ty's case, however, another significant barrier is his sense of not having a "right" to speak in scholarly conversations. He wrote:

> When I think of submitting an editorial or an article on a topic, I immediately feel that there is little to justify my taking up "space"—I can't formulate an author bio that says "X is a professor of —— at ——" or "X is director (or assistant director or other title) of —— program/project at ——." There's just "X has a lot of undocumentable knowledge about this topic." Similarly, for me to blog about a topic, I'm addressing friends who aren't necessarily in the same field and who are probably not all that interested in why Shi'a Islam's support of sex changes is theoretically wonderful but in practice sometimes actually oppressive to women, gay men and transgender people; or a serious consideration of the effect of Facebook, Twitter and even blogging communities like LiveJournal, on composition (as opposed to writing). I could definitely write on those topics and cultivate an audience of like-minded independent and academic scholars, but that again gets into "what right do I have to present my views and perceptions as having merit beyond myself and friends who are hopefully inherently interested (to some extent) in what I think?"

From the way he describes this internal process, it's clear that Ty is not presenting a straightforward assertion that he doesn't have a right to speak in academic contexts. Rather, using scare quotes and other discursive markers, he is conducting an analysis of the feeling itself. As I have argued throughout this book, access is constructed through attitudes as well as physical structures. Attitudes may come directly from others, or may come from the imagined audience to, or for which, one composes. And if the audience Ty imagines is asking questions such as "What right do you have?" it's unsurprising that he feels reluctant to begin the process of inquiry. Throughout our interview, I was repeatedly struck by the fact that Ty and I viewed his work—including work that would meet even the conservative definition of "scholarship" offered by Gross and Gross—quite differently. For example, at one point, when explaining why he doesn't consider most of his writing scholarly, he said, "Most of my knowledge is derived from reading others' work. I do, sometimes, take that a step further in synthesizing that information and posing (and trying to answer) new questions. Yet, ultimately, it feels less like building on others' scholarship and more like simply knowing about it." To me, the process Ty describes—reading others' work, synthesizing it, raising and addressing questions that stem from it—is a textbook (so to speak) definition of scholarly writing. But the key word in his description, I believe, is *feel:* what I or anyone else thinks of his writing matters less than how he feels about it. And this feeling, in turn, sometimes prevents him from beginning potentially scholarly projects, such as editorials or articles.[14]

Interestingly, while Ty does not feel particularly welcome in traditional academic arenas, he does a great deal of work in community-building efforts that combine his skills in service, teaching, and research. His work with Al-Fatiha and True Spirit are two examples; in addition, at his local Unitarian Universalist (UU) congregation he carries out a great range of activities. These have included speaking on interfaith panels; presenting at Nehirim (a Jewish LGBT organization); doing teach-ins on Islam; and serving on many committees, including the UU's new Committee on Gender and Sexual Identities. He is also one of the most active members of the Stonewall Center Speakers Bureau at UMass-Amherst. Ty commented that his work in these arenas feels, in some ways, "more important" than traditional academic work, in the sense that his audiences for such activities "will take the information I offer and use it on the ground, with people in real-life situations." Although community organizing is a different endeavor than academic work, it is striking how similar Ty's chosen responsibilities are to a conventional academic job: teaching, research, and service (and collegiality).

A Way to Move: In/ter/dependent Scholarship

As I researched the history and present status of independent scholarship in the United States, I found myself reminded repeatedly of the tradition's prestigious history and of the importance, for many in this group, of identifying *as* independent. For example, in "The Noble Legacy (and Present Eclipse) of Independent Scholarship," Toni Vogel Carey notes the "inessential role of the university" in the lives of thinkers including Pythagoras, Plato, Aristotle, Jesus, Galileo, Newton, Adam Smith, Jefferson, Darwin, and Einstein (8). And in "An Independent Scholar by Any Other Name," Barbara Currier Bell suggests that the advantages accruing to professors emeriti might "sound familiar" to independent scholars, including (quoting from Richard Wentz) "speak[ing] to the designs of scholarship and education without fear of obsolescence, methodological ostracism, tenure reprisals, salary rebuffs, or other forms of political disdain" (3). Work by independent scholars does acknowledge a level of interdependence, and the existence of groups such as NCIS and CIS indicates that communal efforts are strongly valued. Yet *independent* retains a strong hold, for, as Mark Hineline puts it, otherwise an independent scholar may be considered "the poor cousin of the affiliated academic scholar" (qtd. in Bell, "An Independent Scholar" 3). It is reasonable that independent scholars wish to emphasize their strengths and advantages; this is a group that is undeniably undervalued in conventional academic discourse. Thus independent scholars *are* independent, and often fiercely so; as one independent scholar wrote in his or her response to Sonenschein's survey, "I live in poverty as a result of insisting on doing things my way . . . Doing satisfying intellectual and creative work, however slim, seems to have required this total idiosyncrasy" (51).

However, I'm concerned about the way that disability—and more to the point, conversations about access—may interact with this insistence on "independence." My concern stems in part from the lack of conversation about disability in studies like Sonenschein's 2004 survey: thus far, disability simply does not seem to be on the radar of organized associations of independent scholars. Indeed, the urge to maintain "independence" at times produces direct disavowals of disability. Quoted in Gross and Gross's 1983 study *Independent Scholarship: Promise, Problems, and Prospects,* psychologist Rachel Lauer has this to say:

> I suggest that you [the study authors] avoid any thought or language that creates the image of independent scholars as needy people whose interests must be served by others who are richer or more powerful. For example, I do not like to think of independent scholars as a "lost generation," "wasted people," "embittered, unemployable intellectuals," "human tragedy," "suffering from severe handicaps," "displaced," "unplaceable," "discriminated against, "unable to get or hold a position in academia," etc. I do

> not like for us to see ourselves as one more minority group victimized by the establishment, outsiders looking in, unappreciated and needy, disadvantaged, etc. I do not want to be part of a group, much less identified with a group, which must be "helped, supported, encouraged, recognized, served" by charitable others. As a psychologist in a "helping profession," I have seen far too much damage—dependency, apathy, self-pity, inertia, paranoia, etc.—created by a helper-helpee reciprocity. (34)

In this comment, Lauer acknowledges the marginality of independent scholars, indicating that they are not the "richer or more powerful" members of the academic community. But then the statement quickly moves to conflate this marginality with dependency, and dependency with charity. Lauer's concern about being seen as part of a "displaced" or "unplaceable" group uses repeated metaphors of disability ("handicap," "paranoia") as well as terms often used to devalue disabled people ("embittered," "tragedy," "needy," "self-pity"). In her passionate argument against treating independent scholars as "one more minority group victimized by the establishment," Lauer assumes that marginalization must lead to dependency, and that dependency must be disabling.

However, her assumption rests upon a fallacy: that the counterpart to independence must be *de*-pendence, and that all dependence is disabling. In contrast to Lauer's view, DS engages in active questioning of the concept of "independence," often resisting this notion in favor of some version of interdependence. Tobin Siebers offers a helpful gloss on this perspective:

> A focus on disability provides another perspective by representing human society not as a collection of autonomous beings, some of whom will lose their independence, but as a community of dependent frail bodies that rely on others for survival. Notice that dependence does not figure here as an individual character trait, as in the social contract model, but as a structural component of human society. . . . We depend on other human beings not only at those times when our capacities are diminished but each and every day, and even at those moments when we may be at the height of our physical and mental powers. (*Disability Theory* 182–83)

The essay in which this quote appears, "Disability and the Right to Have Rights," argues for establishment of disability, or "the fragility of the mind and body" (183), as the theoretical cornerstone of human rights. While Western liberal traditions of thought posit that humans ought to have rights because of their prowess as individuals—whether that prowess is framed as being a "rational" thinker (Aristotle 1098a) or a "good man skilled in speaking" (Quintilian) or as having a "self-reliant" and "private" heart (Emerson 259)—Siebers upends this deep-seated ideology to suggest that humans ought to have rights precisely because of our *lack* of wholeness, our fragilities, our very dependence upon one another.[15]

As Siebers and other DS scholars have argued, the counterpart to independence could well be understood as *inter*-dependence, and could be seen as enabling—even empowering.[16] Moreover—and more salient to the present study—Lauer's stance on the rhetorical position of an independent scholar disavows the possibility that such scholars might be *systematically* denied access to full participation in academic spaces such as classrooms, conferences, or university presses. Here again, we see the rhetoric of "choice": if one does not teach for pay, the assumption goes, one must have chosen not to do so. However, given the inaccessibility of teaching (and speaking, and writing) spaces available in academe, it becomes evident that avoidance of these spaces may be a survival strategy rather than a true choice. That is, it may be a "choice" only in the sense of Hobson's choice—the refusal of an intolerable option.

Numerous calls for ways to revalue independent scholarship have come from both inside and outside academe. For example, in *The Independent Scholar,* Stephen Shapiro has proposed the formation of "microcolleges," institutions formed by small groups of independent scholars and run as nonprofits (47). In the *Chronicle of Higher Education,* Elizabeth Welt Trahan has called for foundations and professional organizations to include a category for independent scholars in their grant applications, and to include independent scholars on their review boards. Some professional organizations have responded to the calls. The Modern Language Association offers a book prize dedicated to works produced by independent scholars, and *Disability Studies Quarterly* recently established itself as one of the few fully open-access peer-reviewed journals. Other journals such as *Kairos* have been open-access from their beginning. I am heartened by these moves, but insist that much work remains to be done. This work must be an interdependent effort, coming from communities of independent scholars, academic institutions, and individuals who are not affiliated with organizations. In his final reflections on this chapter, Ty made a similar argument, in words more eloquent than I could muster:

> When I finished reading, I was thinking about the fact that our (or at least my) lack of academic affiliation is a factor in participating in a study like this, where disability and challenges are being discussed frankly. It seems a little like the SSDI/SSI catch-22: if I were affiliated with a university, I'm not sure I'd be as willing to put vulnerable information about my challenges out there for public—especially professional peer—digestion. The availability of that information to academic employers and peers could (to use Cal's great semantic distinction) create a disability (i.e., an imposed barrier) out of a limitation. Yet it also seems crucial for this kind of information to be available so that accessibility can be improved.

Conclusion

Mental disabilities permeate our cultural landscape with frequency and intensity. On network television, we have Monk, who has obsessive-compulsive disorder, and House, who commits himself to a psychiatric hospital at the close of the show's fifth season. On premium cable, there's Showtime's *The United States of Tara,* whose protagonist is a housewife with dissociative identity disorder (DID); meanwhile, on HBO, *In Treatment* depicts a therapist's sessions with his clients, including a traumatized fighter pilot and a suicidal gymnast, while the therapist himself has a panic attack at one point. In the nonfictional world of celebrities, Kirsten Dunst, Brooke Shields, and Halle Berry have announced that they have depression, while Axl Rose has discussed his bipolar disorder, and Herschel Walker has published a book about having DID. The onrush of attention to mental disability goes beyond the world of television and celebrities, entering the academic realm as well. Books such as *Rampage: The Social Roots of School Shootings* and *Binge: What Your College Student Won't Tell You* proliferate on bookstore shelves, and a recent study by Richard D. Kadison and Theresa Foy DiGeronimo announces in its title that we are experiencing a "campus mental health crisis."

Kadison and DiGeronimo's *College of the Overwhelmed: The Campus Mental Health Crisis and What to Do About It* is one of the more measured of recent publications on this newly discovered "crisis." Sensibly, the authors recommend that parents take steps such as evaluating schools' mental health programs as carefully as they would examine "inadequate chemistry labs or athletic facilities" (201); they also encourage students not to regard mental distress as "a personal weakness or character flaw" (232). While much of what appears in *College of the Overwhelmed* is simply common sense, its practical tone is a welcome change from alarmist screeds that seek to diagnose "nutters" or "whack jobs" in order to bar them from the classroom. Mental disability should no longer be considered the affliction of an aberrant few, but a regular feature of our contemporary culture.

Despite this encouraging sign, and despite the glut of information on mental disability in popular and academic culture, we are still missing a careful examination of the ways that higher education clings to the notion that mental disability *must* be an aberration, something that emerges only rarely and, when it does emerge, should be stifled or expunged as quickly as possible. In this book, I have investigated the ways that mental disability is cast out of academic discourse—sometimes by rhetorical means as subtle as our educational debt to Cicero's "right reason," sometimes by means as blatant as the refusal to accommodate students with mental illnesses in college classrooms. Often, the instruments of oppression are difficult to discern because they are simply the way academic life operates "normally": of course students should come to class; of course scholars should stand and deliver their research in front of groups (in a "collegial" manner); of course it's okay to use terms like *idiot, crazy,* or even *academic psycho-killer. Mad at School* is a rhetorical study because I am fascinated by the ways that rhetoric can affect (and effect) relations of power, but also because I am heartened by the belief that attention to rhetoric gives us opportunities to intervene in systems of oppression and change those systems for the better.

This book is intended to begin a conversation, not to serve as the final or authoritative word on mental disability in academe. As I wrote, I came across many research questions and topics that I hope will be taken up by similarly interested researchers. These include the following:

- The intersectional operation of mental disability with factors including class, race, gender, and sexuality. Race and mental disability, for example, is an extraordinarily rich area for continued rhetorical work. Anna Stubblefield's impassioned "The Entanglement of Race and Cognitive Disability" points out that black Americans are overrepresented in diagnoses of cognitive disability, yet underrepresented in inclusive education and support services. Stubblefield's response is that we ought to "dispense with cognitive ability labeling" (533). I admire her conviction, although I am not persuaded this is the best course of action, given my belief in naming—and even diagnosis, sometimes—to empower individual persons and pave a way toward liberation. But

I am hesitant making this argument, and know that much more work is needed in this area, as well as in many other areas that address the intersection of mental disabilities with other identity markers and labels.

- Postcolonial and transnational studies of madness, violence, and "terrorism." At the 2009 Society for Disability Studies conference, I was inspired to hear Shaista Patel speak on the construction of the "Brown Muslim body as 'mentally ill.'" Patel argues:

> I am concerned with grasping how the category of madness is invoked today, specifically in the post-9/11 geopolitical context of the "West." What is this invoking of "mental illness" doing in order to render the body of the so-called terrorist as knowable? What are the cultural implications of the act of questioning the category of madness?

The overlaps between colonialism, nation, race, and mental disability are tremendously complex and, so far, not studied nearly enough. A welcome exception is a 2007 special issue of *Wagadu,* edited by Pushpa Parekh and including a range of articles that address gendered and postcolonial perspectives on disability, including James Overboe's "Vitalism: Subjectivity Exceeding Racism, Sexism, and (Psychiatric) Ableism." Another welcome exception is Ethan Watters's *Crazy Like Us: The Globalization of the American Psyche,* which argues that American technologies of mental illness, and DSM in particular, force Western paradigms of disability and "illness" on all cultures and nations.

- The uneasy relationship between queer and crip identities. Robert McRuer's *Crip Theory* provides a groundbreaking foray into this issue, but further research is needed, especially as it pertains to the intersection of mental disability and queer identity. To be queer (or, more exactly, "homosexual") was, until 1973, classified as a mental illness by the *Diagnostic and Statistical Manual of Mental Disorders.* In the current revision of DSM, "Gender Identity Disorder" (GID) occupies a range of diagnostic spaces, and while this classification as a mental disorder is viewed by some as stigmatizing and oppressive, at the same time

> it can provide a path to access. Persons diagnosed with GID may be able to access needed medical treatments, including hormone therapy and surgeries. This is the case because some health care providers will not provide treatment without first making a GID diagnosis, and because the few insurance companies that do cover sex reassignment treatments often make such coverage contingent upon a GID diagnosis. Moreover, courts have ruled in favor of transgender litigants, including youth and prisoners, when their GID diagnosis is presented as a "legitimate" medical condition for which treatment is medically necessary.

Writing this book has brought me into the wildly divergent and often conflictual worlds of Mad Pride, the *Journal of Orthopsychiatry,* life writing on intellectual disability, and the International Conference on Human-Computer Interaction. Often I have felt like an outsider, unqualified to participate in a given space; just as often, I have felt like too much of an insider, someone whose personal history with mental disability might cloud my judgment and make of me an overly biased apologist. My own disciplinary homes, rhetoric/composition and disability studies, have sustained me, because both disciplines are filled with people who care deeply about access, about what it means when theory lurches into life, about how to teach and communicate and learn. Also sustaining me have been the constant reminders that the questions I am raising *need* to be raised. This work has brought me into contact with students and colleagues, friends and family, near-strangers on listservs and complete strangers represented in popular media, all recognizing that mental disability is an important part of schooling, and that attention must be paid.

I am afraid. I'm afraid that the attention paid will wind up reinforcing the powerful forces that wish to expel persons with mental disabilities from academic discourse. But I am also hopeful—equally hopeful, maybe even a little bit more hopeful. My hope is that persons with mental disabilities will remain a part of academe, as we have been for thousands of years, and that deeper understanding of our abilities and limitations, our place in the human world, might reshape academic culture.

If academic discourses—especially kairotic spaces—are revised to become more accessible for people with mental disabilities, it will create changes that have been needed for a long time. For all its lofty and egalitarian ideals, American academic culture generally operates as a "rich get richer" system, using grades, tenure, and rankings (of persons as well as institutions) to construct and further its workings (Rhode). Calls for change to this system have been many. I argue that strong and thoughtful attention to mental disability in academic culture—*not* as a deficit or problem to be solved, but as a potentially rich source of knowledge—can help in this project. If we take access for mental disabilities seriously, we cannot help but consider changes such as greater reliance on structural collegiality (Philip Lewis); a proliferation of academic jobs beyond the conventional research-teaching-service triad; more flexible classroom structures; vigorous questioning of the ways that mental dis/ability is policed; and, in general, broader possibilities for the pace, structure, and content of our academic "productivity." For quite some time people have been saying, "There are a lot of things wrong with the current academic climate"; the changes I am calling for are ones that can help redress some of these problems.

If we wish to change the educational system, we will need all our minds.

Appendix A

Course Objectives with Space for Annotation (English 286, "Investigation," Spring 2008)

Your thoughts on this objective (January)	*Your thoughts on this objective (April)*	*Objective*
		Identify an issue that you perceive to be important and underexplored. Shape your thoughts on this issue into a clear, focused research question.
		Identify audiences and publications for whom your research question is relevant.
		Gather and evaluate appropriate evidence through various methods, including textual research, interviews, and observation.
		Analyze evidence by means of methods including textual analysis, coding, or thematic grouping.
		Develop and articulate a considered stance (thesis) stemming from your research question.
		Incorporate evidence effectively into your writing, with attention to audience, genre, ethical and stylistic considerations, and accurate citation.
		Write up research in styles appropriate for various genres/contexts, including academic and journalistic.

Appendix B

Instructions on Annotation

"To annotate" means to write on something as you read it. I will construe "write" broadly: in other words, *annotation* may or may not mean physically placing pen to page. If you would like to use an alternative method, such as tape-recording your thoughts as you read, please let me know so we can set up a way for me to access your annotations.

The purpose of annotating is to record your own ideas, questions, and interpretations as you read. That way, you won't look at something a few weeks after reading it and wonder, "What was this about again? What did I think of it?"

Annotation is one of the best strategies you can use as a student—or a reader of any text—to get the maximum possible "bang for your buck." You'll develop your own method as you get more experienced in annotation. If you would like a step-by-step method, try this one:

- *What is my response to each paragraph?* Responses can be paraphrases, comments, or questions. Record your thoughts as you read—at least a few lines per paragraph. It's fine if a "thought" is somewhat unformed, such as "I don't get this." (Try to include some information about exactly what you don't get, or why you don't get it. Is the language getting in the way? Is the author referring to other works, people, or ideas you aren't familiar with? Do you disagree with what's being said, and/or have an alternate interpretation?)
- *What are the author's sources of evidence?* Note them as you go along.

- *How does the author structure this article?* Note structural cues as you go along. (For example, "The analysis of this topic can be divided into two parts." Or, "First I discuss . . . then I discuss . . .")
- When you've finished, *write a two- or three-sentence summary* of the article. My personal preference is to write this somewhere on the first page, so I can easily see it when I look back at the article.
- *What is the thesis or major argument of this article?* Write a paraphrase (not a quote!).
- Finally, if you haven't already written down some *questions*, list two or three questions the article inspires you to ask.

Notes

Introduction

1. Interestingly, stories of encounters with mentally ill persons often take place on public transportation. This is ironic in view of the fact that public transit is notoriously inaccessible to persons with disabilities—and, although general opinion may not recognize it, this includes persons with mental disabilities. For an account of the problem and accommodation suggestions, see "Getting There: Helping People with Mental Illnesses Access Transportation," www.samhsa.gov.

2. The supposed relationship between mental illness and violent behavior has been copiously studied. A review of the literature over the last decade or so indicates that the most significant risk factors for violent behavior include "demographic characteristics, socioeconomic status, [and] past violence," while "psychiatric symptoms such as delusional beliefs are relatively weak or inconsistent predictors" (Skeem et al.). However, the commonsense link between mental disability and violence not only remains firm, but is actually strengthening. In their study of mental health policy in the United States since 1950, Richard G. Frank and Sherry A. Glied found that the percentage of people who perceived a link between mental illness and violent behavior nearly doubled between 1950 and 1996, from 7.2 to 12.1 percent (136–37). The madness-violence relationship is discussed at more length in chapter 4.

3. Chapter 1 examines in detail the economic, social, and political structures that have motivated various revisions of DSM.

4. My definition of "academic discourse" draws upon the theories of Michel Foucault, James Paul Gee, and Norman Fairclough, and is elaborated more fully in chapter 1. Briefly, I understand academic discourse to be the languages, symbols, genres, practices, and ways of knowing that govern relations of power and knowledge in spaces of learning. For the purposes of this book, the "spaces of learning" examined are mainly those of U.S. higher education. Although I generally refer to "academic discourse" in the singular, it should be understood that academic discourse is not monolithic; it is an interconnected web of discourses, and overlaps with various other discourses, including medical discourse.

5. I am indebted to the members of the DS_RHET-COMP listserv, especially Cynthia Lewiecki-Wilson, for helping me work out the connection between topoi and rhetorics of mental disability.

6. Within this 46 percent, the most common disorders were alcohol use disorders (20 percent), followed by personality disorders (18 percent), anxiety disorders (12 percent), and mood disorders (11 percent).

7. Although this rise has sensationally been labeled an "epidemic," in fact it may simply be an "epidemic of discovery" (Grinker 37). The increase in diagnoses has been closely studied and appears to be due to a number of factors, including legislation that led to extensive mainstreaming of students with various kinds of disabilities; the 1990 addition of a specific category to identify autism-spectrum disorders within special education (Shattuck); and the potential for social networks to influence whether or not a child is identified as autistic (Liu, King, and Bearman).

8. See Christensen; Dajani; Linton, chap. 2; Titchkosky, "Disability"; Trent, introduction; and Zola.

9. I use the term *bodymind* to emphasize that although "body" and "mind" usually occupy separate conceptual and linguistic territories, they are deeply intertwined. This theory is drawn in part from Babette Rothschild's *The Body Remembers.* Although Rothschild's usage refers to persons who have experienced trauma, I believe it can be usefully applied to persons with mental disabilities of all kinds, for—as I argue throughout this book—our problems are in no sense "all in our minds." If it weren't so unwieldy, I would be tempted to use something like *psychobiosocialpoliticalbodymind.*

10. Just as this book was going to press, the autism clock was removed from the website. When I wrote to inquire, I received a notice that it has "been brought to our attention that the autism clock was offensive to some members of the autism community." In addition, the domain name of the website was changed from fightingautism.org to thoughtfulhouse.org. While limited, these measures indicate that the hard work of neurodiverse activists is being noticed.

11. *Stimming,* short for "self-stimulating," is a self-soothing repetitive activity that may be practiced by persons with a variety of disabilities, including autism, obsessive-compulsive disorder, or anxiety.

12. For more on the apparitional nature of mental disabilities, see Montgomery, "Critic of the Dawn" and "A Hard Look at Invisible Disability," and Samuels. For more on the apparitional nature of disability and illness generally, see Myers, "Coming Out" and Siebers, "Disability as Masquerade."

Chapter 1

1. Facilitated communication (FC) is a method of linguistic support that fosters the communicative abilities of persons who do not use more conventional communication methods, such as oral speech, signed language, or writing. Often, these are persons with cognitive or psychiatric disabilities. The Facilitated Communication Institute at Syracuse University explains that FC "entails learning to communicate by typing on a keyboard or pointing at letters, images, or other symbols to represent messages. Facilitated communication involves a combination of physical and emotional support to an individual who has difficulties with speech and with intentional pointing (i.e., unassisted typing)." Further informa-

tion is available from sources including the Institute on Communication and Inclusion at Syracuse University.

2. In CDA, *text* is often construed broadly to mean something akin to "communicative practice." For example, Gunther Kress and Theo van Leeuwen have conducted extensive discourse analyses of images, websites, and other multimodal forms of discourse. Fairclough's own analyses are usually linguistic.

3. See Linton's *Claiming Disability,* chap. 2 ("Reassigning Meaning"), for a fuller discussion of the ways that these and other linguistic features affect the construction of disability through discourse.

4. For an insightful analysis of the "good man speaking well" in terms of Deaf politics, see Brueggemann's *Lend Me Your Ear.*

5. Periodically, revisions of editions appear; for instance, DSM-III-R (3rd ed., revised) was published in 1987, and DSM-IV-TR (4th ed., text revision) was published in 2000.

6. Critiques of DSM-IV have followed. For example, Marie Crowe argues that DSM-IV constructs an implicit standard of normality based upon four unstated criteria: productivity, unity, moderation, and rationality.

7. Rosemarie Garland-Thomson's *Staring: How We Look* discusses in detail the ways that the power relations of "the gaze" are transformed when one considers the power of the gazed-upon subject to stare back.

8. Although Ellsworth does not reference disability in this passage, her article acknowledges disability as another factor that disrupts the presumption of the "reasonable" classroom subject (300).

9. As the following discussion shows, rhetorical studies are rife with metaphors based upon sensory abilities, particularly seeing and hearing. To the extent possible, I have tried to use language such as "perceive" or "receive"; where I use terms such as "listen" or "race-blind," these usually come from the author under discussion. Further discussion of the habit of conflating sensory ability with knowledge can be found in Vidali, "Seeing What We Know."

10. While Lee's study focuses primarily on classroom discourse, Ratcliffe's examines arenas including public debate and scholarly writing as well as classroom exchanges.

11. This concern is also addressed in chapter 4, which focuses on school shootings.

12. I elaborate the significance of the nondisabled "view from nowhere" in "Accessing Disability."

13. Aided by the insights of Melanie Yergeau, described below, I have begun to think of this aspect of teacherly discourse as "the reveal." For example, in "From Trauma to Writing," Marian M. MacCurdy introduces a student as follows: "[A] tall, handsome, but mute young man sat with his arms crossed in my classroom for weeks without saying a word—to me or to anyone else . . . In office hours, he finally told me what was troubling him" (177). During this revelation, which turned out to be the death of a sibling, "he stared at me with brittle eyes" (177). In the same volume, an article titled "Writing about Suicide" indicates that the teacher of a course, Jeffrey Berman, "sought to determine the identity of the

unknown diarist" from a class titled "Literary Suicide" in order to see if the student would be willing to coauthor an essay exploring the issue further (Berman and Schiff 294). I do not dispute the authors' claims that writing can have healing properties for students with mental disabilities, and I applaud Berman's desire to coauthor with his student rather than simply render him as a character in the article. However, I also want to call attention to the rather avid energy with which we, as teacher-scholars, seem to seek out these students, to identify or diagnose them, and the regularity with which we fail to identify or diagnose ourselves. It seems to me that, at times, our efforts to "listen" are in fact a form of nonconsensual fetishization. While this is not always the case, I am troubled by how seldom teacher-scholars writing on mental disability even pause to consider this possibility.

14. For further discussion of the problem now commonly referred to in minority studies as "add-and-stir," see Erevelles, "In Search of the Disabled Subject"; Harding; Martin.

Chapter 2

1. This statement is meant to indicate the *general* habit of educational studies to omit mental disability; by no means is it unqualified. Studies and narratives that do focus on mental disability are included below.

2. I discuss online learning spaces in the next section, "Participation."

3. It should be noted that the NEO PI-R is designed for use on individuals without "overt pathopsychology" (Costa and McCrae). However, a critique of it in terms of mental disability remains relevant, for its very design is rooted in the notion that humans can be divided into two camps: the "normals" and those with "psychopathology." In other words, the instrument reinforces an individualized and medicalized model of disability while also claiming to leave disability out of the equation.

4. Tobin Siebers has explored in depth the problems of presuming that persons with disabilities are narcissistic in the article "Tender Organs, Narcissism, and Identity Politics."

5. For the purposes of this chapter, I am referring to "participation" as what takes place once a student enters the classroom, whether virtually or physically. In some educational literature, "participation" is used to refer to whether students actually come to class or not—an issue I have identified as "presence."

6. Feldmann's study was published in fall 2001, and hence predates the new discursive aura that has arisen around *terrorism* since September 11, 2001; it also predates the mass shootings at Virginia Tech (2007), Northern Illinois University (2008), and the U of Alabama–Huntsville (2010). I discuss the recent emphasis on violence in academic discourse in chapter 4.

7. Although not cited by Nussbaum et al., many works explore the possibilities of listening, agreement, and locating common ground in the classroom. Examples include *Teaching Community: A Pedagogy of Hope* (bell hooks) and *Rhetorical Listening: Identification, Gender, Whiteness* (Krista Ratcliffe).

8. I am grateful to Timile Brown for reading and commenting upon this chapter, including my account of her, which has been revised in response to her feedback.

9. I give full credence to Timile's account, but also note that I have had different experiences with this school's support services, and have served as a member of its Office of Disability Services Community of Practice. My efforts to foster greater recognition and more effective accommodations for students with mental disabilities have been met with interest and concrete efforts. I also note that my privilege as a faculty member may be a factor in the differences between my and Timile's experiences.

10. I have elaborated further on the value of "overcoming" stories as potential gestures of agency by students with disabilities in the article "Disability Studies Methodology."

11. Although Adam J. Banks's *Race, Rhetoric and Technology* does not engage disability directly, his multidimensional theory of access and approach to design as an emancipatory practice offer important insights for all teachers, especially those interested in accessible classroom design.

12. Disclosure is highly charged and complex. Other aspects of disclosure are addressed in the introduction, which discusses language and terminology, and chapter 3, which discusses disclosure from the faculty member's point of view. Further rhetorical consideration of this issue as it pertains to students is available from Amy Vidali's qualitative study "Rhetorical Hiccups: Disability Disclosure in Letters of Recommendation," which focuses on an unusual data set: letters of recommendation written on behalf of a student with a traumatic brain injury.

13. Sometimes an unfamiliar mode will lead to humorous exchanges. For example, I once exchanged a couple of text messages with a student who was searching for the room where her final project had been stored. I gave her directions, then walked into our classroom two days later to find her regaling a group of her peers with the tale of what it was like to receive a TM from a professor: "It was like getting a text message from *Moses.*" Although I enjoy being compared to Moses, I also look forward to the day when my TMs with students are seen as a more ordinary part of our communication together.

14. When I was taking tenth-grade chemistry (and struggling miserably), my teacher, Francis Broadway, gave us an unexpected assignment: "Illustrate Le Chatelier's Principle in a short story." Le Chatelier's Principle states, basically, that a system at equilibrium, when subjected to a change, will reach a new and different equilibrium. I received an A+ on my story (and a C in the class). More to the point, I cannot describe how affirmed I felt by this assignment, and the fact that I was able to perform it successfully. Perhaps even more to the point, I still remember—twenty-five years later—the name of the principle and what it means.

15. See also Dunn's cowritten webtext with Kathleen Dunn De Mers, "Reversing Notions of Disability and Accommodation." This article provides many examples of multimodal exercises as well as a section on accessible web design.

16. This device is called a frequency-modulation (FM) microphone.

Chapter 3

1. The official press release announcing this measure may or may not be indicative of the Bush administration's general attitude toward disability rights. However, it is interesting to note that the release, titled "President Bush Signs S. 3406 into Law," is one sentence long. By contrast, a proclamation made on the following day, to designate September 27 "National Hunting and Fishing Day," is six paragraphs long.

2. Carol Moeller has written and spoken insightfully about the intersections of "productivity" with academic discourse and mental disability. One such presentation was "'Psychiatric'/Psycho-Social Disabilities for Critical Consciousness: Human Costs of 'Productivity' and 'Speed,'" presented at the Society for Disability Studies Conference in 2009.

3. I discuss this commonsense belief in more detail in chapter 4.

4. Based on my own anecdotal experience, I have found that students are more likely to be amenable to this suggestion than are faculty colleagues. However, I have had successful meetings with both students and colleagues via instant-message. The impact of instant-messaging in workplace environments, including academic spaces, is receiving increasing attention. Examples include the several contributions to the panel "I Think, Therefore IM" from the 2002 Conference on Human Factors in Computing Systems, as well as Joseph M. McCarthy and danah m. boyd's research on the use of a "chat" program at an academic conference (discussed in more detail below). There is also a long-standing stream of research in educational disciplines, including rhetoric and composition, regarding the use of online synchronous communication ("chat") in the classroom, an issue discussed at more length in chapter 2.

5. The Affordable Care Act, signed in March 2010, is designed to prevent denial of coverage based on pre-existing conditions: for children starting in 2010, and for adults starting in 2014.

6. Lecturers at the University of Michigan have since unionized, and have won significant gains. See http://www.leounion.org for more information.

7. I leave "violent behavior" aside for now, although I note the familiar way it is coupled with mental illness. Chapter 4 addresses the supposed link between mental disability and violence in detail.

8. A similar rhetorical separation often occurs when the topic is students with mental disabilities; see chapters 2 and 4 for more discussion of this phenomenon.

9. An extended discussion of SDS access efforts, including the materials access center and the personal assistance service, appears in "Making Conferences Accessible: Experiences from 1995 SDS" by Susan Stoddard, Devva Kasnitz, and Lisa Wahl. Further commentary on SDS accessibility appears in chapter 6.

10. SDS is not experienced so positively by all persons. Cal Montgomery, whose work is discussed further in chapter 6, has called SDS an "access nightmare." In addition, each annual meeting of SDS is regularly followed by discussion on its listserv of various access problems that occurred. However, the very existence of such conversations, which are usually absent from other professional societies' discussions of conferences, is encouraging.

11. The APHA publishes a different "Accessibility Guide" each year for its annual conference. The version used in this study was the 2007 guide for a meeting taking place in Washington, DC.

12. This assumption that the agonistic exchange is a key—even the only—path to knowledge is often reflected in pedagogical as well as conference designs. I discuss its application in pedagogical designs in chapter 2.

13. For a more detailed description of proactive displays, see McDonald et al., "Proactive Displays."

14. In the six years between the "backchannel" experiment and this book's publication, the emergence of Twitter has created a digital backchannel at virtually every academic conference. Some conferences, including the Conference on College Composition and Communication, establish a hashtag and display the feed at the conference.

15. Actual numbers are no doubt higher than reported numbers. However, it's pretty evident that faculty with disabilities are underrepresented. Moreover, as discussed in more detail below, the low reportage rate indicates other possible concerns, including fear of disclosure.

16. In the final chapter of *Moving Beyond Prozac, DSM, and the New Psychiatry,* "Epilogue: Postpsychiatry Today," Bradley Lewis offers a similar pragmatic and paradigmatic sketch of ways to change the discipline and profession of psychiatry, arguing that smaller "strategic efforts" can effect immediate change while also "lay[ing] the groundwork for a future larger-scale paradigm switch" (165).

17. In 2008, Sean P. Murphy published an edited collection of ethnographies by instructors at teaching-intensive schools (*Academic Cultures: Professional Preparation and the Teaching Life*). Murphy's introduction cites the Carnegie Foundation for the Advancement of Teaching classification, which reported in 2005 that, of the 4,382 schools it counted, only 278 (about 6 percent) were classified as "research university"; the remaining 94 percent were classified as "associate's colleges, master's colleges and universities, baccalaureate colleges, special focus institutions, tribal colleges, and other institutions" (8). Murphy argues that we should value this diversity in higher-education employment, rather than consider it "a problem to redress," and that we should better prepare graduate students to make choices in the current academic culture, rather than pretend that everyone is headed toward—or would prefer—a research-intensive job (7–9).

Chapter 4

1. Since these two highly publicized events, more mass attacks have occurred in the United States, some of them in academic settings. The shootings by Amy Bishop at the University of Alabama–Huntsville (UAH) occurred as this book was going to press. A bit earlier, in April 2009, seventeen people were shot at the American Civic Association in Binghamton, New York, by "Vietnamese immigrant" Jiverly Wong (McFadden). The politics of stigmatization, especially along lines of disability and race, continue to unfold. For example, shortly after

the UAH shootings, a commenter, posting under the name "mainiac" on a blog sponsored by the *Chronicle of Higher Education,* referred to "ACADEMIC PSYCHO-KILLERS." And shortly after the shootings at the American Civic Association, a website with the domain name jiverlywong.com was launched, with the apparent purpose of publicizing hate speech about Wong. One of the "email comments" printed on the site read, "Herro, My name is Jiverly Wong, can please herp me rearn engrish so people stop raughing at me, STOP RAUGHING AT ME." As of this writing, jiverlywong.com has been taken down; the "ACADEMIC PSYCHO-KILLERS" comment remains.

2. I am grateful for the comments on this chapter by an anonymous reader from the Virginia Tech faculty, as well as for "insider" accounts like Kathleen Jones's and Patricia Mooney Nickel's. Such responses and accounts have helped me work through many questions and concerns while working on this chapter. Like Nickel, I believe that "organizational life, including academia, disguises normative violence as personal failure" (175; see also Butler, *Precarious Life*). Consideration of the normative violence that surrounds sudden violent events may help bring needed change to our educational institutions. However, narratives of individual blame, mythologies of mad violence, and elaborate "preparedness" scenarios will not.

3. This phenomenon is not confined to school shootings. For example, in August 2008 the *New York Times* published an article headlined "In Anthrax Scientist's E-mail, Hints of Delusions." The article acknowledges that the scientist in question, Bruce E. Ivins, had not yet been convicted of the crime of sending anthrax through the mail and killing five people in 2001, but immediately adds, "The messages do, however, show that Dr. Ivins privately confided to an unidentified co-worker that he was deeply troubled" (Lipton).

4. Tanya Titchkosky has commented insightfully on the ways that headlines direct the attention of their audiences: headlines, according to Titchkosky, "explicitly participate in *governing* our ways of noticing, taking interest in something, and explaining it" (*Reading* 120). This study is indebted to her careful analysis of both popular media and governmental reports in *Reading & Writing Disability Differently.*

5. Although outside the scope of this chapter, it should be noted that similar moves, particularly in reference to the intersectional operation of madness, race, and nationality, have been made in popular media accounts of Muslim "terrorists." Shaista Patel has pointed out that in such accounts "the bounded space of the nation, as a vulnerable nation, is produced in relation to the body of the 'insane terrorist' who has crossed the borders and is now amidst the bodies which must be protected."

6. For more on the use of darkness and goth imagery to stigmatize school shooters, with specific focus on the Columbine High School shootings, see Berres, "Everybody is their Enemy."

7. Other sources that address this inequity, in addition to Patterson, are Michael Eric Dyson's "Uglier Than Meets the Eye" (*Chicago Sun-Times*) and the film *Tough Guise: Violence, Media & the Crisis in Masculinity,* directed by Sut Jhally (Media Education Foundation).

8. Large-scale studies have confirmed that there is a significant gap between the number of college students with mental disabilities and the number who seek treatment. Blanco et al. found, in a 2008 analysis of the National Epidemiologic Survey on Alcohol and Related Conditions (numbering over 43,000 respondents), that about 46 percent of college-attending individuals reported having had a psychiatric disorder in the year prior to data collection. Yet fewer than 25 percent overall had sought treatment in that year.

9. See the next section for a discussion of research on the possible link between mental illness and violence.

10. A less extreme stance has been proposed by some in the social-work and public-health fields: self-reporting by students with mental disabilities. Researcher Anna Scheyett is in the process of conducting a study of students at the University of North Carolina Chapel Hill who have completed "advance directives" regarding their mental health. An advance directive is a document, not unlike a living will, that allows one to record instructions for future mental-health care or to name a proxy who can serve as decision-maker if one experiences an "incapacitating psychiatric crisis" (Elbogen et al. 274). Whether or not such directives will be used in ways that respect their authors' civil rights remains to be seen.

11. A recent study that examines such perceptions, and reviews much of the relevant literature, is *Better but Not Well: Mental Health Policy in the United States Since 1950* by Richard G. Frank and Sherry A. Glied, especially chapter 7, "Assessing the Well-Being of People with Mental Illness." Studies that focus on media depictions include "Media Depictions of Mental Illness: An Analysis of the Use of Dangerousness" by Ruth Allen and Raymond G. Nairn, and "People Never See Us Living Well: An Appraisal of the Personal Stories about Mental Illness in a Prospective Print Media Sample" by Raymond G. Nairn and John H. Coverdale.

12. The "ECA study" is Swanson et al., "Violence and Psychiatric Disorder in the Community."

13. Patricia Mooney Nickel astutely points out that, in an atmosphere of normative violence (Butler), everyday traumas may become more evident when a highly visible shared trauma has just occurred. In the days and weeks following the shooting at Virginia Tech, she writes, "Suddenly I heard from varying VT faculty members about heartbreak, stress, guilt, rage, difficulties sleeping, financial troubles, over-medication, alcoholism, extramarital affairs, fatigue, and career suicide; none of these expressions of pain were specifically related to the shootings, but were instead preexisting—only the permission to discuss them was new" (170).

14. Although "academic" and "creative" writing are arguably separate domains, in this situation they come together, as the topic of concern is students and teachers in creative writing classrooms.

15. See Miller, "Fault Lines in the Contact Zone" (1994) and "The Nervous System" (1997).

16. Miller's extended meditation on the U.S. "war on terror" as it relates to campus shootings invites consideration of another point that went largely un-

acknowledged in the many representations of the events at Virginia Tech and NIU: that the literal wars being waged by the United States are exacting a heavy price, not only in lives and physical injuries, but in mental wounds as well. In 2004, the *New England Journal of Medicine* published an article titled "Combat Duty in Iraq and Afghanistan, Mental Health Problems, and Barriers to Care" that found that members of U.S. combat infantry units returned from duty in Iraq and Afghanistan with extraordinarily high rates of major depression, generalized anxiety, and PTSD. The study also found significant barriers to care, including stigmatization (Hoge et al.). In 2007, two veterans' groups filed suit against the Department of Veterans Affairs alleging inadequate care. Among the evidence presented in the trial was an email written by Ira Katz, the VA's mental health director, which read in part, "Shh! Our suicide prevention coordinators are identifying about 1000 suicide attempts per month among the veterans we see in our medical facilities. Is this something we should (carefully) address ourselves in some sort of release before someone stumbles on it?" (Leopold). U.S. district judge Samuel Conti heard and eventually dismissed the case on the grounds that there was no existing consensus on what "timely" processing of benefits and care should mean. As of this writing, the veterans' groups have filed an appeal.

Chapter 5

1. Examples include Janz; Mintz; Miner; Rimmon-Kenan; and Garland-Thomson, "Shape Structures Story."

2. I refer to each text's author-narrator by authorial name, although, as I will show, each works that hyphen in her own way.

3. Visual structure is an important part of some of the works discussed; in block quotations, I have included double paragraph breaks, typefaces, and symbols as the authors use them.

4. As Slater elaborates her metaphorical choice, noting that her past diagnoses have included BPD, PTSD, bipolar disorder, OCD, depression, and Munchausen's, she also expresses an apparent revulsion for having once been diagnosed with autism: "Doctors saw [my symptoms] . . . once, even, as autism. Autism!" (220). I do not share or condone this perspective.

5. None of the works studied here uses the gender-subversive third-person pronoun *ze;* however, gender-subversive pronouns including *ze* and *hir* are a rich area for future work in discourse analysis and disability studies.

6. The author's website states, "I have an alter ego named Susanne Antonetta, who writes much of the prose." www.suzannepaola.com.

7. These works include *Prozac Diary* (1999) and *Love Works Like This* (2002), and *Opening Skinner's Box* (2004).

Chapter 6

1. I want to express my deep thanks to Barbara Currier Bell and Katalin Kádár Lynn, both of whom patiently answered my questions and sent me materials.

2. This has also raised a number of important questions regarding the ethics

of this study. Please see the section "Disability Studies Methodology" for more discussion of my efforts to conduct this study of "intimate others" (Ellis, "Telling Secrets") in a mindful and ethical way.

3. In one of our conversations about this chapter, Cal pointed out that this paradox exists for students as well as employees: "There are interesting parallels here with people who have IQ scores in the 'low-normal' (70–85) range. Either they aren't really disabled and they do not qualify for accommodations, or they are really disabled but in a way that means they don't qualify as students."

4. Longmore did obtain a tenure-track job, and before his death in August 2010, held the rank of full professor at San Francisco State University. However, he emphasizes that his story should not be seen as an "overcoming" narrative (which he succinctly calls "individualistic claptrap") but rather the result of "the *political* tenacity and perseverance of our disability community" (257).

5. In fact, Kessler said, his team's estimate was "probably conservative" because the survey from which they drew their findings, the National Comorbidity Survey Replication (NCS-R), did not include participants in prisons or hospitals, and included "very few" with autism or schizophrenia (NIMH, "Mental Disorders").

6. Both *independent scholar* and *mental disability* are terms I brought to the study. The participants have their own ways of naming and identifying themselves, which are discussed below.

7. The fact that we're all white and queer was a coincidental rather than an intentional feature of the study. However, it is an important limitation to note. Toni Morrison has said that whiteness in the American literary imagination tends to function as "mute, meaningless, unfathomable, pointless, frozen, veiled, curtained, dreaded, senseless, implacable" (59), and this has too often been true in qualitative research as well. In this study I regard whiteness, not as a taken-for-granted or invisible feature, but as a limiting and complicating factor.

8. Readers will notice that, in the discussion of the three themes, the amount of text varies between participants. That is, one participant may have had more to say than another in reference to a particular topic; and overall, the three participants' responses to questions varied tremendously in length. I struggled with this unevenness a bit, wondering whether I should attempt to "smooth it out" in the write-up and try to provide a roughly equal amount of text from each participant. Ultimately, I was guided by my belief that DS research must be sensitized to a nonhierarchical approach to difference. The fact that one participant happened to have more words is not an indication of the importance of his or her voice; it simply means that each one took a different approach to the interview, and those differences are reflected in the write-up. Here, again, the importance of "co-interpretation" (Newkirk) is obvious. If a participant finds him- or herself with little to say in the context of an interview, the different context of reading and commenting on a draft of analysis may provide a more accessible opportunity to elaborate further.

9. Although the True Spirit conference has been discontinued, American Boyz remains active. American Boyz is a social and support group that serves transmasculine persons and their significant others, families, friends, and allies.

10. Cal later elaborated this definition as "people with aphasia or dysphasia, some people with cerebral palsy, many deaf people in any place where signing or cued speech or some other visual system is not commonplace, many blind people in places where written texts and/or body language are important, people without a workable communication system at all, people who tend to be literal, etc. (but perhaps not all people with Williams Syndrome?), people whose first language is not commonly used where they live and who have disability-related trouble learning a second language."

11. The language used here is a parody of Internet-specific language, commonly called *LOLspeak*. Roughly translated, it means "I've just received a diagnosis and I'm happy about that."

12. Some scholars have begun to experiment with fictional forms in their academic work (see Ellis, *The Ethnographic I;* Stewart), but this practice is far from established.

13. Fan fiction (also called *fanfic*) is defined by Rebecca Black as "a unique form of writing in which fans base their stories on the characters and plotlines of existing media and popular culture" (398). Phinnia's fanfic most often focuses on characters from the television series *House*. Flash fiction (also called *flashfic* or *nanofic*) is extremely short fiction, generally less than 1,000 words, and sometimes as short as 50 or 100 words.

14. Cal noted that this point resonated with her, explaining, "One thing that you get in grad school is the experience of having people who know their stuff offer feedback on your own mastery of the material. When you are self-educated (whether or not this takes the form of attending 'the University of Google'), there is always that possibility that you have no clue what you're going on about, and that [that] is evident to many people."

15. Related work has suggested other ways we might approach minoritized/oppressed identities to form a basis for connection and collective action. One of these is "The Vulnerability Project," part of the Race and Difference Initiative at Emory University (http://www.gs.emory.edu/vulnerability). Another thematic/political base, "vitalism," is suggested by James Overboe in "Vitalism: Subjectivity Exceeding Racism, Sexism, and (Psychiatric) Ableism."

16. For more on disability and in/ter/dependence, see Davis, *Bending over Backwards;* Durgin; and Lewiecki-Wilson.

Works Cited

Abram, Suzanne. "The Americans with Disabilities Act in Higher Education: The Plight of Disabled Faculty." *Journal of Law and Education* 32.1 (2003). September 21, 2008. http://findarticles.com/p/articles/mi_qa3994/ is_200301/ai_n 9186921.

Aho, Kevin. "Medicalizing Mental Health: A Phenomenological Alternative." *Journal of Medical Humanities* 29 (2008): 243–59.

Allan, Julie. "Inclusion as an Ethical Project." Tremain 281–97.

Allen, Ruth, and Raymond G. Nairn. "Media Depictions of Mental Illness: An Analysis of the Use of Dangerousness." *Australian and New Zealand Journal of Psychiatry* 31 (1997): 375–81.

American Association of University Professors. "On Collegiality as a Criterion for Faculty Evaluation." November 1999. September 1, 2008.

American Psychiatric Association. *Diagnostic and Statistical Manual of Mental Disorders*. Text revision. 4th ed. Arlington, VA: APA, 2000.

American Public Health Organization. *APHA Accessibility Guide*. October 9, 2007. http://www.apha.org/meetings/access/AccessibilityPolicy.htm.

Americans with Disabilities Act. http://www.ada.gov/pubs/ada.htm.

Anderson, Charles M., and Marian M. MacCurdy. "Introduction." Anderson and MacCurdy, 1–22.

Anderson, Charles M., and Marian M. MacCurdy, eds. *Writing and Healing: Toward an Informed Practice*. Urbana, IL: NCTE, 2000.

Anderson, Robert C. "Faculty Members with Disabilities in Higher Education." Vance, 183–200.

Andre, Linda. *Doctors of Deception: What They Don't Want You to Know about Shock Treatment*. Piscataway, NJ: Rutgers UP, 2009.

Angelique, Holly, Ken Kyle, and Ed Taylor. "Mentors and Muses: New Strategies for Academic Success." *Innovative Higher Education* 26.3 (2002): 195–209.

Anson, Chris M. "What's Writing Got to Do with Campus Terrorism?" *Academe Online*. November–December 2007. August 22, 2008.

Antonetta, Susanne. *A Mind Apart: Travels in a Neurodiverse World*. New York: Penguin, 2005.

Aristotle. *The Complete Works of Aristotle*. Jonathan Barnes, ed. and trans. Bollingen Series LXXI: 1–2. Princeton, NJ: Princeton UP, 1984.

Aristotle. *The Nicomachean Ethics*. Trans. J. A. K. Thomson. Rev. Hugh Tredennick. Intro. Jonathan Barnes. New York: Penguin, 2004.

Avinger, Charles, Edith Croake, and Jean Kearns Miller. "Breathing Underwater in Academia: Teaching, Learning and Working with the Challenges of Invisible Illnesses and Hidden (Dis-)Abilities." Vance, 201–15.

Banks, Adam J. *Race, Rhetoric & Technology: Searching for Higher Ground.* Mahwah, NJ: Lawrence Erlbaum; Urbana, IL: NCTE, 2006.

Barnes, Colin. "What a Difference a Decade Makes: Reflections on Doing 'Emancipatory' Disability Research." *Disability & Society* 18.1 (2003): 3–17.

Barnett, Timothy. "Politicizing the Personal: Frederick Douglass, Richard Wright, and Some Thoughts on the Limits of Critical Literacy." *College English* 68.4 (2006): 356–81.

Barron, Monica. "Creative Writing Class as Crucible." *Academe Online.* November–December 2007. August 22, 2008.

Bartholomae, David. "Writing with Teachers: A Conversation with Peter Elbow." *College Composition and Communication* 46.1 (1995): 62–71.

Barton, Ellen. "Inductive Discourse Analysis: Discovering Rich Features." *Discourse Studies in Composition.* Ed. Ellen Barton and Gail Stygall. Cresskill, NJ: Hampton Press, 2002. 19–42.

Baumlin, James S., and Tita French Baumlin. "Psyche/Logos: Mapping the Terrains of Mind and Rhetoric." *College English* 51.3 (1989): 245–61.

Bell, Barbara Currier. "An Independent Scholar by Any Other Name." *Newsletter of the Center for Independent Study* 20.5 (April 2002): 3.

Bell, Barbara Currier. "Independent Scholarship: In a Reciprocal Spirit." *ADE Bulletin* 77 (1984): 38–43.

Bell, Barbara Currier. "Independents and Faculty Redeployment." *Newsletter of the Center for Independent Study* 22:1 (February 2004): 1.

Beresford, Peter. "Including Everyone's Knowledge and Experience." National Conference of University Professors Prize Essay 2004. August 22, 2008.

Beresford, Peter. "Violence and Psychiatry: Rethinking Relationships." Paper presented at the Centre for Disability Studies, University of Leeds, UK. December 5, 2007.

Berlin, James A. "Contemporary Composition: The Major Pedagogical Theories." *College English* 44.8 (December 1982): 765–77.

Berman, Jeffrey, and Jonathan Schiff. "Writing about Suicide." Anderson and MacCurdy, 291–312.

Berres, Allen. "'Everybody is their Enemy': Goths, Spooky Kids, and the American School Shooting Panic." *Children's Folklore Review* 24.1–2 (2002): 43–53.

Beverley, John. "The Margin at the Center: On Testimonio (Testimonial Narrative)." *Modern Fiction Studies* 35 (1990): 11–28.

"Beyond Greco-Roman Rhetorics: Breaking Precedent, Revising Stories Home." Wiki begun by students in Qwo-Li Driskill's History of Rhetoric (English 353) course at Texas A&M University. Spring 2009. http://breakingprecedent.wetpaint.com.

Bishop, Wendy. "Writing Is/And Therapy? Raising Questions about Writing

Classrooms and Writing Program Administration." *JAÇ: A Journal of Composition Theory* 13.2 (1993): 503–16.

Black, Rebecca W. "Online Fan Fiction, Global Identities, and Imagination." *Research in the Teaching of English* 43.4 (2009): 397–425.

Blanco, Carlos, Mayumi Okuda, et al. "Mental Health of College Students and Their Non-College Attending Peers: Results from the National Epidemiologic Study on Alcohol and Related Conditions." *Archives of General Psychiatry* 65.12 (2008): 1429–37.

Bloom, Lynn Z. "Collegiality, the Game." *symplok* 13.1–2 (2005): 207–18.

Booth, Tim. "Sounds of Still Voices: Issues in the Use of Narrative Methods with People who Have Learning Difficulties." *Disability and Society: Emerging Issues and Insights*. Ed. Len Barton. London: Longman, 1996. 237–55.

Borrowman, Shane, ed. *Trauma and the Teaching of Writing*. New York: SUNY P, 2006.

Boudreau, Abbie, and Scott Zamost. "Girlfriend: Shooter Was Taking Cocktail of 3 Drugs." CNN.com. February 20, 2008. August 22, 2008. http://www.cnn.com/2008/CRIME/02/20/shooter.girlfriend/index.html.

Bracken, Patrick, and Philip Thomas. "Postpsychiatry: A New Direction for Mental Health." *British Medical Journal* 322 (2001): 724–27.

Bracken, Patrick, and Philip Thomas. "Time to Move Beyond the Mind-Body Split." *British Medical Journal* 325 (2002): 1433–34.

Brandzel, Amy L., and Jigna Desai. "Race, Violence and Terror: The Cultural Defensibility of Heteromasculine Citizenship in the Virgina Tech Massacre and the Don Imus Affair." *Journal of Asian American Studies* 11.1 (2008): 61–85.

Brennan, Karen. "The Managed Teacher: Emotional Labour, Education, and Technology." *Educational Insights* 10.2 (2006). March 23, 2009. http://www.ccfi.educ.ubc.ca/publication/insights/v10n02/html/brennan/brennan.html.

Brooke, Robert. "Underlife and Writing Instruction." *College Composition and Communication* 38.2 (1987): 141–53.

Broughton, Walter, and William Conlogue. "What Search Committees Want." *Profession* (2001): 39–51.

Brown, Timile. "Drawn Out of Dejection." *Disability Studies Quarterly* 28.4 (2008).

Brownlow, Charlotte. "Re-presenting Autism: The Construction of 'NT Syndrome.'" *Journal of Medical Humanities* 31 (2010): 243–55.

Brueggemann, Brenda Jo. *Lend Me Your Ear: Rhetorical Constructions of Deafness*. Washington, DC: Gallaudet P, 1999.

Brueggemann, Brenda Jo. "Still-Life: Representations and Silences in the Participant-Observer Role." Mortensen and Kirsch, 17–39.

Brueggemann, Brenda Jo, Linda Feldmeier White, Patricia A. Dunn, Barbara A. Heifferon, and Johnson Cheu. "Becoming Visible: Lessons in Disability." *College Composition and Communication* 52 (2001): 368–98.

Butler, Judith. *Precarious Life: The Powers of Mourning and Violence*. London & New York: Verso, 2004. Print.

Carey, Toni Vogel. "The Noble Legacy (and Present Eclipse) of Independent Scholarship." *Independent Scholar* 14.1 (1999–2000): 8–13.

Caspi, Avner, Eran Chajut, Kelly Saporta, and Ruth Beyth-Marom. "The Influence of Personality on Social Participation in Learning Environments." *Learning and Individual Differences* 16 (2006): 129–44.

Chandler, Sally. "Fear, Teaching Composition, and Students' Discursive Choices: Re-thinking Connections between Emotions and College Student Writing." *Composition Studies* 35.2 (2007): 53–70.

Cho, David, and Amy Gardner. "An Isolated Boy in a World of Strangers." *Washington Post.* April 21, 2007. September 2, 2008.

Choe, Jeanne Y., Linda A. Teplin, and Karen M. Abram. "Perpetration of Violence, Violent Victimization, and Severe Mental Illness: Balancing Public Health Concerns." *Psychiatric Services* 59.2 (2008): 153–64.

Christensen, Carol. "Disabled, Handicapped or Disordered: What's in a Name?" *Disability and the Dilemmas of Education and Justice.* Ed. Carol Christensen and Fazal Rizvi. Buckingham: Open UP. 63–77.

Cicero. *De Re Publica: Selections.* Ed. James E.G. Zetzel. New York: Cambridge UP, 2008.

Clark, Hilary. "Invisible Disorder: Passing as an Academic." Myers, 123–30.

Cohen, Jodi S., and Stacy St. Clair. "Emotional Struggles Detailed in Essays: Writings Offer Candid Look at NIU Shooter." *Chicago Tribune.* April 20, 2008. September 9, 2008.

"Collegiality: A Roundtable." *Profession* (2006): 100–118.

"Collegiality: Statements from Chairs." *Profession* (2006): 95–99.

Collins, Mary Elizabeth, and Carol T. Mowbray. "Higher Education and Psychiatric Disabilities: National Survey of Campus Disability Services." *American Journal of Orthopsychiatry* 75.2 (2005): 304–15.

Conard, Maureen A. "Aptitude Is Not Enough: How Personality and Behavior Predict Academic Performance." *Journal of Research in Personality* 40.3 (2006): 339–46.

Costa, Paul T., Jr., and Robert R. McCrae. *The NEO Personality Inventory Manual.* Odessa, FL: Psychological Assessment Resources, 1985.

Couser, G. Thomas. "Conflicting Paradigms: The Rhetorics of Disability Memoir." Wilson and Lewiecki-Wilson, 78–91.

Couser, G. Thomas. "Disability as Metaphor: What's Wrong with *Lying.*" *Prose Studies* 27.1–2 (2005): 141–54.

Couser, G. Thomas. *Recovering Bodies: Illness, Disability and Life Writing.* Madison: U of Wisconsin P, 1997.

Couser, G. Thomas. *Signifying Bodies: Disability in Contemporary Life Writing.* Ann Arbor: U of Michigan P, 2009.

Couser, G. Thomas. *Vulnerable Subjects: Ethics and Life Writing.* Ithaca, NY: Cornell UP, 2004.

Crowe, Marie. "Constructing Normality: A Discourse Analysis of the DSM-IV." *Journal of Psychiatric and Mental Health Nursing* 7 (2000): 69–77.

Crowley, Sharon. *Toward a Civil Discourse: Rhetoric and Fundamentalism.* Pittsburgh: U of Pittsburg P, 2006.

Dajani, Karen Finlon. "What's in a Name? Terms Used to Refer to People with Disabilities." *Disability Studies Quarterly* 21.3 (2001).

Davidovitch, Nitsa, and Dan Soen. "Class Attendance and Students' Evaluation of Their College Instructors." *College Student Journal* 40.3 (2006): 691–703.

Davis, Lawrence J. "The Encyclopedia of Insanity." *Harper's Magazine* 294.1761 (Feb. 1997): 61–66.

Davis, Lennard J. *Bending over Backwards: Disability, Dismodernism, and Other Difficult Positions*. New York: New York UP, 2002.

Davis, Lennard J. *Obsession: A History*. Chicago: U of Chicago P, 2008.

Deletiner, Carole. "Crossing Lines." *College English* 54.7 (1992): 809–17.

Derrida, Jacques. *Speech and Phenomena: And Other Essays on Husserl's Theory of Signs*. Trans. David B. Allison. Evanston, IL: Northwestern UP, 1973.

Diller, Matthew. "Judicial Backlash, the ADA, and the Civil Rights Model of Disability." Krieger, 62–97.

Dixon, Kathleen, and William Archibald. "Outbursts: The Theory and a Guide to Reading." *Outbursts in Academe: Multiculturalism and Other Sources of Conflict*. Ed. Kathleen Dixon. Portsmouth, NH: Boynton/Cook, 1998. ix–xv.

Dolmage, Jay. "Mapping Composition: Inviting Disability in the Front Door." Lewiecki-Wilson and Brueggemann, 14–27.

Druger, Marvin. "Being There: A Perspective on Class Attendance." *Journal of College Science Teaching* 32.5 (2003): 350–51.

Dubrow, Heather. "Collegiality: Introduction." *Profession* (2006): 48–59.

Dunn, Patricia A. *Talking, Sketching, Moving: Multiple Literacies in the Teaching of Writing*. Portsmouth, NH: Boynton/Cook, 2001.

Dunn, Patricia A., and Kathleen Dunn De Mers. "Reversing Notions of Disability and Accommodation: Embracing Universal Design in Writing Pedagogy and Web Space." *Kairos* 7.1 (2002).

Durgin, Patrick F. "Psychosocial Disability and Post-Ableist Poetics: The 'Case' of Hannah Weiner's *Clairvoyant Journals*." *Contemporary Women's Writing* 2:2 (2008): 131–54.

Dyson, Michael Eric. "Uglier Than Meets the Eye." *Chicago Sun-Times*. March 13, 2001: 25.

Eakin, Paul John. *How Our Lives Become Stories: Making Selves*. Ithaca, NY: Cornell UP, 1999.

Ehrenreich, Barbara. "Our Broken Mental Health System." *This Land Is Their Land: Reports from a Divided Nation*. New York: Holt, 2008.

Elbogen, Eric B., et al. "Effectively Implementing Psychiatric Advance Directives to Promote Self-determination of Treatment among People with Mental Illness." *Psychology, Public Policy, and Law* 13.4 (2007): 273–88.

Ellis, Carolyn. *The Ethnographic I: A Methodological Novel about Autoethnography*. Walnut Creek: Alta Mira, 2004.

Ellis, Carolyn. "Evocative Ethnography: Writing Emotionally about Our Lives." *Representation and the Text: Re-framing the Narrative Voice*. Ed. William G. Tierney and Yvonna S. Lincoln. New York: SUNY P, 1997. 115–39.

Ellis, Carolyn. "Telling Secrets, Revealing Lives: Relational Ethics in Research With Intimate Others." *Qualitative Inquiry* 13.3 (2007): 3–29.

Ellsworth, Elizabeth. "Why Doesn't This Feel Empowering? Working Through the Repressive Myths of Critical Pedagogy." *Harvard Educational Review* 59.3 (1989): 297–324.

Emerson, Ralph Waldo. *Emerson: Essays & Lectures*. Ed. Joel Porte. Washington, DC: Library of America, 1983.

Engel, David M., and Frank W. Munger. "Narrative, Disability and Identity." *Narrative* 15.1 (2007): 85–94.

Engelhardt, H. Tristram, Jr. *The Foundations of Bioethics*. New York: Oxford UP, 1986.

Erevelles, Nirmala. "In Search of the Disabled Subject." Wilson and Lewiecki-Wilson, 92–111.

Erevelles, Nirmala. "Signs of Reason: Rivière, Facilitated Communication, and the Crisis of the Subject." Tremain, 45–64.

"Ex-Classmates Say Gunman Was Bullied." MSNBC.com. April 19, 2007. September 10, 2008.

Faigley, Lester. *Fragments of Rationality: Postmodernity and the Subject of Composition*. Pittsburgh: U of Pittsburgh P, 1992.

Fairclough, Norman. *Analysing Discourse: Textual Analysis for Social Research*. New York: Routledge, 2003.

Fairclough, Norman. *Discourse and Social Change*. Cambridge: Polity P, 1992.

Falco, Edward. "Creative Writing and the Virginia Tech Massacre." *Chronicle of Higher Education* 53.36 (2007): 60.

Farrell, Elizabeth F. "Asperger's Confounds Colleges." *Chronicle of Higher Education* 51.7 (2004): 35–36.

Fast, Jonathan. "Steve Kazmierczak: The Secret Life." *Huffington Post*. February 16, 2008. September 1, 2008.

Feldmann, Lloyd J. "Classroom Civility Is Another of Our Instructor Responsibilities." *College Teaching* 49.4 (2001): 137–40.

Fine, Michelle. "Working the Hyphens: Reinventing Self and Other in Qualitative Research." *Handbook of Qualitative Research*. Ed. Norman K. Denzin and Yvonna S. Lincoln. Thousand Oaks, CA: Sage, 1994. 70–82.

Fine, Michelle, Lois Weis, Susan Weseen, and Loonmun Wong. "For Whom? Qualitative Research, Representations and Social Responsibilities." *Handbook of Qualitative Research,* 2nd ed. Ed. Norman K. Denzin and Yvonna S. Lincoln. Thousand Oaks, CA: Sage, 2000. 107–31.

Fitzsimmons, Anne. "Annotation as an Ethical Practice." *Reflections in Writing* 18 (1998). January 31, 2002.

Flynn, Elizabeth. "Strategic, Counter-Strategic and Reactive Resistance in the Feminist Classroom." *Insurrections: Approaches to Resistance in Composition Studies*. Ed. Andrea Greenbaum. Albany: SUNY, 2001. 17–34.

Foley, John P., ed. *The Jeffersonian Cyclopedia: A Comprehensive Collection of the Views of Thomas Jefferson*. New York: Funk & Wagnalls, 1900. [Accessed via Google Books.]

Foucault, Michel. *The Archaeology of Knowledge and the Discourse on Language*. Trans. A. M. Sheridan Smith. New York: Pantheon, 1972.

Foucault, Michel. "Governmentality." *The Foucault Effect: Studies in Govern-*

mentality. Ed. Graham Burchell, Colin Gordon, and Peter Miller. Chicago: U of Chicago P, 1991. 87–104.

Foucault, Michel. *Madness and Civilization: A History of Insanity in the Age of Reason*. Trans. Richard Howard. New York: Vintage, 1988.

Fox, James Alan. "Campus Shootings: A Prevention Primer." *Chronicle of Higher Education* 54.43 (2008): 64.

Friedman, Emily. "Who Was the Illinois School Shooter?" ABC News. February 15, 2008. August 22, 2008.

"Framing the Virginia Tech Tragedy." *Rockridge Nation*. April 17, 2007. August 22, 2008.

Frank, Richard G., and Sherry A. Glied. *Better but Not Well: Mental Health Policy in the United States Since 1950*. Baltimore: Johns Hopkins UP, 2006.

Friedman, Paul, Fred Rodriguez, and Joe McComb. "Why Students Do and Do Not Attend Class: Myths and Realities." *College Teaching* 49.4 (2001): 124–33.

Gale, Xin Liu. " 'The Stranger' in Communication: Race, Class, and Conflict in a Basic Writing Class." *JAC: A Journal of Composition Theory* 17.1 (1997): 53–68.

Gappa, Judith M., and David W. Leslie. *The Invisible Faculty: Improving the Status of Part-Timers in Higher Education*. San Francisco: Jossey-Bass, 1993.

Garland-Thomson, Rosemarie. "Integrating Disability Studies into the Existing Curriculum: The Example of 'Women and Literature' at Howard University." *Radical Teacher* 47 (1995): 15–21.

Garland-Thomson, Rosemarie. "Shape Structures Story: Fresh and Feisty Stories about Disability." *Narrative* 15.1 (2007): 113–23.

Garland-Thomson, Rosemarie. *Staring: How We Look*. New York: Oxford UP, 2009.

Gecker, Ellen. "How Do I Know If My Student Is Dangerous?" *Academe Online*. November–December 2007. August 22, 2008.

Gendlin, Eugene T. *Focusing*. 2nd ed. New York: Bantam, 1982.

Gill, Carol J. "A Psychological View of Disability Culture." *Disability Studies Quarterly* 15.4 (1995). N.p.

Gilligan, Carol. *In a Different Voice: Psychological Theory and Women's Development*. Cambridge: Harvard UP, 1993.

Gilmore, Leigh. *Autobiographics: A Feminist Theory of Women's Self-Representation*. Ithaca, NY: Cornell UP, 1994.

Giorgio, Grace. "Traumatic Truths and the Gift of Telling." *Qualitative Inquiry* 15.1 (2009): 149–67.

Glenn, Cheryl. *Rhetoric Retold: Regendering the Tradition from Antiquity Through the Renaissance*. Carbondale: Southern Illinois UP, 1997.

Glenn, Cheryl. *Unspoken: A Rhetoric of Silence*. Carbondale: Southern Illinois UP, 2004.

Goffman, Erving. *Asylums: Essays on the Social Situation of Mental Patients and Other Inmates*. New York: Anchor, 1961.

Goffman, Erving. *Stigma: Notes on the Management of a Spoiled Identity*. New York: Simon and Schuster, 1963.

Goggin, Peter N., and Maureen Daly Goggin. "Presence in Absence: Discourses and Teaching (In, On and About) Trauma." Borrowman, 29–51.

Goggin, Gerard, and Christopher Newall. "Foucault on the Phone: Disability and the Mobility of Government." Tremain, 261–77.

Goldberg, Susan G., Mary B. Killeen, and Bonnie O'Day. "The Disclosure Conundrum: How People with Psychiatric Disabilities Navigate Employment." *Psychology, Public Policy, and Law* 11.3 (2005): 463–500.

Golden, Daniel. "From Disturbed High Schooler to College Killer." *Wall Street Journal*. August 20, 2007. September 10, 2008.

Goldsworthy, Kerryn. "Creative Writing and the Virginia Tech Massacre." *Chronicle of Higher Education* 53.36 (2007): 60.

Gouge, Catherine, Laura Brady, and Nathalie Singh-Corcoran. "What Counts? The Changing Realities of Scholarship." Conference on College Composition and Communication. New Orleans. April 4, 2008.

Gouvier, W. Drew, Sara Sytsma-Jordan, and Stephen Mayville. "Patterns of Discrimination in Hiring Job Applicants with Disabilities: The Role of Disability Type, Job Complexity, and Public Contact." *Rehabilitation Psychology* 48.3 (2003): 175–81.

Grabill, Jeffrey T. "On Divides and Interfaces: Access, Class, and Computers." *Computers and Composition* 20.4 (2003): 455–72.

Graham, Charles R., Tonya R. Tripp, Larry Seawright, and George L. Joeckel III. "Empowering or Compelling Reluctant Participators Using Audience Response Systems." *Active Learning in Higher Education* 8.3 (2007): 233–58.

Granger, David. "Editor's Letter: Men and Murder." *Esquire* (August 2008): 16.

Grinker, Roy Richard. *Unstrange Minds: Remapping the World by Autism*. New York: Basic Books, 2007.

Gross, Ronald, and Beatrice Gross. *Independent Scholarship: Promise, Problems and Prospects*. New York: College Entrance Examination Board, 1983.

Gump, Steven E. "The Cost of Cutting Class: Attendance as a Predictor of Student Success." *College Teaching* 53.1 (2005): 21–26.

Guy-Sheftall, Beverly. "Shared Governance, Junior Faculty, and HBCUs." *Academe* 92.6 (2006). September 25, 2008.

Hacking, Ian. *Mad Travelers: Reflections on the Reality of Transient Mental Illness*. Cambridge, MA: Harvard UP, 1998.

Halawah, Ibtesam. "The Impact of Student-Faculty Informal Interpersonal Relationships on Intellectual and Personal Development." *College Student Journal* 40.3 (2006): 670–78.

Haraway, Donna. "Situated Knowledges: The Science Question in Feminism and the Privilege of Partial Perspective." *Simians, Cyborgs, and Women: The Reinvention of Nature*. New York: Routledge, 1991. 183–201.

Harding, Sandra. *Whose Science? Whose Knowledge? Thinking From Women's Lives*. Ithaca, NY: Cornell UP, 1991.

Harker, Michael. "The Ethics of Argument: Rereading *kairos* and Making Sense in a Timely Fashion." *College Composition and Communication* 59.1 (2007): 77–97.

Harrison et al. "Assessing Candidate Disposition for Admission into Teacher Education: Can Just Anyone Teach?" *Action in Teacher Education* 27.4 (2006): 72–80.

Harry, Beth, and Janette K. Klingner. *Why Are So Many Minority Students in Special Education? Understanding Race and Disability in Schools.* New York: Teachers College P, 2005.

Harvey, Gordon. "Presence in the Essay." *College English* 56 (1994): 642–54.

Heilker, Paul. "Comment on 'Neurodiversity.'" *College English* 70.3 (2008): 319–21.

Herrington, Anne J., and Marcia Curtis. *Persons in Process: Four Stories of Writing and Personal Development in College.* Urbana, IL: National Council of Teachers of English, 2000.

Hochschild, Arlie Russell. *The Managed Heart: Commercialization of Human Feeling.* Berkeley: U of California P, 1983.

Hoge, Charles W., Carl A. Castro, Stephen C. Messer, Dennis McGurk, Dave I. Cotting, and Robert L. Koffman. "Combat Duty in Iraq and Afghanistan, Mental Health Problems, and Barriers to Care." *New England Journal of Medicine* 351.1 (2004): 13–22.

hooks, bell. *Teaching Community: A Pedagogy of Hope.* New York: Routledge, 2003.

Hoover, Eric. "Colleges Wade Into Survival Training for Campus Shootings." *Chronicle of Higher Education* 54:42 (2008): 1.

Hughes, Stephanie, Rebecca J. White, and Giles Hertz. "A New Technique for Mitigating Risk on U.S. College Campuses." *Journal of Higher Education Policy and Management* 30.3 (2008): 309–18.

Hurlbert, C. Mark, and Michael Blitz, eds. *Composition and Resistance.* Portsmouth, NH: Boynton/Cook, 1991.

Hurlbert, C. Mark, and Michael Blitz, eds. "Resisting Composure." Hurlbert and Blitz, 1–8.

Ingram, Richard A. "Double Trouble." Myers, 209–19.

Jackson, Vanessa. "In Our Own Voice: African-American Stories of Oppression, Survival and Recovery in Mental Health Systems." MFI Portal. April 4, 2009. http://www.mindfreedom.org/kb/mental-health-abuse/Racism/InOurOwn Voice/view.

Jacobs, Dale, and Laura R. Micciche, eds. *A Way to Move: Rhetorics of Emotion & Composition Studies.* Portsmouth, NH: Boynton/Cook, 2003.

Janz, Heidi L. "Crip-Academic, Disabled-Writer, Sparrow on Wheels and Other Split-Identities: Reflections on the Oxymoronic Aspects of Writing an Auto/Biographical Novel About Disability." *Disability Studies Quarterly* 28.1 (2008).

Johnson, Cheryl L. "Participatory Rhetoric and the Teacher as Racial/Gendered Subject." *College English* 56.4 (1994): 409–19.

Jones, Kathleen W. "The Thirty-third Victim: Representations of Seung Hui Cho in the Aftermath of the 'Virginia Tech Massacre.'" *Journal of the History of Childhood and Youth* 2.1 (2009): 64–82.

Jurecic, Ann. "Neurodiversity." *College English* 69.5 (2007): 421–42.

Kadison, Richard, and Theresa Foy DiGeronimo. *College of the Overwhelmed:*

The Campus Mental Health Crisis and What to Do About It. San Francisco: Jossey-Bass, 2004.

Kang, K. Connie, Bob Drogin, and Faye Fiore. "Bright Daughter, Brooding Son: Enigma in the Cho Household." *Los Angeles Times*. April 22, 2007. September 2, 2008.

Kessler, Ronald C., et al. "Individual and Societal Effects of Mental Disorders on Earnings in the United States: Results from the National Comordibity Survey Replication." *American Journal of Psychiatry* 165.6 (June 2008): 703–11.

King, Stephen. "Creative Writing and the Virginia Tech Massacre." *Chronicle of Higher Education* 53.36 (2007): 60.

Kinneavy, James L. "*Kairos:* A Neglected Concept in Classical Rhetoric." *Rhetoric and Praxis*. Ed. Jean Dietz Moss. Washington, DC: Catholic University of America P, 1986.

Kirsch, Gesa E. *Ethical Dilemmas in Feminist Research: The Politics of Location, Interpretation, and Publication*. New York: SUNY P, 1999.

Kleinfield, N. R. "Before Deadly Rage, a Life Consumed by a Troubling Silence." *New York Times*. April 22, 2007. September 2, 2008.

Kress, Gunther, and Theo Van Leeuwen. *Multimodal Discourse: The Modes and Media of Contemporary Communication*. New York: Oxford UP, 2001.

Kress, Gunther, and Theo Van Leeuwen. *Reading Images: The Grammar of Visual Design*. 2nd ed. London: Routledge, 2006.

Krieger, Linda Hamilton, ed. *Backlash Against the ADA: Reinterpreting Disability Rights*. Ann Arbor: U of Michigan P, 2003.

Laden, Vicki A., and Gregory Schwartz. "Psychiatric Disabilities, the Americans with Disabilities Act, and the New Workplace Violence Account." Krieger, 189–220.

Lather, Patti. *Getting Smart: Feminist Research and Pedagogy Within/in the Postmodern*. New York: Routledge, 1991.

LaCapra, Dominick. *Writing History, Writing Trauma*. Baltimore: Johns Hopkins UP, 2000.

Lavooy, Maria J., and Michael H. Newlin. "Online Chats and Cyber-Office Hours: Everything but the Office." *International Journal on E-Learning* 7.1 (2008): 107–16.

Lee, Amy. *Composing Critical Pedagogies: Teaching Writing as Revision*. Urbana, IL: NCTE, 2000.

Lejeune, Philippe. "Autobiography in the Third Person." *New Literary History* 9.1 (1977): 27–50.

Lejeune, Philippe. *On Autobiography*. Trans. Katherine Leary. Minneapolis: U of Minnesota P, 1989.

Leopold, Jason. "Veterans Administration Tried to Conceal Extent of Attempted Veteran Suicides, Email Shows." *Global Research*. Centre for Research on Globalization. May 11, 2008. Accessed August 26, 2008.

Lewiecki-Wilson, Cynthia. "Rethinking Rhetoric through Mental Disabilities." *Rhetoric Review* 22.2 (2003): 156–67.

Lewiecki-Wilson, Cynthia, and Brenda Jo Brueggemann, with Jay Dolmage. *Dis-*

ability and the Teaching of Writing: A Critical Sourcebook. Boston: Bedford / St. Martin's, 2008.

Lewiecki-Wilson, Cynthia, and Jay Dolmage. "Comment on 'Neurodiversity.'" *College English* 70.3 (2008): 314–18.

Lewin, Tamar. "After Campus Shootings, U.S. to Ease Privacy Rules." *New York Times*. March 25, 2008. September 6, 2008.

Lewis, Bradley. *Moving Beyond Prozac, DSM, & the New Psychiatry*. Ann Arbor: U of Michigan P, 2006.

Lewis, Bradley. "Narrative Psychiatry." *Comprehensive Textbook of Psychiatry*, 9th ed. Ed. Benjamin J. Sadock and Virginia A. Sadock. Philadelphia: Lippincott, 2009. 2934–39.

Lewis, Philip. "From the Institutional Text to Bicollegiality." *Profession* (2006): 75–86.

Lightfoot, Brenda J. "Disclosing Disability in an Academic Job Search: Reflections on Two Approaches with Different Outcomes." Vance, 97–103.

Linde, Charlotte. *Life Stories: The Creation of Coherence*. New York: Oxford UP, 1993.

Link, Bruce G., John Monahan, Ann Stueve, and Francis T. Cullen. "Real in Their Consequences: A Sociological Approach to Understanding the Association Between Psychotic Symptoms and Violence." *American Sociological Review* 64 (1999): 316–32.

Linton, Simi. *Claiming Disability: Knowledge and Identity*. New York: New York UP, 1998.

Lipson, Carol S., and Roberta A. Binkley, eds. *Rhetoric Before and Beyond the Greeks*. New York: SUNY P, 2004.

Lipton, Eric. "In Anthrax Scientist's E-Mail, Hints of Delusions." *New York Times*. August 7, 2008. August 7, 2008.

Lissner, L. Scott. "Congressional Reset of the ADA: How Will the ADA Amendments Affect Your Policy & Practice?" Association on Higher Education and Disability (AHEAD) audioconference. October 10, 2008.

Liu, Ka-Yuet, Marissa King, and Peter S. Bearman. "Social Influence and the Autism Epidemic." *American Journal of Sociology* 115.5 (2010): 1387–1434.

Loftus, Brian. "Speaking Silence: The Strategies and Structures of Queer Autobiography." *College Literature* 24.1 (1997): 28–44.

Long, Mark C. "Reading, Writing and Teaching in Context." *Academic Cultures: Professional Preparation and the Teaching Life*. Ed. Sean P. Murphy. New York: MLA, 2008. 121–46.

Longmore, Paul K. *Why I Burned My Book: And Other Essays on Disability*. Philadelphia: Temple UP, 2003.

Luna, Catherine. "Learning from Diverse Learners: (Re)writing Academic Literacies and Learning Disabilities in College." *Journal of Adolescent & Adult Literacy* 45.7 (2002): 596–605.

MacCurdy, Marian M. "From Trauma to Writing: A Theoretical Model for Practical Use." Anderson and MacCurdy, 158–200.

Malinowitz, Harriet. *Textual Orientations: Lesbian and Gay Students and the Making of Discourse Communities*. Portsmouth, NH: Boynton/Cook, 1995.

Mancuso, Katherine. *Invisible in Disabled Country.* Dir. Lori Teague. Perf. Katherine Mancuso. Fieldwork Showcase. Schwartz Center for Performing Arts, Atlanta. April 29, 2007.

Marks, Deborah. "Introduction: Counselling, Therapy and Emancipatory Praxis." *Disability Studies Quarterly* 22.3 (2002).

Martin, Deb. "Add Disability and Stir: The New Ingredient in Composition Textbooks." Lewiecki-Wilson and Brueggemann, 74–91.

McCarthy, Joseph F., and danah m. boyd. "Digital Backchannels in Shared Physical Spaces: Experiences at an Academic Conference." Conference on Computer-Human Interaction. Portland, OR. April 7, 2005.

McCarthy, Joseph F., David W. McDonald, Suzanne Soroczak, David H. Nguyen, and Al M. Rashid. "Augmenting the Social Space of an Academic Conference." ACM Conference on Computer-Supported Cooperative Work. Chicago. November 8, 2004. 39–48.

McCarthy, Lucille Parkinson, and Joan Page Gerring. "Revising Psychiatry's Charter Document DSM-IV." *Written Communication* 11.2 (1994): 147–92.

McCrae, Robert R., and Oliver P. John. "An Introduction to the Five-Factor Model and Its Applications." *Journal of Personality* 60 (1992): 175–215.

McDonald, David W., Joseph F. McCarthy, Suzanne Soroczak, David H. Nguyen, and Al M. Rashid. "Proactive Displays: Supporting Awareness in Fluid Social Environments." *Transactions on Computer-Human Interaction* 14.4 (2008). Web. 2 April 2010.

McFadden, Robert D. "13 Shot Dead During a Class on Citizenship." *New York Times.* April 4, 2009: A1, A13.

McRuer, Robert. *Crip Theory: Cultural Signs of Queerness and Disability.* New York: NYUP, 2006.

Mercer, Geof. "Emancipatory Disability Research." Ed. Colin Barnes, Mike Oliver, and Len Barton, *Disability Studies Today.* Cambridge: Polity, 2002. 228–49.

Micciche, Laura R. *Doing Emotion: Rhetoric, Writing, Teaching.* Portsmouth, NH: Boynton/Cook, 2007.

Michalec, Paul, and Hilary Burg. "Transforming Discussions from Collegiate to Collegial." *Curriculum and Teaching Dialogue* 9.1–2 (2007): 311–26.

Michalko, Rod. *The Difference that Disability Makes.* Philadelphia: Temple UP, 2002.

Milanés, Cecilia Rodríguez. Hurlbert and Blitz, 115–25.

Miller, Richard E. "Fault Lines in the Contact Zone." *College English* 56 (1994): 389–408.

Miller, Richard E. "The Fear Factor." *Academe Online.* November–December 2007. August 22, 2008.

Miller, Richard E. "The Nervous System." *College English* 58.3 (1996): 265–86.

Millet, Kate. *The Loony-Bin Trip.* New York: Simon and Schuster, 1990.

Miner, Madonne. "'Making Up the Stories as We Go Along': Men, Women and Narratives of Disability." Mitchell and Snyder, 283–95.

Mintz, Susannah B. *Unruly Bodies: Life Writing by Women with Disabilities.* Chapel Hill: U of North Carolina P, 2007.

Minwalla, Omar, B. R. Simon Rosser, Jamie Feldman, and Christine Varga. "Identity Experience Among Progressive Gay Muslims in North America: A Qualitative Study Within Al-Fatiha." *Culture, Health & Sexuality* 7.2 (2005): 113–28.

Mitchell, David T., and Sharon L. Snyder. *The Body and Physical Difference: Discourses of Disability.* Ann Arbor: U of Michigan P, 1997.

Modern Language Association. "Report of the MLA Task Force on Evaluating Scholarship for Tenure and Promotion." *Profession* (2007): 9–71.

Moeller, Carol. "'Psychiatric'/Psycho-Social Disabilities for Critical Consciousness: Human Costs of 'Productivity' and 'Speed.'" Society for Disability Studies Conference. Tucson, AZ. June 17, 2009.

Monahan, John. "Mental Disorder and Violent Behavior: Perceptions and Evidence." *American Psychologist* 47 (1992): 511–21.

Monastersky, Richard. "Is There an Autism Epidemic?" *Chronicle of Higher Education* (May 11, 2007). July 16, 2008.

Montgomery, Cal. "Critic of the Dawn." *Ragged Edge Online* 22.3 (May 2001). http://www.ragged-edge-mag.com/0501/0501cov.htm.

Montgomery, Cal. "A Hard Look at Invisible Disability." *Ragged Edge Online* 22.2 (March 2001). http://www.ragged-edge-mag.com/0301/0301ft1.htm.

Moore, Randy. "Attendance and Performance: How Important Is It for Students to Attend Class?" *Journal of College Science Teaching* 32.6 (2003): 367–71.

Moran, Stephen T. "Autopathography and Depression: Describing the 'Despair Beyond Despair.'" *Journal of Medical Humanities* 27 (2006): 79–91.

Moran, Terry. "Inside Cho's Mind." ABC News. August 30, 2007. September 2, 2008.

Morey, Leslie C., and Mary C. Zanarini. "Borderline Personality: Traits and Disorder." *Journal of Abnormal Psychology* 109.4 (2000): 733–37.

Morrison, Linda J. *Talking Back to Psychiatry: The Psychiatric Consumer/Survivor/Ex-Patient Movement.* New York: Routledge, 2005.

Morrison, Toni. *Playing in the Dark: Whiteness and the Literary Imagination.* Cambridge: Harvard UP, 1992.

Mortensen, Peter, and Gesa E. Kirsch. *Ethics and Representation in Qualitative Studies of Literacy.* Urbana, IL: National Council of Teachers of English, 1996.

Mowbray, Carol T., James M. Mandiberg, Catherine H. Stein, Sandra Kopels, Caroline Curlin, Deborah Megivern, Shari Strauss, Kim Collins, and Robin Lett. "Campus Mental Health Services: Recommendations for Change." *American Journal of Orthopsychiatry* 76.2 (2006): 226–37.

Murphy, Michael. "New Faculty for a New University: Toward a Full-Time Teaching-Intensive Faculty Track in Composition." *College Composition and Communication* 52.1 (2000): 14–42.

Murphy, Sean P., ed. *Academic Cultures: Professional Preparation and the Teaching Life.* New York: MLA, 2008.

Murray, Stuart. "On Autistic Presence." *Journal of Literary Disability* 2.1 (2008): 1–10.

Myers, Kimberly R. "Coming Out: Considering the Closet of Illness." *Journal of Medical Humanities* 25.4 (2004): 255–70.

Myers, Kimberly R., ed. *Illness in the Academy: A Collection of Pathographies by Academics.* West Lafayette, IN: Purdue UP, 2007.

Nagel, Thomas. *The View from Nowhere.* New York: Oxford UP, 1986.

Nairn, Raymond G., and John H. Coverdale. "People Never See Us Living Well: An Appraisal of the Personal Stories about Mental Illness in a Prospective Print Media Sample." *Australian and New Zealand Journal of Psychiatry* 39 (2005): 281–87.

National Institute of Mental Health. "The Numbers Count: Mental Disorders in America." July 16, 2008. http://www.nimh.nih.gov/health/publications/the-numbers-count-mental-disorders-in-america/index.shtml.

National Institute of Mental Health. "Mental Disorders Cost Society Billions in Unearned Income." May 1, 2009. http://www.nimh.nih.gov/science-news/2008/mental-disorders-cost-society-billions-in-unearned-income.shtml.

Newall, Christopher. "Flourishing Rhetorically: Disability, Diversity and Equal Disappointment Opportunity." Vance, 117–27.

Newkirk, Thomas. "Seduction and Betrayal in Qualitative Research." Mortensen and Kirsch, 3–16.

Newman, Katherine S. "Before the Rampage: What Can Be Done?" *Chronicle of Higher Education* 53.35 (2007): B20.

Newman, Katherine S., Cybelle Fox, David J. Harding, Jal Mehta, and Wendy Roth. *Rampage: The Social Roots of School Shootings.* New York: Basic Books, 2004.

Nickel, Patricia Mooney. "There Is an Unknown on Campus: From Normative to Performative Violence in Academia." *There Is a Gunman on Campus: Tragedy and Terror at Virginia Tech.* Ed. Ben Agger & Timothy W. Luke. Lanham, MD: Rowman & Littlefield, 2008.

Nicki, Andrea. "The Abused Mind: Feminist Theory, Psychiatric Disability, and Trauma." *Hypatia* 16.4 (2001): 80–104.

Noddings, Nel. *Educating Moral People: A Caring Alternative to Character Education.* New York: Teachers College P, 2002.

Nussbaum, E. Michael, Kendall Hartley, Gale M. Sinatra, Ralph E. Reynolds, and Lisa D. Bendixen. "Personality Interactions and Scaffolding in On-line Discussions." *Journal of Educational Computing Research* 30.1–2 (2004): 113–37.

Okolo, Cynthia M., Ralph P. Ferretti, and Charles A. MacArthur. "Talking about History: Discussions in a Middle School Inclusive Classroom." *Journal of Learning Disabilities* 40.2 (2007): 154–65.

Oliver, Mike. "Changing the Social Relations of Research Production." *Disability, Handicap & Society* 7.2 (1992): 101–14.

O'Rourke, William. "Creative Writing and the Virginia Tech Massacre." *Chronicle of Higher Education* 53.36 (2007): 60.

Overboe, James. "Vitalism: Subjectivity Exceeding Racism, Sexism, and (Psychi-

atric) Ableism." *Intersecting Gender and Disability Perspectives in Rethinking Postcolonial Identities.* Ed. Pushpa Parekh. *Wagadu* 4 (2008): 37–50.
Palmeri, Jason. "Disability Studies, Cultural Analysis, and the Critical Practice of Technical Communication Pedagogy." *Technical Communication Quarterly* 15.1 (2006): 49–65.
Patel, Shaista. "Encountering the Terrorism of Madness: Nation's Normal Race to the Culture of Categories." Society for Disability Studies Conference. Tucson, AZ. June 20, 2009.
Patterson, Orlando. "When 'They' Are 'Us.'" *New York Times.* April 30, 1999. September 7, 2008.
Payne, Michelle. *Bodily Discourses: When Students Write about Abuse and Eating Disorders.* Portsmouth, NH: Boynton/Cook, 2000.
Perl, Sondra. *Felt Sense: Writing with the Body.* Portsmouth, NH: Boynton/Cook, 2004.
Perreault, Jeanne. *Writing Selves: Contemporary Feminist Autography.* Minneapolis: U of Minnesota P, 1995.
Petrila, John, and Thomas Brink. "Mental Illness and Changing Definitions of Disability Under the Americans with Disabilities Act." *Psychiatric Services* 52.5 (2001): 626–30.
"Portrait of a Killer." *Guardian.* August 30, 2007. August 31, 2008.
Powell, Annette Harris. "Access(ing), Habits, Attitudes, and Engagements: Rethinking Access as Practice." *Computers and Composition* 24 (2007): 16–35.
Power, Tynan. "Lifting." *Pinned Down by Pronouns.* Ed. Toni Amato and Mary Davies. Jamaica Plain, MA: Conviction Books, 2003. 146.
Pratt, Mary Louise. "Arts of the Contact Zone." *Profession* (1991): 33–40.
Prelli, Lawrence J. "The Rhetorical Construction of Scientific Ethos." *Landmark Essays on Rhetoric of Science: Case Studies.* Ed. Randy Allen Harris. Mahwah, NJ: Lawrence Erlbaum, 1997. 87–104.
Prendergast, Catherine. "On the Rhetorics of Mental Disability." Wilson and Lewiecki-Wilson, 45–60. *Also* in *Towards a Rhetoric of Everyday Life: New Directions in Research on Writing, Text, and Discourse.* Ed. Martin Nystrand and John Duffy. Madison: U of Wisconsin P, 2003. 189–206.
Prendergast, Catherine. "The Unexceptional Schizophrenic: A Post-Postmodern Introduction." *Journal of Literary Disability* 2.1 (2008).
"President Bush Signs S. 3406 into Law." White House News Release. September 25, 2008. http://www.whitehouse.gov/news/releases/2008/09/20080925-8.html.
Price, Margaret. "Access Imagined: The Construction of Disability in Policy Documents." *Disability Studies Quarterly* 29.1 (2009).
Price, Margaret. "Accessing Disability: A Nondisabled Student Works the Hyphen." *College Composition and Communication* 59.1 (2007): 53–76.
Price, Margaret. "Disability Studies Methodology." *Practicing Research in Writing Studies: Reflections on Ethically Responsible Research.* Ed. Pamela Takayoshi and Katrina M. Powell. Forthcoming from Hampton Press.
Price, Margaret. "Then You'll Be Straight." *Creative Nonfiction* 28 (2006): 84–101.
Probyn, Elspeth. *Blush: Faces of Shame.* Minneapolis: U of Minnesota P, 2005.

"Professor: Shooter's Writing Dripped with Anger." CNN. April 18, 2007. August 27, 2008.

"Profile of Undergraduates in U.S. Postsecondary Educational Institutions 2003–04." Institute of Education Sciences. United States Department of Education. July 16, 2008.

Quintilian. *Institutio Oratoria.* 4 vols. Trans. H. E. Butler. Cambridge: Harvard UP, 1980.

Ratcliffe, Krista. *Rhetorical Listening: Identification, Gender, Whiteness.* Carbondale: Southern Illinois UP, 2005.

Reaume, Geoffrey. "Mad People's History." *Radical History Review* 94 (2006): 170–82.

Reda, Mary M. *Between Speaking and Silence: A Study on Quiet Students.* New York: SUNY P, 2009.

Reda, Mary M. "Re-Seeing Resistances: Telling Stories." *Composition Studies* 35.2 (2007): 31–52.

Reiss, Benjamin. "Madness after Virginia Tech: From Psychiatric Risk to Institutional Vulnerability." *Social Text* 105, vol. 28, no. 4 (Winter 2010): 25–44.

Reynolds, J. Fred. "The Rhetoric of Mental Health Care." *Rhetoric of Healthcare: Essays Toward a New Disciplinary Inquiry.* Ed. Barbara Heifferon and Stuart C. Brown. Cresskill, NJ: Hampton P, 2008. 149–57.

Rhode, Deborah L. *In Pursuit of Knowledge: Scholars, Status, and Academic Culture.* Stanford, CA: Stanford UP, 2006.

Richmond, Kia Jane. "Repositioning Emotions in Composition Studies." *Composition Studies* 30.1 (2002): 67–82.

Rimmon-Kenan, Shlomith. "The Story of 'I': Illness and Narrative Identity." *Narrative* 10.1 (2002): 9–27.

Rinaldi, Jacqueline. "Rhetoric and Healing: Revising Narratives about Disability." *College English* 58.7 (1996): 820–34.

Roberts, Alison, and Keri Iyall Smith. "Managing Emotions in the College Classroom: The Cultural Diversity Course as an Example." *Teaching Sociology* 30 (2002): 291–301.

Robertson, Scott Michael, and Ari Daniel Ne'eman. "Autistic Acceptance, the College Campus, and Technology: Growth of Neurodiversity in Society and Academia." *Disability Studies Quarterly* 28.4 (2008).

Rose, Sarah F. "Disability and the Academic Job Market." *Disability Studies Quarterly* 28.3 (2008).

Roth, Geneen. *Appetites: On the Search for True Nourishment.* New York: Dutton, 1996.

Rothschild, Babette. *The Body Remembers: The Psychophysiology of Trauma and Trauma Treatment.* New York: Norton, 2000.

Ryden, Wendy. "Conflict and Kitsch: The Politics of Politeness in the Writing Class." Jacobs and Micciche, 80–91.

Saks, Elyn R. *The Center Cannot Hold: My Journey Through Madness.* New York: Hyperion, 2007.

Samuels, Ellen. "My Body, My Closet: Invisible Disability and the Limits of Coming-out Discourse." *GLQ* 9.1 (2003): 233–55.

Sanders, Lisa. "Hidden Clues." *New York Times Magazine*. 6 Dec. 2009. 22–23.

Schell, Eileen E. *Gypsy Academics and Mother-Teachers: Gender, Contingent Labor, and Writing Instruction*. Portsmouth, NH: Boynton/Cook, 1998.

Schell, Eileen E., and Patricia Lambert Stock. "Working Contingent Faculty in(to) Higher Education." *Moving a Mountain: Transforming the Role of Contingent Faculty in Composition Studies and Higher Education*. Ed. Eileen E. Schell and Patricia Lambert Stock. Urbana, IL: National Council of Teachers of English, 2001. 1–44.

Scott, Evelyn. "On Falling Up." Myers, 198–208.

Seitz, David. *Who Can Afford Critical Consciousness? Practicing a Pedagogy of Humility*. Cresskill, NJ: Hampton P, 2004.

Shalom, Celia. "The Academic Conference: A Forum for Enacting Genre Knowledge." Ventola, Shalom, and Thompson, 51–68.

Shapiro, Stephen. "A Tennis Court Oath for Independent Scholars." *Independent Scholar* 14.1 (1999–2000): 44–48.

Shattuck, Paul T. "The Contribution of Diagnostic Substitution to the Growing Administrative Prevalence of Autism in U.S. Special Education." *Pediatrics* 117.4 (2006): 1028–37.

Sheard, Cynthia Miecznikowski. "*Kairos* and Kenneth Burke's Psychology of Political and Social Communication." *College English* 55.3 (1993): 291–310.

Sheehan, Eugene P., Teresa M. McDevitt, and Heather C. Ross. "Looking for a Job as a Psychology Professor? Factors Affecting Applicant Success." *Teaching of Psychology* 25.1 (1998): 8–11.

Shields, Stephanie A. "The Politics of Emotion in Everyday Life: 'Appropriate' Emotion and Claims on Identity." *Review of General Psychology* 9.1 (2005): 3–15.

Siebers, Tobin. "Disability as Masquerade." *Literature and Medicine* 23.1 (2004): 1–22.

Siebers, Tobin. *Disability Theory*. Ann Arbor: U of Michigan P, 2008.

Siebers, Tobin. "Tender Organs, Narcissism, and Identity Politics." *Disability Studies: Enabling the Humanities*. Ed. Sharon L. Snyder, Brenda Jo Brueggemann, and Rosemarie Garland-Thomson. New York: MLA, 2002. 40–55.

Silver, Patricia, Andrew Bourke, and K. C. Strehorn. "Universal Instructional Design in Higher Education: An Approach for Inclusion." *Equity & Excellence in Education* 31.2 (1998): 47–51.

Skeem, Jennifer L., Joshua D. Miller, Edward Mulvey, Jenny Tiemann, and John Monahan. "Using a Five-Factor Lens to Explore the Relation Between Personality Traits and Violence in Psychiatric Patients." *Journal of Consulting and Clinical Psychology* 73.3 (2005): 454–65.

Slater, Lauren. *Love Works Like This: Moving from One Kind of Life to Another*. New York: Random House, 2002.

Slater, Lauren. *Lying: A Metaphorical Memoir*. New York: Random House, 2000.

Slater, Lauren. *Opening Skinner's Box: Great Psychological Experiments of the Twentieth Century*. New York: W. W. Norton, 2004.

Slater, Lauren. *Prozac Diary*. New York: Penguin, 1999.

Smith, Sidonie. *Subjectivity, Identity, and the Body: Women's Autobiographical Practices in the Twentieth Century.* Bloomington: Indiana UP, 1993.

Social Security Administration. "Annual Statistical Report on the Social Security Disability Insurance Program, 2007." Released September 2008. February 19, 2009.

Snelgrove, Sue. "Bad, Mad and Sad: Developing a Methodology of Inclusion and a Pedagogy for Researching Students with Intellectual Disabilities." *International Journal of Inclusive Education* 9.3 (2005): 313–29.

Snyder, Sharon L., and David T. Mitchell. *Cultural Locations of Disability.* Chicago: U of Chicago P, 2006.

Sonenschein, David. *Independent Together: The 2004 Membership Survey.* Berkeley: National Coalition of Independent Scholars, 2004.

"Source: Gunman Angry at 'Rich Kids.'" CNN.com. April 18, 2007. August 27, 2008.

Stanley, Liz. *The Auto/Biographical I: The Theory and Practice of Feminist Auto/biography.* Manchester: Manchester UP, 1992.

Stanton, Domna C. "Autogynography: Is the Subject Different?" *The Female Autograph: Theory and Practice of Autobiography from the Tenth to the Twentieth Century.* Ed. Domna C. Stanton. New York: New York Literary Forum, 1984. 5–22.

Stewart, Kathleen. "Cultural Poesis: The Generativity of Emergent Things." *Handbook of Qualitative Research,* 3rd ed. Ed. Norman K. Denzin and Yvonna S. Lincoln. Thousand Oaks, CA, 2005. 1027–42.

Stoddard, Susan, Devva Kasnitz, and Lisa Wahl. "Making Conferences Accessible: Experiences from 1995 SDS." *Disability Studies Quarterly* 18.1 (1998): 36–38.

Stone, Elizabeth T. "A Sketch of My Life." *Women of the Asylum: Voices from Behind the Walls, 1840–1945.* Ed. Jeffrey L. Geller and Maxine Harris. New York: Anchor, 1994. 32–41.

Stone, Emma, and Mark Priestley. "Parasites, Pawns and Partners: Disability Research and the Role of Non-disabled Researchers." *British Journal of Sociology* 47.4 (1996): 699–716.

Stubblefield, Anna. "The Entanglement of Race and Cognitive Dis/ability." *Metaphilosophy* 40.3–4 (2009): 531–51.

Sunderland, Steve. "Opening the Door to Higher Education: The Rights of the Intellectually Different to Access and Peace." *Disability Studies Quarterly* 28.4 (2008).

"Suzanne Paola." July 22, 2010.www.suzannepaola.com.

Swanson, Jeffrey W., Charles E. Holzer III, Vijay K. Ganju, and Robert Tsutomu Jono. "Violence and Psychiatric Disorder in the Community: Evidence from the Epidemiologic Catchment Area Surveys." *Hospital and Community Psychiatry* 41 (1990): 761–70.

Tharp, Julie. "When the Body Is Your Own: Feminist Film Criticism and the Horror Genre." *Autobiographical Writing Across the Disciplines: A Reader.* Ed. Diane P. Freedman and Olivia Frey. Durham, NC: Duke UP, 2003. 281–91.

Theis, Jeffrey. "Collegiality and the Department Mailbox: Subdivide and Conquer." *Profession* (2006): 87–94.

Thiher, Allen. *Revels in Madness: Insanity in Medicine and Literature.* Ann Arbor: U of Michigan P, 2004.

Thomas, Cornell, and Douglas J. Simpson. "Community, Collegiality, and Diversity: Is There a Conflict of Interest in the Professoriate?" *Journal of Negro Education* 64.1 (1995): 1–5.

Thompson, Wendy Marie. "Her Reckoning: A Young Interdisciplinary Academic Dissects the Exact Nature of Her Disease." Myers, 373–80.

Tichenor, Kristin Ruth. "High Schools Need to Give Colleges More Information About Troubled Students." *Chronicle of Higher Education* 54.34 (2008): B21.

Tillmann-Healy, Lisa M. "Friendship as Method." *Qualitative Inquiry* 9.5 (2003): 729–49.

Tincani, Matt. "Improving Outcomes for College Students with Disabilities: Ten Strategies for Instructors." *College Teaching* 52.4 (2004): 128–32.

Titchkosky, Tanya. "Disability: A Rose by Any Other Name? 'People-First' Language in Canadian Society." *Canadian Review of Sociology and Anthropology* 38.2 (2001): 125–40.

Titchkosky, Tanya. *Reading and Writing Disability Differently: The Textured Life of Embodiment.* Toronto: U of Toronto P, 2007.

Tough Guise: Violence, Media & the Crisis in Masculinity. Dir. Sut Jhally. Perf. Jackson Katz. Media Education Foundation, 1999.

Toth, Emily. "Can I Dazzle Them With My Energy?" *Chronicle of Higher Education* (August 22, 2005). August 22, 2008.

Trahan, Elizabeth Welt. "Every University Should Support Independent Scholars As a Matter of Principle." *Chronicle of Higher Education* (May 16, 1990). February 8, 2009.

Tremain, Shelley. "Foucault, Governmentality, and Critical Disability Theory: An Introduction." Tremain, *Foucault,* 1–24.

Tremain, Shelley, ed. *Foucault and the Government of Disability.* Ann Arbor: U of Michigan P, 2005.

Trent, James W., Jr. *Inventing the Feeble Mind: A History of Mental Retardation in the United States.* Berkeley: U of California P, 1994.

Trower, Cathy A., and Richard P. Chait. "Faculty Diversity: Too Little for Too Long." *Harvard Magazine* (March–April 2002). September 28, 2008.

United States Department of Education. "U.S. Department of Education Awards 13 Grants to Higher Education Institutions to Plan and Prepare for Campus Emergencies." July 30, 2008. September 6, 2008.

"University Shooter Interested in 'Peace and Social Justice.'" CNN.com. February 16, 2008. August 31, 2008.

Van Dyne, Linn. "Mentoring Relationships: A Comparison of Experiences in Business and Academia." *Rhythms of Academic Life: Personal Accounts of Careers in Academia.* Ed. Peter J. Frost and M. Susan Taylor. Thousand Oaks, CA: Sage, 1996. 159–63.

Vance, Mary Lee. "Introduction." *Disabled Faculty,* Vance, 5–8.

Vance, Mary Lee, ed. *Disabled Faculty and Staff in a Disabling Society: Multiple*

Identities in Higher Education. Ed. Mary Lee Vance. Huntersville, NC: AHEAD, 2007.

Vann, David. "Portrait of the School Shooter as a Young Man." *Esquire* (August 2008): 114–26.

Ventola, Eija, Celia Shalom, and Susan Thompson, eds. *The Language of Conferencing.* Frankfurt am Main: Peter Lang, 2002.

Vidali, Amy. "Rhetorical Hiccups: Disability Disclosure in Letters of Recommendation." *Rhetoric Review* 28.2 (2009): 185–204.

Vidali, Amy. "Seeing What We Know: Disability and Theories of Metaphor." *Journal of Literary and Cultural Disability Studies* 4.1 (2010): 33–54.

Virginia Tech Review Panel. *Mass Shootings at Virginia Tech: Report of the Review Panel.* Presented to Governor Kaine, Commonwealth of Virginia. August 2007. September 2, 2008.

Vital Signs: Crip Culture Talks Back. Dir. David Mitchell and Sharon Snyder. Marquette, MI: Brace Yourselves Productions, 1997.

Wallace, David L. "Transcending Normativity: Difference Issues in 'College English.'" *College English* 68.5 (2006): 502–30.

Walmsley, Jan. "Normalisation, Emancipatory Research and Inclusive Research in Learning Disability." *Disability & Society* 16.2 (2001): 187–205.

Warhol, Robyn R. *Gendered Interventions: Narrative Discourse in the Victorian Novel.* New Brunswick, NJ: Rutgers UP, 1990.

Watters, Ethan. *Crazy Like Us: The Globalization of the American Psyche.* New York: Free Press, 2010.

Watts, Ivan Eugene, and Nirmala Erevelles. "These Deadly Times: Reconceptualizing School Violence by Using Critical Race Theory and Disability Studies." *American Educational Research Journal* 41.2 (2004): 271–99.

"We Have Common Cause Against the Night: Voices from the WPA-L, September 11–12, 2001." Borrowman, 201–29.

Webb-Johnson, Gwendolyn. "Are Schools Ready for Joshua? Dimensions of African-American Culture among Students Identified as Having Behavioral/Emotional Disorders." *Qualitative Studies in Education* 15.6 (2002): 653–71.

Webber, Pauline. "The Paper Is Now Open for Discussion." Ventola, Shalom, and Thompson, 227–53.

Wells, Susan. "Notes on Handling Difficult Faculty Members." *ADE Bulletin* 143 (2007): 32–33.

Wendell, Susan. "Unhealthy Disabled: Treating Chronic Illnesses as Disabilities." *Hypatia* 16.4 (2001): 17–33.

Wentz, Richard E. "The Merits of Professors Emeriti." *Chronicle of Higher Education* 48:6 (2001): B5.

Wesling, Donald. "Scholarly Writing and Emotional Knowledge." *Papers on Language and Literature* 43 (2007): 363–89.

Wharton, Amy S. "The Psychosocial Consequences of Emotional Labor." *Annals of the American Academy of Political and Social Science* 561 (1999): 158–76.

Wilson, Anne, and Peter Beresford. "Madness, Distress and Disability: Putting the Record Straight." *Disability/Postmodernity: Embodying Disability The-*

ory. Ed. Mairian Corker and Tom Shakespeare. London: Continuum, 2002. 143–58.

Wilson, James C. *Weather Reports from the Autism Front: A Father's Memoir of His Autistic Son*. Jefferson, NC: McFarland, 2008.

Wilson, James C., and Cynthia Lewiecki-Wilson, eds. *Embodied Rhetorics: Disability in Language and Culture*. Carbondale: Southern Illinois UP, 2001.

Wilson, Mitchell. "DSM-III and the Transformation of American Psychiatry: A History." *American Journal of Psychiatry* 150.3 (1993): 399–410.

Wittig, Monique. *Le Corps Lesbien*. Trans. Peter Owen. New York: William Morrow, 1973.

Wodak, Ruth. "What CDA is About: A Summary of its History, Important Concepts and Its Developments." *Methods of Critical Discourse Analysis*. Ed. Ruth Wodak and Michael Meyer. London: Sage, 2001. 1–13.

Woodfield, Ruth, Donna Jessop, and Lesley McMillan. "Gender Differences in Undergraduate Attendance Rates." *Studies in Higher Education* 31.1 (2006): 1–22.

Worsham, Lynn. "Going Postal: Pedagogic Violence and the Schooling of Emotion." *JAC: A Journal of Composition Theory* 18.2 (1998): 213–45.

Yergeau, Melanie. "Aut(hored)ism." *Computers and Composition Online* (Spring 2009). http://www.bgsu.edu/cconline/dmac/index.html.

Yergeau, Melanie. "Narrating Telepresence, or Composing High-Functioning Autism." Conference on College Composition and Communication. San Francisco. March 14, 2009.

Zembylas, Michalinos. *Beyond Cartesian Dualism: Encountering Affect in the Teaching and Learning of Science*. New York: Springer, 2005.

Zembylas, Michalinos. *Teaching with Emotion: A Postmodern Enactment*. Charlotte, NC: Information Age, 2005.

Zink, Christy. "Teaching Writing through Grief: Getting Up for Class when the Professor is Down." Conference on College Composition and Communication. San Francisco. March 12, 2009.

Zola, Irving Kenneth. "Self, Identity and the Naming Question: Reflections on the Language of Disability." *Social Science and Medicine* 36.2 (1993): 167–73.

Index